LEADERSHIP IN EDUCATION

LEADERSHIP IN EDUCATION
The Power of Generative Dialogue

Pamela Adams

Carmen Mombourquette

David Townsend

CANADIAN
SCHOLARS

Toronto | Vancouver

Leadership in Education: The Power of Generative Dialogue
By Pamela Adams, Carmen Mombourquette, and David Townsend

First published in 2019 by
Canadian Scholars, an imprint of CSP Books Inc.
425 Adelaide Street West, Suite 200
Toronto, Ontario
M5V 3C1

www.canadianscholars.ca

Library and Archives Canada Cataloguing in Publication

Title: Leadership in education : the power of generative dialogue / Pamela Adams, Carmen Mombourquette, David Townsend.
Names: Adams, Pamela, 1959- author. | Mombourquette, Carmen, 1960- author. | Townsend, David, 1942- author.
Description: Includes index.
Identifiers: Canadiana (print) 20190172363 | Canadiana (ebook) 20190172444 | ISBN 9781773381572 (softcover) | ISBN 9781773381589 (PDF) | ISBN 9781773381596 (EPUB)
Subjects: LCSH: Educational leadership. | LCSH: Communication in education.
Classification: LCC LB2806 .A33 2019 | DDC 371.2—dc23

Page layout by S4Carlisle
Cover design by Lauren Wickware

Printed and bound in Ontario, Canada

Canada

"Our lives are not our own." To DJ and B, who persevered to live it beside me with patience, joy, and love.

PA

Throughout my career as a vice-principal, principal, and now, university professor specializing in educational leadership, it has been my life's partner and wife, Sharon, who has kept me grounded in doing the work that I do. It is for her unwavering support that I dedicate this book with all my love.

CM

Thanks to all those educators who have worked with us over many years. Your sustained commitment to leadership, learning, and school improvement has made a difference in the lives of thousands of students. I hope your contributions of time, effort, and expertise are fairly represented in the pages of this text.

DT

Contents

Figures and Tables

FIGURES

TABLES

Acknowledgements

This book could not have been written without the help, support, guidance, and ongoing commitment of many people. We would like to acknowledge the tireless efforts of two research assistants, Dr. Sharon Allan and Leonard Sproule, who worked on various stages of the research, literature review, and writing of technical pieces of this text. Thank you for always saying "yes" even to all the last-minute requests we made of you both. Your work truly added value to our scholarship.

The members of the Leaders of Learning Network also require mention as to the role they played in helping us solidify our ideas about generative leadership, generative dialogue, inquiry-guided professional learning, collaboration, and the interplay between each and all. By listening to your stories of how each of these big ideas impacts your professional lives, we were able to clarify in our own minds the ways in which we should put this book together.

The publishing team at Canadian Scholars, led by our editorial/production manager, Nick Hilton, is also to be acknowledged and applauded for the way in which they helped us from the conceptualization of the idea of the book to its actual publication. Throughout each stage of the publication process, we marvelled at your commitment to the work and talent in doing it. Thanks also to our copy editor, Cindy Angelini.

And to the thousands of teachers, vice-principals, principals, directors, and system leaders who so willingly entered into dialogue with us about teaching, leading, and learning, we say—thank you for what you do each and every day of your professional lives.

Foreword

It is an honour and a privilege to be invited to write the foreword for this book. I first met David Townsend in 2011. It was a remarkably casual encounter. He contacted me in my capacity as head of the School of Education at Southern Cross University in Australia to say he was visiting from Canada and would like to have a brief chat. After 30 minutes, I began to appreciate that what David was telling me about his work in Alberta was very significant. The discussion continued for a long time. In many respects, it is a discussion that never reached a point of closure.

David described how he and his colleagues in Alberta were using a process referred to as collaborative inquiry and generative dialogue to build a new framework for leadership in schools in various parts of Canada. I wanted to hear more. I also wanted my colleagues in the education community on the North Coast of New South Wales in Australia to hear more. We began to chat about a follow-up visit, and then about more follow-up visits, and then about establishing a North Coast Initiative for School Improvement, and then about study tours by Australians to Canada and by Canadians to Australia.

Fairly soon, David's insights were becoming of interest to authorities responsible for the state system of education in New South Wales. Ways of integrating collaborative inquiry and generative dialogue with school leadership development policies across the state were being discussed. Soon, collaborative inquiry and generative dialogue were being implemented across an ever-increasing number of schools.

Various scholarly papers describing these developments in New South Wales have been published, and many papers have also been published by scholars from Canada. Missing, though, was a comprehensive account of the notion of *generative leadership*. Pamela Adams, Carmen Mombourquette, and David Townsend have now addressed this need. These three distinguished scholars provide a comprehensive and compelling account of the nature of generative leadership. Their account is informed not only by years of research experience, but also by their depth of engagement with schools. Pamela brings to the book her skills as an accomplished academic author. Carmen brings to the book his vast experience in school leadership, including service as a school principal in Alberta and Ontario. David brings to the book his mastery of the ability to enable schools to become extraordinary.

Their book marks, in my view, an important point of transition in the literature on educational leadership, moving the discussion of educational leadership forward from a concern about change management to a concern about professional effectiveness and growth. Though it is too early yet to make a definitive pronouncement on the matter, the book seems likely to represent a paradigm shift in the literature on educational leadership.

The book is especially welcome for its detailed and systematic exposition of the nature of generative leadership. Its eight chapters provide a fascinating account of what generative leadership seeks to achieve, how it is practised, how skills in generative leadership can be developed, and how generative leadership can achieve an impact in educational settings.

The book is authoritative, with all aspects of its message firmly grounded conceptually and with examples from practice. It is professionally relevant and authentic, drawing extensively on the experiences of educators in North America and Australia. It is also remarkably engaging to read, drawing upon personal accounts by a wide range of educational leaders from across these two continents. The values it espouses are those of respect, trust, reflection, partnership, and the use of inquiry to guide action.

It is an elegant book, and I commend it to a wide readership.

Dr. Martin Hayden
Former Head and Dean, School of Education
Southern Cross University, Australia

Preface

This is a book about **growth** and how to shift the mindsets of leaders, teachers, students, and any members of educational organizations who may be striving to achieve higher levels of introspection, insight, and effectiveness. Growth is often viewed to be synonymous with change and improvement. However, our experiences in thousands of classrooms and in dozens of school systems has taught us that the semantics of growth do not create the same type or degree of emotive reaction in educators. *Change* and *improvement* are words frequently associated with deficit: a teacher's standardized test results are not up to expectations, so he must improve; a principal's accountability measures are stagnant, so she must change. The pejorative vocabularies of change and improvement can be a powerful obstacle to the forward-looking work of leaders in undertaking the complex task of overcoming the inertia of decades of satisfaction with "good enough."

Growth, on the other hand, is interpreted as organic, more gently sustained, and more able to accommodate an agenda of personalization and personal empowerment. We have observed schools and systems evolve and transform at impressive speeds and extents with little fear, defensiveness, or obstruction, but only in the presence of a clarion leadership message of growth rather than change.

Semantics aside, we are certain that growth in people and organizations will not occur without impetus. This trigger comes from an external source in the form of political policies or legislation; sometimes it originates from a crisis or catastrophic event that mobilizes action. In a less reactionary way, we contend that the most impactful growth that we have seen in education has resulted from a **provocation**: a niggling irritant that is relentless in requiring attention and that causes **reflection**, a shift in thinking, and a variation in the course of action. Merriam-Webster Online defines the word *provoke* as an emotional incitation to respond and describes someone who causes this movement as a *provocateur*. Historically, the profile of a provocateur has been surreptitious and criminal, someone who leads illegal activities as a way of disrupting the status quo. However, we imagine a much less clandestine role of the provocateur, one that is more akin to the actions spurred by a grain of sand in an oyster shell. In our experiences, the healthy disruption that can be planted by a knowledgeable and skilled **provocateur** can result in pearls rather than protests.

Before we begin an exploration of the processes and structures that effective leaders can adopt to promote individual and organization growth, let us be clear about what provocation *does not* look like: it does not purposefully create conflict of the type that results in winners and losers; it does not encourage competitiveness or one-upmanship; it does not involve strategies that question judgment, worth, or value, nor does it inflame vengefulness or disenfranchisement. Rather, as we will explain, a **leader-as-provocateur** demonstrates a nuanced skillset of **Socratic questioning** that affirms mutual respect, builds trust, stimulates reflection, strengthens partnerships, and uses inquiry to guide action.

For us, exploring the multi-faceted and nuanced links between educational leadership, school improvement, teaching effectiveness, and student learning has been a career-long endeavour. After decades of examination and exploration, we have gathered increasing evidence of the value of a core set of concepts, processes, and structures that, when supported with commitment and skill, can help schools and districts experience meaningful growth. Four of these principles include the value of collaboration, the centrality of **teams**, the importance of relationships, and, above all, the power of inquiry. Most powerfully, these principles are enacted by leaders whom we refer to as provocateurs: educators who, having spent considerable time and skill building a wealth of social capital, are able to evoke inspiration to grow, and can present incongruence as an opportunity to shift thinking.

At the heart of this work, we assert that professional practice, by definition and design, is most effectively enhanced when these leaders-as-provocateurs promote and demonstrate authentic forms of inquiry (often referred to as **authentic curiosity**); that essential and clear guiding questions initiate and sustain successful professional growth; and that conversations about teaching and learning are the primary means by which educators reflect on, understand, and expand their skills and knowledge. In recent years, we have observed skilled provocateurs causing hundreds of educators to achieve higher levels of competence by facilitating reflective action. In this book, we refer to this skill set as the *generative dialogue*. In our interpretation, the generative dialogue is grounded in active listening; avoiding criticism and judgment; nurturing trust and reciprocal respect; patiently practising Socratic reflective questioning; and, ultimately, adopting an ethos of usefulness in achieving professional goals. At its best, the generative dialogue promotes reflection-on-action, which, in turn, leads to shifts in perspective, purposeful growth, and enhanced competence.

We contend that much being written about educational leadership, school improvement, and **professional learning** may overemphasize the "what"—leadership characteristics, management programs, teaching strategies, assessment practices, policies, checklists, and even technology tools. Some of these writings adopt a panacean tone, leaving teachers and leaders with the impression that improved practice can be achieved through purchase. In this text, we focus more on *how* and *how well*: in what ways and to what extent real people responsible for leading learning in real schools and systems have been able to build commitment to professional growth, clearly articulated goals, and partnerships that have resulted in increased numbers of students receiving an enhanced quality of teaching and learning.

The assertions we make in this book have resulted from our research into successful leadership and leadership development, school improvement, and professional learning based on a series of research and development projects conducted over the past 16 years: first, in 148 schools over a period of 11 years (2000 to 2011), later, in 105 schools over a period of 5 years (2011 to 2016), and at present in 108 schools over 3 years. Data gathered from a variety of school districts, ranging in size from 13 to 41 schools, show remarkable thematic consistency around complex issues such as system-level leadership, school leadership, and distributed leadership. One enduring finding is that school improvement is more likely to ensue when the central or system leadership team is unequivocally committed to providing continuous support and high levels of expectation to school leadership teams and teachers through regular, purposeful presence in their schools. These activities form the basis of our definition of the educational provocateur.

Our research shows, repeatedly, that the formation of functional teams of educators in schools is a powerful indicator of increased effectiveness in teaching, leading, and learning. Equally important, this text shines a light on key elements of the implementation process used by provocateurs to cause individual and organizational growth. In particular, it describes the role of formal leaders in modelling skillful use of the generative dialogue; the crucial importance of clear messaging and commitment to high expectations; the need for achievement timelines that reflect long-standing theory and best practices in the professional learning process; and the impact that attitudes of trust and supportive responsibility have in contributing to sustained and purposeful growth.

During our research, we have observed many examples of initiative implementation in education that appear to be a form of paradoxical intention gone awry. It is as if those most responsible for implementing a new idea, program, curriculum, or policy begin by asking the question "If we had to guarantee that this would never be successfully implemented, or was ultimately doomed to fail, what would we do?" Then, unfortunately, the process takes on a life of its own, and the answers to that misguided question multiply as various stakeholders assume roles as if following a script.

We have found that when those educators most affected by the introduction of any new initiative are engaged as active participants, have multiple opportunities to voice their ideas and concerns, and are given the necessary time and resources to build their commitment, success is highly likely. More specifically, when educators are provided site-embedded time and are *expected* to form functional teams, when those teams are able to convert their goals into guiding questions that form ongoing inquiry into an aspect of their professional practice they deem important, and when supported through regular conversations with colleagues and leaders, levels of confidence, competence, improvement, and learning (their own and their students') are exemplary.

FEATURES OF THIS BOOK

This book was written to serve as both an academic resource and an interactive manual. The literature reviews, suggested readings, and academic references are important aspects of each chapter. These features are meant to provide a scholarly foundation and context for our thinking about the expansive concepts contributing to our understanding of generative leadership and generative dialogue.

Yet, this is also a book of questions. Each chapter is infused with dozens of ideas meant to provoke your current understandings, to persuade you to think deeper, or to entice you to engage in journal writing and reflection. Whether you participate in the case study analyses alone or with a team, whether you use the sidebar questions to consider your own leadership experiences or to engage others in organizational reflections, or whether you find yourself adding to our list of unhelpful assumptions, we hope you will find that the book encourages your curiosity and engagement.

Throughout each chapter, you will come across words in **bold type**. These are words that have unique definitions, words that are used idiosyncratically, or words that require further explanation or citation. Information about these words or phrases is contained in the glossary at the back of the book. In addition, we acknowledge that some terms we use are distinctive of countries or regions and, to the extent that we are able, we have attempted to maintain an international neutrality when explaining leadership positions and educational organizational structures unique to places such as Australia, the United Kingdom, and America.

In developing this text, we have participated in literally thousands of conversations with teachers and school and system leaders as they have explained and examined their practice in regularly scheduled monthly meetings in their school sites and central offices. As a result, we make a case in this text for a stronger role for the leader-as-provocateur: someone who subtly arouses curiosity and inquiry in the professional lives of educators; someone humbly bold enough to construct structures that offer direct and sustained support for formal and informal school leaders; someone who models and promotes a robust method that guides powerful collaboration around the most important work of schools and districts; and someone who orchestrates and champions an elegant process for enhancing the likelihood of greater learning and growth in educators.

OVERVIEW

Each chapter of this text focuses on the key activities mastered by an educational provocateur. The chapters include a short section on relevant research; one or more case studies related specifically to the chapter title; the inclusion, where appropriate, of biographical information about those school and district educators who have been most involved in this work; evidence of success; and templates or other materials we have used over the course of our research. Importantly, the text guides the reader through the skills of a generative dialogue by making suggestions about when and what questions an effective provocateur might ask that will cause reflection, conversation, collaboration, and action.

Chapter 1 begins with a review of the progress we have experienced over the last 16 years, with close attention to an understanding of growth versus change, leadership competence, and professionalism. It identifies and describes ways that school districts can promote growth from within, build capacity, and become healthier learning organizations.

Chapter 2 focuses on cultural considerations at the school and district level. It contains a critical examination of what we have called a generative organization, and the place of such an organization within the public education system. It concludes with an overview of conditions essential to organizational growth and long-term success.

Chapter 3 shows how a relentless focus on the leadership of learning—for staff and students alike—can ignite the passion of educators, bring greater clarity of meaning and purpose to their work, and contribute in comprehensive ways to heightened levels of efficacy, responsibility, and confidence. The chapter offers a view of leadership that works across an organization, from the district office out to schools, and from each school into the center. It is a model in which trust, respect, and the quality of relationships are every bit as important as positional authority; a model in which people's behaviour *is* the message they want to share; and, above all, a model in which rhetoric and reality are fused together in an unambiguous commitment to the success of every student.

Chapter 4 explains in detail why we have come to put so much credibility in the power of the question. It explores the strengths of the collaborative inquiry process as it is harnessed in support of professional growth and school improvement. It includes specific examples of the relationship between goals and guiding questions, the value of a focus on evidence, and the impact of the monthly review-and-reflection process on educators' growth and commitment. Sample growth plan templates and other data collection instruments are presented in this chapter.

Chapter 5 asks the questions: To what extent can reflection enhance practice? In what ways can leaders promote reflective practice? We explore in this chapter some of the semantics and rhetoric around professional learning and professional development. We also offer several strategies that promote reflective practice and make the case that leading individual and collective reflection is a difficult but necessary skillset that is at the heart of an effective provocateur.

Chapter 6 represents an attempt to capture key findings about collaboration and the role that effective teams play in promoting school improvement. It contains a comprehensive overview of schools and districts as learning organizations and posits some explanations as to why they may be more or less capable of setting and achieving goals. We also present a set of suggestions for providing schools and districts with the knowledge, skills, and resources to tackle such challenges as continuous growth, steady improvement, the implementation of new ideas, and capacity building.

Chapters 7 and 8 address issues of scalability and extrapolation; that is, we explore ways that the generative leadership model and the use of generative dialogues are being enacted in leadership practices outside a metro-urban or Canadian context. These chapters offer a rich description of how organizations, including systems and schools, have used the foundational principles of an "ask, don't tell" approach as a starting point to meet the challenges in school improvement and leading professional learning. Importantly, we remind readers of the ethical responsibility of all educators, regardless of context, to focus all decisions and practices on optimal learning for all students. In doing so, each chapter offers compelling evidence of the impact that this model can have on student learning.

Throughout this text, we have avoided outrageous extrapolations, suggestions of quick fixes, or gratuitous criticisms of approaches by other authors. It is our hope that readers will be intrigued by the methods we have observed and the evidence of success that we offer. We also hope that readers will come to see that our descriptions can be adapted and distilled into a form of professional practice that can contribute mightily to an enhanced quality of teaching and learning in every school. Lastly, we hope to provoke a bit of incongruence that will cause readers to think differently about how to cause shifts in thinking and doing in the leading of learning in schools and through systems.

CHAPTER ONE

Why Grow from the Inside Out?

Temet nosce!
Know thyself
   —Plato

Some of the real positives for me are increased collaboration between schools and senior administrators; increased accountability for the goals we set; the modelling we observe that helps us ask better questions and engage in better conversations with staff; the development of leadership capacity; and our leadership growth. We were told that the answer is within the organization and we are starting to believe it.
   —Elementary school principal

GROWING FROM THE INSIDE OUT

A time-honoured model of organizational growth, leadership development, and enhanced teaching has been one characterized by incessant—often punitive—evaluative processes, inordinate value on standardized measures of success, externally mandated goals, and accountability measures that are disproportionate to assurance and responsibility. Accurate or not, we often hear educators point to these realities as reasons for teachers feeling that their professional goals are developed as compliance documents; for principals engaged in terminal fixedness and competition; and for district leaders building or entrenching hierarchical structures that are almost certain to limit system health and effectiveness.

In this chapter, we examine some of the assumptions that advocate for a renewed examination of *building from within*: of identifying, locating, and highlighting the people and practices that presently exist within schools and districts, and creating the support structures and processes that will grow effectiveness of the type that develops an internal locus of control. We often refer to this approach as "finding the answer in the room." In effect, the very resources that can resolve some of a school's or system's most pressing issues are already part of existing expertise; what is missing is a process to identify who has the answers, a structure to harness the knowledge and skills of those who are committed to the pursuit of achieving organizational goals, and a transparent mechanism to disseminate this expertise in an efficacious and consistent way.

We first discuss the importance of developing an **educational vision** and **mission** that inspires all stakeholders, with particular attention to the sometimes tenuous relationship between leaders' actions and rhetoric. We offer the case study of Superintendent Goodman and consider the lessons of her experiences in understanding some of the complexities of system transformation. Key to these actions, we contend, is the extent to which leaders model an unshakable belief in the primacy of learning for all students and teachers (Bottoms & Schmidt-Davis, 2010; Fullan & Hargreaves, 2016; Schnellert & Butler, 2014). In this regard, we use the work of Daniel Goleman to describe how visionary leaders set the stage by working from the inside out. As we will explain, attitudes of authentic organizational introspection are a mandatory minimum requisite for asking the powerful questions that will result in enhanced leadership and transformed schools and systems.

Why do we challenge you, as a leader, to ask questions rather than simply provide answers?

Case Study: Alice Goodman Gets beyond the Nameplate

When I was appointed superintendent, it was humbling to know I was following in the footsteps of some legendary leaders, people who had earned honours and respect within the district and across the broader educational community. Yet, I felt there was still much work to be done if our district was to realize its full potential. Most of our school leaders and teachers were knowledgeable, skillful, confident, and caring. Our students came from families with average or above average socioeconomic advantages and, while we performed reasonably well on almost all the external measures of organizational effectiveness, there were no areas in which we truly excelled. It seemed that we had become satisfied with being a fairly good school district, having settled into patterns of behaviour and expectation that consistently reinforced the status quo.

I knew we had to do something different, but I didn't know what. I also knew I would not be able to do it on my own, but I simply didn't know where to start. I recalled the words my mentor had said as I was leaving my previous school jurisdiction: "Remember that your nameplate on the door is only the beginning of the work, not the end." In the earliest days, I think I had a clear idea of what the big picture should look like, but I was very hazy on the specifics of "the work"—how to get a team of 8 district leaders, 70 school leaders, and 600 teachers all pulling in the same direction. Still, I told myself "Clarity will come."

The notion of *teamness* was one of the unshakable principles that guided my work as district leader. I began trying to influence all members of the central office staff to see themselves as a team: to communicate openly with each other; to share equally in opportunities to develop plans, strategies, and policies; and to explore new ways of thinking about our jobs. Yet, the fact that site-based decision making was so deeply embedded in the culture of the system seemed to be at odds with my preferred model of a common mission, vision, and goals, and my cherished belief that a school district could best achieve excellence by making an all-out commitment to the success of every student.

Within the first three months of making efforts to reconcile these differences, I became increasingly aware that two district office leaders were intent on maintaining the personal networks and relationships with schools that they had built up over the years. It became glaringly obvious that some school leaders, too, wanted to preserve those historical partnerships. Loyalties were dividing, and misunderstandings arose. We seemed, at times, to be spinning our wheels. I sensed that part of the way forward lay in making ourselves a more functional system overall, but I could not have predicted how complicated the situation was to become.

> How should a new leader work with the people she inherits? When should a leader look at moving people into new roles to "disrupt" existing practices? When should a leader encourage people to find new positions?

Dale, an associate superintendent, had been with the district for 14 years and had much more central office experience than I had. Jane had six years of experience as an associate (again, far more than I had) and had nurtured rich personal and professional relationships with several long-time principals. In addition, she had been an unsuccessful candidate for the position I now held. I had many long and frank discussions with both educators, clearly outlining my expectations for members of the district leadership team and how these expectations aligned with the district mission and vision statements that were being drafted at the time. I listened to the educators' concerns. I acknowledged their personal views about leadership and constantly invited them to enter into a more productive collaboration with me and the rest of the district leadership team.

This was a lonely time for me. I realized that I was the only one who could see this conflict through to its resolution. I could not involve other members of the team. So much of these discussions could not be shared. The situation got worse as Dale made it clear he was not about to change his ways. Fortunately, around the same time, Jane began finding healthy and productive ways to participate in the work of our increasingly more collaborative district office team.

Here was my dilemma: Dale was almost openly working against our best efforts. I worried often that I might have to initiate steps to terminate his position.

continued

But how could I get rid of a member of the central office staff while maintaining the support and goodwill of the rest of the team? Exactly four months to the day from when I was appointed superintendent, Dale and I had what proved to be our most difficult conversation. Running out of patience and empathy, I asked Dale what he wanted to get out of his work with the district and, to my great surprise, he blurted, "I just want to get out!"

With a sense of relief, and appreciation for his personal courage, I agreed to help Dale seek out new employment opportunities. I knew the way I dealt with his departure would become part of my own legacy within the district, and I knew it had to be done with respect and dignity. It was. In less than three weeks, Dale was recruited by an energy exploration company and immediately installed as the vice-president of human resources.

Those early months of work flew by. I had my own schedule of conversations with school leaders, board members, bus drivers, community members, government officials, and teachers, paired against frequent team meetings, reports, district planning sessions, budget meetings, celebrations, and the minutiae of the daily life of a school district. Everyone was busy. Busy-ness was just the way we did our work. At one point, I decided to find out just how busy I was by taking stock of what I did every half-hour for one full week of work. What a lesson! My time audit indicated that less than 20 percent of my weekly time was actually related to the important work I knew I should be doing to move the district forward.

I had always admired educators who were able to combine their work in schools and districts with an ability to present at conferences, complete graduate studies, keep up with current research, and otherwise engage in continuous professional learning. Nevertheless, as I became more immersed in the work of a superintendent, I was drawn increasingly to the conclusion that many of the answers we were looking for would be found within our own organization. In the matter of leadership in particular, I was convinced we needed to shine a light on our own leadership practices.

So, our district leadership team helped create and refine a model of community visits involving representatives of all stakeholders; an innovative model of school effectiveness; new mission and vision statements; and new three-year plans. We were becoming a more active district and, slowly, we were achieving a balance between those elements of education that could be done best in individual schools and those that needed the support and commitment of the whole district. In addition, we promoted the creation of a team of teachers who would meet with the superintendent four times per year to discuss their concerns. We made almost all of these decisions about structure and process through team discussions. I recall one day when I realized how far we had come as a team. Sitting around my office one afternoon, late, we were brainstorming ways of being more present in schools. Jane came up with the idea that we could all have a "family of schools" to which we were most connected—our liaison schools. One of the associates proposed that we start that process by personally delivering copies of the newly-minted mission and vision statements to every classroom. In short order, that schedule was planned and the liaison process got off to a strong start.

After much discussion with my school board members and the central leadership team, we decided to enlist the help of a team of researchers from the university. Through a carefully designed research and development initiative, together we would discover those areas of practice in which we were growing and those that needed greater attention. The research model we adopted matched up well with our district's emerging ethos of collaboration and engagement that reflected the values of **shared responsibility**.

The upcoming fall retreat would mark my first year as a superintendent. We decided to begin the university/school district partnership at that event by demonstrating the *generative dialogue*, an element of the **collaborative inquiry** process that was central to the work of the university researchers. A primary purpose of the generative dialogue would be to encourage all our school leaders to reflect on their goals and commit to specific actions. "Who should be our first volunteer?" I wondered. But not for long. It became perfectly clear to me that, if I was going to be asking everyone else to suspend their disbelief and get involved in this bold new initiative, I had better be willing to be the first to take the risk. So I did. I really had no idea what I was getting into when I stepped onto the stage at the retreat to be interviewed by one of those university people. I had been asked to think about my own goals for the year and some of the strategies I planned to use. After 20 minutes of deep thought, fear, humility, courage, self-deprecation, insight, reflection, and moments of great ambiguity, I had a clear goal for the year, a seemingly-magical question to guide my professional work, and some strategies that I had not considered before the conversation began. I also had a bit of an intuition that our district and the university researchers had just entered into a powerful partnership that would propel our district down a path of continuous growth.

If presented with a similar decision—to be onstage to open your practice to public scrutiny—how would you react? Would you embrace it as an opportunity to lead by example? Or would you invite another member of staff to take this opportunity in your place?

Case Study Reflections: Building the Backdrop

- What attitudes or beliefs might have guided Alice's actions in building the backdrop for an improved school jurisdiction?
- What obstacles arose in short order after Alice's appointment?

continued

- What were Alice's key strategies to increase cohesiveness within the district?
- What behaviours did Alice display that demonstrated her commitment to relational leadership?
- What are some potential risks associated with Alice demonstrating her vulnerability at the fall retreat? What are some advantages?
- What do you think Alice meant by "shine a light on our own leadership practices"? What are the gains and limitations to starting down this path of system examination?
- What is your opinion about Alice's strategies to gather information about the system?
- What are the limitations of *teamness* and where do you stand on the spectrum of collaboration?

THE CORE OF BUILDING FROM WITHIN: LOOKING FOR VISION

In our work with school and system leaders, we have observed a wide range of opinions regarding the role of school vision and mission. This is so, despite some compelling literature documenting the impact of school vision on student learning (Bottoms & Schmidt-Davis, 2010; Chappuis, Chappuis, & Stiggins, 2009; Gronn, 2002; Lambert, 2005; Leithwood, 2013; Marzano, Waters, & McNulty, 2005; Murphy, Elliott, Goldring, & Porter, 2007; Naseer, 2011; Seashore Louis, Dretzke, & Wahlstrom, 2010; Ylimaki, 2006).

Some leaders view vision statements as required decorations whose parameters and content have been externally mandated at the level of the ministry, then painted or hung on the entrance walls to contribute to the building's aesthetics. On the other hand, some vision statements are so rooted in local folklore and history that even the suggestion that their meaning be clarified or revisited is tantamount to questioning the very existence of the community!

> How are vision and mission statements treated in your school? Are they critical to the school's growth and evolution?

We have been fortunate to work with some school and system leaders who have walked the tightrope of incorporating both internal and external elements to generate a functional and living vision that communicates students', teachers', parents', and community members' beliefs about education. In developing such a document, these leaders have demonstrated how a broadly developed mission and vision can strengthen the core of the organization in ways that allow for critique, questions, and dialogue.

Why Is a Vision Necessary?

Ylimaki (2006) examined a variety of definitions for the term *vision*, noting that the most often used definition relates to a leader's ability to imagine and articulate a compelling future (Bennis & Nanus, 1985; Westley & Mintzberg, 1989). She also identified another category of definitions that outline organizational goals (Boyd, 1992; DuFour &

Eaker, 1998). Ylimaki classified the former definition as leader-driven and internal, while the latter is collective and, often, external.

Effective leaders are guided by a belief system and educational philosophy based on reflection in balance with sound research. A key to the beliefs of school and system leaders is that all students can learn and, accordingly, that the leaders' role is to impact that learning to the greatest extent they are directly able. Bandura (1993) and Tschannen-Moren (2009) referred to this as efficacy in making a difference in others' lives. Hallinger and Heck (1996) linked this efficacy directly to community needs, thus reconciling the internal with the external in a fluid and sustained way (see also Fullan, Rincon-Gallardo, & Hargreaves, 2015).

Indeed, school and system leaders play an important role in translating community needs into those that enhance student learning. Leithwood, Mascall, and Strauss (2009) contended that mediating community priorities with that of student learning can be achieved by *distributing* leadership responsibilities and that, in the process, school and system leaders can assess relative strengths and areas of growth (see also Pan, Nyeu, & Cheng, 2017; White, Cooper, & Anwaruddin, 2017). To do so, effective leaders analyze a diversity of data to arrive at a vision that is inclusive, yet contextualized.

Many authors point to the important role of data in actualizing the vision, and ensuring that its premises remain focused on student learning (Barnes, Camburn, Sanders, & Sebastion, 2010; Bowers, 2009; Copland, 2003; Datnow, Park, & Wohlstetter, 2007; Knapp, Copland, & Swinnerton, 2007; Luo, 2008; Mombourquette, 2017). Such data can take many forms, but most can be loosely clustered as *external* or *internal*. For example, standardized tests are externally mandated but can also result from, and in, practices that are school-specific. Of most importance is that effective leaders interpret and create opportunities to align data with that which has been collaboratively and collectively defined as the broadly understood mission and vision.

Once what is important to the school community has been determined, as informed by internal and external sources of data, leaders begin working to sustain the organization as a culture that learns and grows. The notion of educational cultures and communities has been written about frequently as a correlate to student learning (see, for example, DuFour & Eaker, 1998; DuFour & Marzano, 2011; DuFour & DuFour, 2012; Owen, 2015), although some authors suggest that the link is unproven or, at best, tenuous (Timperley, 2011). Waters, Marzano, and McNulty (2003) included fostering culture as one of 21 leadership responsibilities they associated with student learning. Their work emphasized the ways that effective leaders enact mission and vision, and the critical role leaders play in communicating the ways and means by which a vision is realized (see also Leithwood, 2013).

Vision for All?

School and system leaders must also address and solve the challenging puzzle of alignment. Bedard, Mombourquette, and Aitken (2013) demonstrated the impact of aligning school, system, and ministry goals and, much like Knapp, Copland, Honig, Plecki, and Portin

(2010), found that focusing school and district goals on student learning resulted in sustained organizational growth and gains in achievement. This alignment entailed, among other things, a redesign of system services to complement rather than replicate the work of schools (Honig, 2012). Bottoms and Schmidt-Davis (2010, pp. iv–v) outlined the following strategies to align system and school vision:

> How is the word *alignment* perceived in your school? District? Province? State? Is it viewed as an imposition on the real work of teachers? Or is it embraced and recognized as supporting growth?

- Work with a cross-section of community and school leaders to create a strategic vision.
- Focus on policies and support services that enhance each school's ability to achieve its strategic vision and plan within the context of the district's vision.
- Develop tools and processes that principals and teachers can use to ensure that instruction for all groups of students is aligned with school and school district goals.
- Invest in high-quality **professional development** for the district staff, school principals, and teachers, along the lines of high-quality teaching and student learning and the role that instructional leadership can play in optimizing these.
- Build capacity in educators to analyze a variety of data—beyond test scores— and discover the root causes behind student attainment/ lack of attainment of learning goals.
- Give school principals real authority in areas of staff selection, school scheduling, instructional programs, and use of and redirection of new and existing resources.
- Consider working with external school improvement researchers to develop a forward-looking strategic vision that can move the district toward a preferred future. Many consistently low-performing districts bring in new superintendents every two to four years. An outside facilitator can help break this cycle by working with district leaders and the school board to identify community goals and create structures that will better serve students' learning.
- Develop a succession plan for school principals. Districts can help themselves by investing in professional development that builds capacity in leaders at all levels.
- Work continually with parents and community leaders to ask and answer a variety of questions related to the common vision for school improvement.

Building from within, then, begins with creating an aligned system and school vision and mission that communicates broad community values, beliefs, and aspirations for and about student learning. The most effective leaders we have worked with also demonstrate a combination of styles and predispositions that incorporate a strong value for introspection in balance with visionary action and what Goleman (2005) refers to as *coaching leadership*, a term that we expand upon in chapter 3 and refer to as generative leadership.

Daniel Goleman: Growth from Within

In the early days of this century, when the Alberta Initiative for School Improvement was having an effect on virtually every school in that Canadian province, our team of educators from the University of Lethbridge was closely involved with educational leaders from 17 school districts and 114 different schools.

Our understanding of the role leaders played in helping schools become more successful had been shaped by the effective schools movement; 30 years of participation in formal evaluations of schools; conclusions drawn from hundreds of books, articles, and conference presentations devoted to the subject; our own doctoral studies; and our personal experiences in a number of elementary, junior high, and high schools.

It probably is not surprising that our background of knowledge, skills, and perceptions proved inadequate to our needs as we strove diligently to help the schools with which we partnered pursue and achieve some highly desirable goals. Schools were even more "cultural" than we first expected them to be, and the cultural norms in many schools tended more toward individualism, separateness, and resistance to new ideas than toward collaboration and trust. Groups of educators did not come together as willingly as we had anticipated they would. In some cases, it took several years before teachers saw much value in working in teams. Many schools proved not to be goal-directed organizations, while others were chasing a new set of goals every year. Few schools were seen to use data with purpose or effect.

Connections between school and district leaders were as varied as the personalities of the educators involved. We worked with two districts in which the principals were clearly the guardians of the district culture, far more influential in setting the direction and manipulating opinion than any central office staff members. They set the agenda for the monthly principals' meeting, to which they invited the superintendent. Vice-principals did not attend. In a few districts, the actual perceptions of district office staff concerning matters of effectiveness, climate, and relationships were so at odds with those of school leaders that they contributed directly to serious dysfunction. In several districts, relations between school and district leaders were cordial—even highly collegial—but, in most cases, matters of management and budget took precedence over concerns about the quality of teaching and the leadership of learning.

In these times of uncertainty, we were attracted to the ideas of Daniel Goleman, especially as they were expressed in the book *Primal Leadership* (Goleman, Boyatzis, & McKee, 2002). In Goleman's assertions about **resonant** and **dissonant** leadership behaviours, for example, we found persuasive analysis of patterns of leadership behaviour we were observing in school districts. As well, in his descriptions of leadership style, we found a framework that helped us better understand the impact of leadership behaviour on some key measures of school improvement.

We developed a questionnaire based on Goleman's concept of emotional intelligence and distributed it to 127 principals and 73 district office staff. Almost ironically, the results of that questionnaire seemed to confirm some of Goleman's key assertions about leadership. Moreover, they offered support to the findings of another influential author of the time, Jim Collins, who wrote *Good to Great*. Of the leaders who completed our survey, superintendents collectively rated themselves lowest in their leadership effectiveness as defined by Goleman. Other central office staff rated themselves higher than superintendents. Principals rated themselves highest in their effectiveness.

Goleman classifies styles of leadership into those that are most likely to generate resonance and those that are most likely to create dissonance within an organization. His most effective leaders are self-aware, in that they are "attuned to their guiding values ... accurate in their self-assessment ... and self-confident" (Goleman et al., 2002, pp. 253–254). They are strong on self-control, transparency, initiative, and optimism. They are socially aware, they listen well, they are available, and they display "an understanding of the guiding values and unspoken rules that operate" (p. 255) within their organizations. Finally, such leaders are seen to be inspirational and influential, adept at catalyzing change, managing conflict, developing the talents of others, and promoting collaboration.

> Think about leaders you consider to be highly effective. In what ways do they conform to Goleman's leadership styles? In what ways do you try to emulate their leadership?

In the period from 2000 to 2017, we had the good fortune to work with many leaders who exhibit most of the qualities of resonant leaders. Upon reflection, we contend there are more effective leaders in schools and districts than have ever been recognized or honoured for their talents and their often enduring contributions to the leadership of learning. The evidence we have been able to accumulate of the impact of adaptive and generative leadership in more than 500 schools in North America and Australia is compelling.

That being said, we must also note that a number of leaders with whom we have worked do not fit easily into any of Goleman's categories. A few leaders are really high on the jocularity scale: they try hard to find humour in virtually everything they encounter in their working lives. Some see their primary role as their school's loudest cheerleaders, while others appear preoccupied with issues of policy, or the minutiae of day-to-day operations, or masses of data. Still others will be seen to tackle any tasks other than making purposeful classroom visits or engaging staff members in focused conversations about teaching and learning. A few leaders are serious micromanagers; a small number come across as aloof, or *un*personal.

However, taken as a whole, the educational leaders with whom we have worked, and continue to work, have shown a genuine and sustained capacity for professional growth, a pronounced willingness to collaborate with colleagues around the pursuit of important goals, appropriate humility in the face of daunting challenges, and a growing determination to be the best they can be in leading the learning in their schools and districts. They have become much more sophisticated in their use of data and evidence to guide decisions and action and, without question, their collective commitment to professional reading and research has been one of the most positive outcomes of these last two decades of our work in school improvement. Our model of generative leadership has evolved, in part, from the evidence we gathered from these remarkable leaders-of-learning.

KEY CONSIDERATIONS TO GROWTH FROM WITHIN

Thus far in this chapter, a pattern of thought has begun to emerge about the key considerations necessary for "growth from within" to occur. Growth from within can apply to individuals (students, teachers, staff, principals, directors, system leaders), as well as to various components of an organization (professional learning communities [PLCs], teacher teams, departments, schools, school system).

Throughout this book, we assert that growth arises from a shared responsibility for student learning. When all the requirements for doing the job of school or system leader are considered, the functions that come to mind as most relevant for growth from within pertain particularly to the role of instructional leadership. Instructional leadership necessitates modelling. **Modelling** requires not only an understanding of what is involved in an actual process, but also the establishment of a mindset in which leaders and learners alike welcome ongoing reflection, feedback through questioning, and a commitment to the refinement of practice. Growth through this process, then, requires system leaders, **directors**, and **executive directors** to model the leadership of learning with school leaders, school leaders to model the leadership of learning with teachers and staff, and teachers to model the leadership of learning with each other in their teams as well as with students.

Inquiry lies at the heart of this work. In practice, all goals associated with student, teacher, and leader growth start with a question rather than a statement. Why a question? Questions employ a set of processes that require deeper thinking and, in turn, necessitate more action than that which is required in response to a statement. Questions also have the power to promote a quality of reflection that leads to informed action. As an example, a teacher's goal statement might be "This year in my class, I would like to work on the implementation of Daily 5." An inquiry question to guide the teacher's pursuit of this goal might read, "In what ways and to what extent will implementing the Daily 5 structure in my literacy program impact my struggling readers?" When an educator's work is guided by an essential question, professional learning can be a likely outcome. Timperley (2011) highlighted the fundamental difference between professional development and professional *learning* as one of having something being done to you versus something that you are doing for yourself. In other words, professional development implies a more passive participation in the process, while professional learning more clearly equates with empowerment (see also Butler, Schnellert, & MacNeil, 2015).

Another key consideration for building the backdrop for growth from within pertains to an understanding of the need for alignment at all levels of the organization. This alignment function is

> Before you read this paragraph, think about a time when you accomplished something about which you are very proud. What led you to do the work? Were you really curious about something? Were you told to do it? Where did the impetus come from?

dependent upon a balance that takes into consideration both the context and the individuals involved. A one-size-fits-all approach will simply not work. Balance also assumes that a provincial/state perspective is embedded in the process of goal identification and articulation. Individual teachers function as part of a school, district, and provincial/state system of education. Very often the alignment shows through in the ways in which vision is developed and shared. School personnel develop a mutually supported vision for education in conjunction and partnership with what the school district has developed and, in turn, what the school district develops as its road map for the way forward is crafted in clear alignment with what the province/state desires education to achieve.

HELPFUL RESPONSES TO UNHELPFUL ASSUMPTIONS ABOUT GROWTH FROM WITHIN

In her TED Talk, Kathryn Schulz refers to herself as a "wrongologist." She contends that there are myriad reasons why organizations and leaders avoid learning, many based on assumptions about success, risk, and growth that are particularly prevalent in Western cultures. These assumptions are especially disposed against growth from within and are enacted by different leaders, in different positions, making various decisions. In the context of effectively building the backdrop for growth from within, these assumptions are damaging, but all too common. Here are several we hear consistently in our work in schools and systems.

Most Educators Just Intuitively Know If or When They Are Doing a Good Job

In our work with thousands of educators, we have come to believe that most do have a general sense of effectiveness, honed over years of practice, failures, and successes. As a matter of fact, the type of work that we do with the generative dialogue model is based on an assumption of competence, and so we accept that there is a general understanding of what constitutes "good enough" in teaching and leading. Yet, as we meet with teachers and leaders at all levels of experience and honorifics, many still ask "Am I doing a good job?" or "How did I do?" or even "What could I do better?" As we continue working with them, we find that the veracity of the claim of "intuitiveness" fades and is replaced by a strong need to be clear about *how* they know that they are competent and what evidence they will accept to ascertain their professional effectiveness.

These questions cue us to at least two observations. The first is that the internal locus of control and accurate calibration of levels of effectiveness lie dormant in many very competent educators. They often don't know what they know or don't know. Furthermore, many don't know how to provide evidence of the enormous scope of their effectiveness; that is, they are unconsciously competent, a state of conceptualization and performance analysis that leads to myths about the "craft" of teaching and leading. The second is that most educators we have worked with are starving for the opportunity to reflect upon their levels of effectiveness. They do not necessarily feel good about making superficial assessments of their practice, nor do they feel that they are provided time or space to engage in authentic inquiry into their strengths, weaknesses, and growth. They are not avoiding doing so. In the impossible demands of the "now," most educators simply cannot imagine a way to carve out a place and time to reflect with purpose on their effectiveness.

> Leaders are essential to building structures that embed reflection into practice. What do these structures look like in your school?

Good Leaders Stay Out of the Way and Let Teachers Do Their Job

In one of the most telling assessments of leadership effectiveness we have heard, one highly respected and effective teacher commented upon the new superintendent in her district. She said that he was doing a great job because it had been two years since he had started in the position, and he had not yet been in her school. This, she assured us, was a good thing, because past superintendents had visited regularly and had "just ended up giving us more work to do."

Our thesis about leaders' roles in enhancing teaching and learning hinges on an *ethos of usefulness*. Some authors refer to this as "**value added leadership**." We prefer to describe it as a skill set in differentiating support and pursuing individual and organizational goals that are unique to each member of the school community. One key is that the *raison d'être* for visiting schools or classrooms, or any other number of educational events in which leaders engage, must focus on the question "How can I be of greatest use in this context?" As we will describe in upcoming chapters, the greatest use often involves asking powerful questions to cause reflective action and growth. Contrary to our Western value for doing and fixing, usefulness is really that simple and, at the same time, that obfuscatory.

System and school leaders achieve greater usefulness, in part, by establishing and maintaining quality professional relationships. The organizations that we have observed to be most healthy and effective in meeting the learning needs of students are those in which children, teachers, leaders, and community members are interacting with attitudes of usefulness rather than independence or isolation.

We're Already Doing Most of This and Have Been for Quite Some Time

The slogan reads, "Been there, done that, got the T-shirt to prove it." As an example, a central office coordinator informed us that they had "done learning communities last year and were moving on to literacy this year." We have observed variations of this mindset in almost every school and initiative in which we have been engaged.

To be fair, there has been a long history of time-honoured "initiative abuse" and **"initiative fatigue"** over the past several decades. We have experienced the cycle as frequently and predictably as many now-skeptical educators have: a high-level official or politician introduces an idea, sometimes with merit and potential; money is spent to buy resources or to stopgap many existing areas of deficit; the initiative is "rolled out" and excitement is built; episodic workshops are provided for a few early adopters who will be charged with converting the masses; and teachers in classrooms are left to do the work. When we go back two or three years later, we find that not much has changed at the level of instruction, while many originators of the initiative have been promoted or have moved on to other opportunities. This cycle serves to further confirm the notion that change and growth are synonymous, both equally annoying to many educators. Worse, it provides a fail-safe excuse for educators who will not engage with curiosity and wonder about their practice.

> Again, think about your school context. What does the "initiative cycle" look like? How accurately does our description apply? In what ways does it not apply?

In our experiences, most educators want to reflect on the times in their careers when they were at their best; most are looking for ways to engage in a different model of professional learning that more accurately honours their challenges and interests. Most educators enter into new initiatives with a healthy degree of skepticism that can best be transformed into enthusiasm when the new initiative meets their needs for professional growth.

I Don't Do Reflection. I Wonder Why We Have to Do It So Often?

We have encountered people at all levels in various types of organizations, from new and directly out of university to seasoned with years of experience. Some are very vocal in making the contention that **reflective practice** is just "a waste of time with all that touchy feely stuff." Many, however, say "I wish I had more time to reflect."

In our work facilitating reflective thinking through the generative dialogue, we have observed that carefully structured and purposeful activities to encourage reflection engender insight, problem solving, critical thinking, interpersonal and intellectual engagement, and analysis. We also note a palpable sense of calm when teachers and leaders deconstruct their practice and arrive at some clear conclusions for action.

As we will discuss further throughout the text, we work through a process that embeds, at various stages, three types of reflection: for practice, in practice, and on practice. Taken together, we find that reflective thinking is under-utilized in tapping into an enormous potential to honour existing expertise while increasing achievement of individual and organizational goals.

Collaboration Is a Nice Idea but, in Reality, It Just Takes Too Much Time
for Too Few Results

We are strident advocates for the power of teams. In all schools and districts with which we have worked, we have seen a measurable shift toward collaborative efficacy that can be evidenced over time by increased student achievement and numerous other indicators of accountability and organizational efficiency. In all our data collected about the work of teams, the message from teachers and leaders has been clear: "Collaborate, collaborate, and then collaborate some more!"[1]

Teachers and leaders enjoy and believe they benefit from multiple regularized opportunities at the school and district levels to share experiences, expertise, and learnings with colleagues; to support each other's goal achievement and celebrate success and growth; to learn how to build and sustain healthy and functional professional communities; and to engage in generative dialogues about actualizing the important work of enhancing student learning. Even students and parents have told us that "Collaborative time has allowed teachers to work together, share strategies, and be creative."

We recommend that collaborative processes and structures be institutionalized and embedded, even as the professional goals and work of educators may be individualized and personalized. Norms and protocols for collaborative work and collaborative learning should be established and articulated repeatedly, in various and diverse contexts. Distinction should be made between **collaborative *learning* time**, **collaborative *work* time**, and **collaborative *social* time**; more of the first, but some of all.

Effective Leaders Keep People Fearful and on the Edge of Their Seats
to Maximize Results

A few principals we have met over the years verbalized beliefs and demonstrated behaviours associated with keeping teachers just on the edge of fear. These beliefs and behaviours were predicated on a desire to keep teachers motivated to always do all that was expected of them.

Fear arises from uncertainty. Fear is a reaction to the unknown by people who don't fully trust that great things can arise from experimentation, trial and error, and a desire to push the limits of current practice. Fear can find an effective place when the old adage of the fight or flight principle occurs. If a teacher is on playground supervision and a bull bison enters the scene (we have been in a school when this happened), then fear for children and their safety takes priority and the teacher gets students moving quickly toward the door. However, fear does not work when a teacher is striving to make guided reading with the children purposeful, meaningful, and organized. If this teacher knows the principal is watching closely and will jump in and "tell them what to do" the minute a mistake is made, if the children are getting too loud, or if fellow teachers start to complain that the teacher is getting too "experimental," then the desire to grow will be diminished and the status quo will prevail. Fear, except in those rare occasions when bull bison are chasing you on a playground, only hinders performance.

Basing Decisions on Evidence Is Just Work to Justify My Existence

Educators are constantly being asked to do something in their working lives because someone else thinks it's a good idea. For many, a first response to any new request is a firm "No." Most educators with whom we work have a healthy skepticism of all new ideas. So, when we first asked teams of educators if they would provide evidence of changes in student learning as a result of changes in teaching practice, we were not particularly surprised when many resisted such an idea. It *was* a new idea. It was more work. It was redundant. It was offensive ("Why can't you just take my word for it?"). It was irrelevant university researcher stuff, not teachers' work. It took precious time away from students.

In our projects covering the last five years especially, we have developed richer meanings for the term *shared responsibility* as it applies to the work of people from within schools in collaboration with people from outside schools. All taken-for-granted assumptions need to be explored carefully and often. The voices of all participants need to be heard. It is no secret that our success in school improvement has been shown to be heavily dependent on the ability of participants to listen more effectively. In fact, a key conclusion in two of our larger initiatives has been that active listening is *the* most important communication skill. If educators get the notion that their voices are being muted or others are not listening to them, they have numerous time-tested strategies for dealing with such situations.

Perhaps a more specific example could enhance this discussion. It is most likely we first encountered the term *evidence-based practice* (as applied to education) in a conference program in the United Kingdom in 1997. It has come into more common use only over the last five years, but, in practice, acceptance for its applicability to the work of schools still faces regular challenge from many educators. Like *clinical supervision* before it, **evidence-based practice** can conjure up such images as white lab coats, clipboards, hierarchies of expertise, sterile conditions, and presumed objectivity that are anathema to the views many teachers have of their classrooms and their practice.

Through the collaborative inquiry process—the methodology that we have adapted for all our school improvement initiatives—we have had some obvious success in helping educators stay true to their own philosophies of teaching, while, at the same time, helping them take increased responsibility for showing how their more purposeful efforts on behalf of their students have actually resulted in the outcomes they intended to achieve.

The collaborative inquiry process encourages educators to pursue their goals with attention to an important guiding question. In reality, as educators work together to find the answers to their questions, they uncover or develop the *evidence* of the extent to which they are achieving their goals. It's an educative approach. Participants in all our projects make a commitment to continuous professional learning; their own learning is as important as the learning of their students. Accordingly, they are more willing to share both the practices and the outcomes of their planned, joint efforts.

Successful collaboration is hard work. We have written about the power of collaboration as *people of goodwill working together to achieve agreed-upon goals*. In our experience, nothing gives school leaders and teams of teachers more satisfaction in their professional work than successful collaboration.

There Is a Right Way and a Wrong Way to Do Leadership from Within

We worked, briefly, with a superintendent who spent inordinate amounts of time working on the district budget and meeting with school board members. He told us he felt that was the best use of his (considerable) financial expertise, his political skills, and his time, so his principals would be freer to perform their instructional leadership roles.

Another superintendent with whom we shared a long professional relationship derived great satisfaction and earned the respect of all his principals when he helped negotiate a new set of relationships between schools and the district office. He worked tirelessly. He won awards. He gained the trust of teachers and custodians alike. However, in the time he was superintendent, the provincially mandated tests of curriculum results in his district continued to decline. He retired, never having been able to build consensus and commitment among his school leaders that they should develop strategies for improving student learning as evidenced by external exam results.

We have worked with principals who have combined book studies and crucial conversations to move their teaching staffs forward successfully. Alternately, we have known one director whose strategies for helping school leaders improve included sending them a new book to read every month and lecturing them on the main points of each book at every principals' meeting.

We have been impressed to the point of wonder at the almost-spiritual leadership of a superintendent who has been able to show care and concern for virtually everyone in the district, and, almost simultaneously, we have watched a central leadership team in another district build the capacity of teachers and principals, influence morale and commitment, and create a sense of *inspiration* among staff and students in their rural school district.

We are often asked to provide lists of things that good leaders can do, or say, or be—lists of questions to ask, lists of attributes, lists of actions—suggesting that many educators may hold the belief that there is one right way to lead from within. It's more likely that there are as many "wrong" ways to lead from within as there are "right" ways, but one thing has become more certain for us as we continue to work on school improvement initiatives; that is, there are *more* effective and *less* effective ways of leading and building leadership capacity. There *is* a body of research and practice that offers guidance and support for those who have the courage to lead, and the leadership *context* is probably every bit as important as any other factor in determining whether leadership from within becomes a reality or remains a dream.

We have maintained, for many years, that school improvement occurs one classroom at a time, one school at a time, and one district at a time. A corollary to that conclusion is that leadership from within succeeds one context at a time.

SYNOPSIS: HOW DO QUESTIONING LEADERS CAUSE GROWTH FROM WITHIN?

- Create inclusive, dynamic documents that are frequently referenced and revised
- Demonstrate and model the spirit of the vision
- Connect goals at all levels with reference to vision
- Encourage reflection on goals and vision
- Honour individual and group values in balance
- Model ethical decision making based on collective vision
- Model growth in teaching and leading
- Excel in interpersonal relationships
- Use evidence to support growth
- Encourage experimentation
- Provide support; don't instill fear

REFLECTIONS AND WRITING PROVOCATIONS FOR GROWTH FROM WITHIN

We often use a strategy of reflective writing to encourage leaders to think more deeply about assumptions and world views that may hinder growth from within. In this regard, free-form writing has been particularly helpful. As we use it, free-form writing requires leaders to make only two commitments to thinking about their leadership experiences: don't stop writing until an agreed-upon time limit is reached; and don't correct, censor, judge, or otherwise evaluate the thoughts that are being written.

We have used the following provocation stems to encourage reflections around growth from within:

- A fundamental belief about my colleagues' levels of effectiveness is that …
- Implementing a vision for a school or system is only as good as …
- The role of reflection in learning is …
- My role in enhancing student learning is …
- Leading learning is a priority that …

Select one of the prompts for yourself. Write for an amount of time that starts to make you feel a little uncomfortable. Read what you wrote. Reflect on what you have written. If you feel comfortable with sharing your writing, please do so with a trusted colleague.

SUGGESTED READINGS FOR GROWTH FROM WITHIN

Argyris, C. (1993). *Knowledge for action: A guide to overcoming barriers to organizational change.*
New York, NY: Jossey-Bass.

Argyris proposes that organizational progress stalls because people don't learn. He also argues that personalities and personal histories evoke defensive routines that prevent effective learning, and he identifies a four-step process to move through this resistance. The process moves through internally motivated investigation to sharing and facilitating change by honouring the voices of individuals and identifying points of impact. Argyris closes by describing situations that could derail organizational change initiatives—such as trust, explosive relationships, dysfunctional routines, and changes in personnel—and offers advice on mitigating risk during transition and transformation.

Collins, J., & Hansen, M. T. (2011). *Great by choice.* New York, NY: Harper Collins.

In this sequel to Collins' *Good to Great* (2001), the authors investigate why some organizations cope well amidst uncertainty while others struggle. They identify the principles required for organizational success amidst chaos by focusing on a group of exemplar organizations they refer to as "10x" in which the best leaders were not risk takers, but rather were disciplined and evidence-based. They contend that the most stellar organizations take a measured approach to change, characterized by clear, measured, creative, and strategic decisions made from within.

Dweck, C. (2006). *Mindset: The new psychology of success.* New York, NY: Random House.

Carol Dweck studied schoolchildren who became discouraged after failure because they believed their failures were due to a lack of ability. She defines mindset as a belief about one's self and one's basic qualities: either fixed or growth. In this book, Dweck reveals how established attitudes can influence organizational effectiveness. Her theory of mindset continues to gain popularity in classrooms, staff rooms, and organizational boardrooms as a way to understand the importance of building from within.

Hallinger, P., & Huber, S. (2012). School leadership that makes a difference: International perspectives, school effectiveness, and school improvement. *An International Journal of Research, Policy and Practice, 23*(4), 359–367.

Researchers Hallinger and Huber examine the impact of school leaders on teaching and learning. In addition to exploring leadership practices and effects in a wide range of national contexts, they identify articles that describe international research on school leadership. The authors posit that such research provides a broader perspective that can help inform the present school reform movement in North America.

Hargreaves, A., & Fink, D. (2004). Seven principles of sustainable leadership. *Educational Leadership, 61*(7), 8–13.

Hargreaves and Fink recognize sustainable leadership as a shared, active, and enduring responsibility to cross-fertilize good ideas and successful practices throughout the school community. The authors argue that, despite the best intentions of many leaders to leave a legacy, it is the *system* that has been failing. If change is to matter and persist, Hargreaves and Fink contend, leaders can further promote sustainability by considering how they approach, commit to, and protect deep learning from within their schools.

Senge, P. M. (2006). *The fifth discipline: The art and practice of the learning organization.* New York, NY: Doubleday.

Peter Senge revisits the concepts introduced in his 1990 book of the same name, adding over 100 pages of experiences. He proposes that the most effective way for organizations to maintain a competitive advantage is to *learn* faster, not *do* faster. He contends that the principal instruments of learning involve five disciplines and that the fifth discipline, systems thinking, is the cornerstone of the learning organization. One foundational concept that Senge explores involves patterns of behaviour, referred to as *archetypes*, that doom organizations to perpetual cycles of ineffectiveness. He contends that learning organizations can break unproductive cycles by finding a leverage point where targeted actions can have large impacts.

Senge, P. M., Smith, B., Kruschwitz, N., Laur, J., & Schley, S. (2008). *The necessary revolution: How individuals and organizations are working together to create a sustainable world.* New York, NY: Doubleday.

This collaborative work brings together a network of authors who contend that leaders employing decades-old habits and thinking processes render organizations unable to grow. The authors propose that new thinking is required to ensure organizational health and that small incremental changes may not be sufficient for transformation. Senge et al. issue a call for collaboration across silos and specialties, encourage systems thinking, and propose a move away from problem solving to creatively thinking about situations in new ways. *The Necessary Revolution* identifies a need to look within to shift the way we envision organizations and leadership.

REFERENCES

Bandura, A. (1993). Perceived self-efficacy in cognitive development and functioning. *Educational Psychologist, 28*(2), 117–148.

Barnes, C., Camburn, E., Sanders, B., & Sebastion, J. (2010). Developing instructional leaders: Using mixed methods to explore the black box of planned change in principals' professional practice. *Educational Administration Quarterly, 46*(2), 242–279. doi:10.1177/1094670510361748

Bedard, J., Mombourquette, C., & Aitken, A. (2013). Calgary Catholic School District. In J. Brandon, P. Hanna, & K. Rhyason (Eds.), *Vision in action: Seven approaches to school system success* (pp. 165–231). Edmonton, AB: Henday.

Bennis, W., & Nanus, B. (1985). *Leaders: The strategies for taking charge.* New York, NY: Harper & Row.

Bottoms, G., & Schmidt-Davis, J. (2010). *The three essentials: Improving schools requires district vision, district and state support, and principal leadership.* Atlanta, GA: Southern Regional Education Board.

Bowers, A. J. (2009). Reconsidering grades as data for decision making: More than just academic knowledge. *Journal of Educational Administration, 47*(5), 609–629. doi:http://dx.doi.org/10.1108/09578230910981080

Boyd, V. (1992). *School context: Bridge or barrier to change?* Austin, TX: Southwest Educational Development Laboratory.

Butler, D., Schnellert, L., & MacNeil, K. (2015). Collaborative inquiry and distributed agency in educational change: A case study of multi-level community of inquiry. *Journal of Educational Change, 16,* 1–26. doi:10.1007/s10833-014-9227-z

Chappuis, S., Chappuis, J., & Stiggins, R. (2009). The quest for quality. *Educational Leadership, 67*(3), 14–19.

Copland, M. (2003). Leadership of inquiry: Building and sustaining capacity for school improvement. *Educational Evaluation and Policy Analysis, 25*(4), 375–395.

Datnow, A., Park, V., & Wohlstetter, P. (2007). *Achieving with data.* Los Angeles, CA: Center on Educational Governance.

DuFour, R., & DuFour, R. (2012). *The school leader's guide to professional learning communities at work.* Bloomington, IN: Solution Tree Press.

DuFour, R., & Eaker, R. (1998). *Professional learning communities at work: Best practices for enhancing student achievement.* Bloomington, IN: NES.

DuFour, R., & Marzano, R. (2011). *Leaders of learning: How district, school, and classroom leaders improve student achievement.* Bloomington, IN: Solution Tree Press.

Fullan, M., & Hargreaves, A. (2016). Bringing the profession back in: Call to action. Oxford, OH: Learning Forward.

Fullan, M., Rincon-Gallardo, S., & Hargreaves, A. (2015). Professional capital as accountability. *Education Policy Analysis Archives, 23*(15), 1–22. http://dx.doi.org/10.14507/epaa.v23.1998

Goleman, D. (2005), *Emotional intelligence: Why it can matter more than IQ.* New York, NY: Bantam.

Goleman, D., Boyatzis, R. E., & McKee, A. (2002). *Primal leadership: Learning to lead with emotional intelligence.* Cambridge, MA: Harvard Business School Press.

Gronn, P. (2002). Distributed leadership as a unit of analysis. *The Leadership Quarterly, 13*(4), 423–451. doi:http://dx.doi.org/10.1016/S1048-9843(02)00120-0

Hallinger, P., & Heck, R. (1996). Reassessing the principal's role in school effectiveness: A review of empirical research, 1980–1995. *Educational Administration Quarterly, 32*(1), 5–44. doi:10.1177/0013161x96032001002

Honig, M. (2012). District central office leadership as teaching: How central office administrators support principals' development as instructional leaders. *Educational Administration Quarterly, 48*, 733–774. doi:10.1177/0013161X12443258

Knapp, M. S., Copland, M., & Swinnerton, J. A. (2007). Understanding the promise and dynamics of data-informed leadership. In P. A. Moss (Ed.), *Evidence and decision making. 106th yearbook of the National Society for the Study of Education* (Part I, pp. 74–104). Malden, MA: Blackwell.

Knapp, M. S., Copland, M. A., Honig, M. I., Plecki, M. L., & Portin, B. S. (2010). Urban renewal: The urban school leader takes on a new role. *Journal of Staff Development, 31*(2), 24–29.

Lambert, L. (2005). Leadership for lasting reform. *Educational Leadership, 62*(5), 62–65.

Leithwood, K. (2013). *Strong districts and their leadership: A paper commissioned by the Council of Ontario Directors of Education and the Institute for Education Leadership*. Retrieved from www.ontariodirectors.ca/ downloads/Strong%20Districts-2.pdf

Leithwood, K., Mascall, B., & Strauss, T. (Eds.). (2009). *Distributed leadership according to the evidence*. New York, NY: Routledge.

Luo, M. (2008). Structural equation modeling for high school principals' data-driven decision making: An analysis of information use environments. *Educational Administration Quarterly, 44*(5), 603–634.

Marzano, R., Waters, T., & McNulty, B. (2005). *School leadership that works: From research to results*. Alexandria, VA: Association for Supervision and Curriculum Development.

Mombourquette, C. (2017). The role of vision in effective school leadership. *International Studies in Educational Administration, 45*(1), 19–36.

Murphy, J., Elliott, S. N., Goldring, E., & Porter, A. C. (2007). Leadership for learning: A research-based model and taxonomy of behaviors. *School Leadership & Management, 27*(2), 179–201. doi:10.1080/13632430701237420

Naseer, A. S. (2011). Successful leadership practices of head teachers for school improvement. *Journal of Educational Administration, 49*(4), 414–432. doi:http://dx.doi.org/10.1108/09578231111146489

Owen, S. (2015). Teacher professional learning communities in innovative contexts: "Ah haha moments", "passion" and "making a difference" for student learning. *Professional Development in Education, 41*(1), 57–74. doi:10.1080/19415257.2013.869504

Pan, H.-L., Nyeu, F.-L., & Cheng, S.-H. (2017). Leading schools for learning: Principal practices in Taiwan. *Journal of Educational Administration, 55*(2), 168–185. doi:10.1108/JEA-06-2016-0069

Schnellert, L., & Butler, D. (2014). Collaborative inquiry: Empowering teachers in their professional development. *Education Canada, 54*(3), 18–22.

Seashore Louis, K., Dretzke, B., & Wahlstrom, K. (2010). How does leadership affect student achievement? Results from a national US survey. *School Effectiveness & School Improvement, 21*(3), 315–336. doi:10.1080/09243453.2010.486586

Timperley, H. (2011). *Realizing the power of professional learning.* Maidenhead, UK: Open University Press.

Tschannen-Moran, M. (2009). Fostering teacher professionalism in schools: The role of leadership orientation and trust. *Educational Administration Quarterly, 45*(2), 217–247. doi:10.1177/0013161x08330501

Waters, T., Marzano, R., & McNulty, B. (2003). *Balanced leadership: What 30 years of research tells us about the effect of leadership on student achievement: Mid-Continent Research for Education and Learning.* Retrieved from http://www.mcrel.org/

Westley, H., & Mintzberg, F. (1989). Visionary leadership and strategic management. *Strategic Management Journal, 10,* 17–32.

White, R., Cooper, K., & Anwaruddin, S. (2017). Canadian contexts in educational leadership: A hermeneutic approach to distributed leadership for teachers' professional learning. *International Journal of Leadership in Education, 20*(6), 682–696. https://doi.org/10.1080/13 603124.2016.1210827

Ylimaki, R. M. (2006). Toward a new conceptualization of vision in the work of educational leaders: Cases of the visionary archetype. *Educational Administration Quarterly, 42*(4), 620–651. doi:10.1177/0013161x06290642

CHAPTER TWO

Where Can Growth Begin?

To build community requires vigilant awareness of the work we must continually do to undermine all the socialization that leads us to behave in ways that perpetuate domination.

—*bell hooks*

Everything I do should support our teachers in their critically important role of building quality learning communities in every classroom. This requires commitment to a comprehensive series of supports to ensure that teachers flourish, feel engaged and part of a community in achieving great teaching.

—*School division superintendent*

BEGINNING THE GROWTH PROCESS

The impact of the *learning community* phenomenon in environments educational and corporate has been profound. What started as a faint metaphor in the mid-1990s for re-structuring workspace, re-allotting task completion, or facilitating employee creativity and brainstorming passed quickly through stages of fad and trend to become, worldwide, one of the most commonly accepted structures and visions of effective organizations. Moreover, it is now generally acknowledged to be an important condition that leaders must create in order that collaborative learning and professional growth can thrive.

This chapter takes up an examination of learning communities as an essential consideration of the extent to which leaders are successful in leveraging the skills, knowledge, and attributes of all members of their organization. Who are these leaders and how do they set the stage for success through promoting a sense of community and collaboration?

After visiting hundreds of self-proclaimed learning communities over the past decade, we have concluded that it is rare for any one school to meet all the criteria of most commonly accepted definitions of the phrase. In several, leaders reorganized aspects of the organizational schedule so that frequent collaboration could occur; in others, leadership is strong and broadly shared; and, in many, leaders' commitment

to evidence-based practice has been exemplary. However, most of these schools unevenly exhibit the critical
characteristics of learning communities. It is true that
most of them have mission and vision statements.
Many are required by law to produce education plans
that incorporate school goals. School districts require all teachers to prepare and follow a professional
growth plan that must be shared with an administrator. Many of these schools attempt
to reflect and honour the values of the communities they serve, even if they are less clear
about incorporating the values of staff members into operating practices consistent with
the learning communities philosophy. And, while a majority claim to be learning communities, they vary widely in their ability to provide appropriate learning opportunities
for all students, involve parents in the work of the school, and come to terms with the
competing value systems of government, district administrators, staff, students, and
parents. In practice, the learning communities model may be based on an ideal that
is unattainable for many schools, even if a majority of leaders actually have a positive
disposition toward it.

As you start this chapter, think about the learning communities in your school(s). How closely do they attend to all the criteria commonly associated with PLCs?

Yet the level of rhetoric and expectation—that leaders will create and sustain the
conditions that characterize effective learning communities—is so great that some feel
compelled to indulge in a form of wishful thinking that has them reporting, sometimes quite fancifully, on the extent to which they see their organizations operating as
functional learning communities. Unfortunately, when the gap grows too wide between
what leaders hope is happening and what's *really* happening in a school, it can trigger
a negatively reinforcing downward spiral of lost opportunity, lowered morale, and increased cynicism. In short, this gap triggers a pattern of response to change that occurs
all too frequently in public education.

And yet most leaders of schools or districts believe they are already operating as
learning communities (or they wish they were). The concept of the learning community is a powerful one, but when it is implemented by executive fiat, or when schools, in
attempting to become learning communities, organize themselves in ways that are in
sharp contradiction to the fundamental principles of the concept itself, trouble ensues.
One of the reasons some schools are unable, or unwilling, to adopt the learning communities' model is that there is too often a mismatch between the implementation process and the culture of the school.

In this chapter, we first offer the case study of Principal John Francis and tell the
story of his success and challenges with using a learning community approach to recalibrate the culture of a school. We then offer a diagnostic tool that many leaders
have administered to get a sense of levels of awareness, readiness, and functioning of
the learning community as they set the stage for implementing a model of leadership
characterized by powerful questions.

Case Study: John Francis Accepts the Challenge of Change

The staff at Concordia Junior High School (CJHS) believed in the axiom "We're okay, you're okay." On the whole, they were a hardy crew of veterans confident in their ability to control and enlighten 650 adolescents, socialize a smattering of neophyte teachers, and neutralize just about any

> As you read the John Francis case study, compare CJHS with your school or a school you know well. What is similar? What is different?

administrator. As head of the math department, Sylvia Hammer was fond of crowing, in reference to school principals, "We've seen 'em come, and we'll see 'em go."

When he was appointed principal of this large junior high school, John Francis replaced a colleague who had held the position for the previous six years. A kind and gentle person, the departing principal was moving into retirement. In his first address to the staff, John's message was naively simple. "I am a different kind of principal and I hope you agree that this can be a different kind of school." Staff members were divided over whether or not to believe him. Most of them were not risk-takers. Collectively, they were comfortable with their principal telling them what to do and then staying out of their way. They had predictable, time-honoured mission and vision statements that they believed represented the will of most members of the community, and they were reluctant to change.

However, almost in spite of their reservations, the staff agreed to participate in some team-building and professional development activities that helped them to coalesce around a new mission, a new vision statement, a new slogan, and a new set of goals for the year. After only two meetings directed by John, quick agreement was reached about these important statements. Then, in a few short months filled with challenges and conversations, a subtle shift began to occur. It was given impetus when the administrative team rearranged the school timetable to accommodate daily grade-level meetings that focused on what (almost) everyone had agreed were the school's two top priorities: student learning and professional growth. Based on the authority he felt he had derived from the evolving staff consensus, John began to ask his whole staff to reconsider many of their assumptions about teaching and learning. For example, in response to a staff member's call for a change in dealing with Indigenous students, John asked, "How does that fit with our new mission and vision?" When a group of teachers raised concerns about student behaviour, they were asked, "What can *you* contribute to help solve this problem?" And, when a grade-level team argued for a new structure for their team meetings, they were first asked, "Can you make this part of your professional growth plan?" and then, "How does this help provide a better learning experience for your students?"

continued

Because they had become used to a previous culture characterized by complaining and blaming, many staff members were surprised by these new conversations: a few were offended, and others were unsure how to respond. Nevertheless, through making immediate and regular contact with all staff, through listening to their concerns, and through encouraging them to identify ways they thought they could contribute to the school, John moved steadily forward, and the staff followed.

Each month during the first year, staff members reconfirmed their commitment to the mission, vision, and goal statements. Monthly professional development meetings began with John asking such questions as "Do we still believe in the spirit and intent of these statements?" "Are these still our goals?" "Do we need to change any of these statements?" Perhaps the biggest change in the first year was a shift to shared language and expectations surrounding student learning and effective teaching. A commitment to trying to do things differently emerged. Student behaviour definitely improved. Incrementally, staff members and students adapted to more effective ways of working together. At the end of the year, a majority of staff members indicated their growing appreciation for John's style of leadership.

The second year could be characterized as the year of the team. Staff members increasingly embraced an ethos of collaboration and responsibility as they realized the principal would ensure that they could align their individual professional interests with the achievement of school goals. For example, sports academies were championed by staff members and, much more quickly than most teachers had thought possible, two academies—one for girls and one for boys—sprang into being. Building on the efforts of staff teams, the fine arts program expanded dramatically. In two grades, the academic program was refined to more effectively accommodate the unique needs of learners. The sharing of instructional materials and assessment instruments across grade levels became more pronounced. Student leadership flourished. Parent involvement escalated. The expansion of Indigenous student programming provided broader services for students whom regular classroom teachers may otherwise not have had the time or skill to help. Each small success seemed to promote another successful initiative. Each team's achievements encouraged the formation of more teams.

Still, there were some staff members who changed very little, and some who resisted collaboration. They carried their wait-and-see attitude through the first two years, not openly challenging John, but clearly not going along willingly with the majority of staff members. Nevertheless, the school community became more inclusive. Month by month, members of the support staff came to realize that they were seriously part of this developing community. Their voices were heard increasingly in every meeting and they became active participants in all professional development opportunities. Representatives of community agencies were seen to be much more involved in the work of the school. Word spread steadily throughout the city that Concordia school was a good place for students, and applications for registration increased accordingly.

During the third year, a broader sharing of strategies, concerns, opinions, and ideas became the way much of the work was done at Concordia. While the more entrenched teachers were taking the longest to adapt, all of them appeared to change aspects of their professional behaviour during this year. For example, one previously resistant teacher stepped forward and made a presentation to colleagues on preparing students for standardized tests. Two others opened their classrooms to student teachers for the first time in many years. Several invested time and effort in a re-examination of the curriculum. Others took a more active interest in community events. All staff moved more willingly toward making decisions about *our* students rather than *my* students. A highlight of the year was a massive and wildly successful fine arts festival that involved hundreds of students and almost every staff member.

In the meantime, the administrative team continued to model shared leadership. Most importantly, they rarely responded to a staff request by saying "You can't do it." Rather, they asked enabling questions, such as "How will you do this?" and "Is this the time to do it?" They created a climate in which it was increasingly okay for teachers to step forward to take reciprocal responsibility for what they thought would help the school better meet its goals.

As increasing numbers of teachers working in teams challenged themselves to become more familiar with curriculum and assessment, student learning was seen to steadily improve. One simple measure of this was observed in the weekly and monthly reviews of students' results shared in team meetings. In discussions leading to decision making, the staff moved from random uses of data to more frequent references to available data: What do we know about attendance? What do we know about parent satisfaction? What do we know about student achievement? Which students require more attention and support? Most staff became comfortable with sharing data, making sense of it, making decisions, and setting goals based on all available and relevant information. Student behaviour continued to improve over three years. Students became increasingly friendly, they interacted with adults in more respectful ways, and incidents of gross misbehaviour, as defined by office visitations and referrals, declined yearly.

The administrative team complemented each other in skills and personality. As well, they supported each other publicly even as they were willing to disagree privately. The team met daily to share information, and kept the staff fully informed about matters that affected the school. Their transparency regarding the school budget was more than most staff members expected, but it proved to be a benefit to the team when they were challenged by their superintendent to make draconian

continued

cuts to their proposed budget for the new school year. The whole staff stood in total support of their administrators, as did the members of their school council, who organized an unprecedented delegation to the school board. In the face of such solidarity, the board changed its decision in favour of the school. Through extensive role-modelling, high expectations, hard work, and a consistency of enthusiasm, caring, and focus, John succeeded, over time, in convincing this staff that he certainly was a different kind of principal. In turn, CJHS became a different kind of school.

And then, as so often happens, John accepted a new position in a new district, creating the very circumstances that can bedevil successful schools. Would his legacy be one of continuing growth and success, or would the school lapse back into its previous culture: benign, passive, and safe? Did Concordia Junior High School truly become a more effective community? Most of the staff claimed it had. Did it become better able to meet the needs of its students? Again, most of the staff were certain it had. Did the school become an exemplary learning community? Most staff members seemed sure they had embarked on a journey of learning. They liked what they were becoming. Some believed they had a ways to go, while others concluded that the journey would never end.

Ironically, when this staff was given the Learning Communities Survey at the beginning of the John Francis era, they rated themselves very high. Midway through John's term, they rated themselves appreciably lower, even as staff satisfaction with their leader and their working conditions had improved considerably. At the end, many staff members were still reluctant to rate themselves too high because, even as they acknowledged how far they had come, most of them were much more aware of how far they could go in becoming the best school they could be.

Case Study Reflections: Beginning the Growth Process
- Which of John's actions in building culture and community caused you to think differently about your own leadership?
- Why do you suppose so many staff members were inclined to go along with John's leadership?
- What was it about John's leadership that influenced the culture of the school?
- As a teacher, how might you have responded to John's questions, such as "Are these still our goals?" and "What can you contribute to help solve this problem?"
- What do you see as the primary actions taken by John that set the stage for change?
- Analyze the ways that the three-year cycle of cultural shift differs from your experiences.
- As a leader, what advice would you offer John to set the stage for change?

THE ESSENCE OF GROWTH: CREATING A CULTURE OF LEARNING

In one of our early studies of secondary schools, school principals were asked to describe the nature of their relationships with district office leaders. Perhaps the most telling response came from a former high school science teacher. He drew a space lab circling high above the earth, with his school far below. He wrote the following:

> They blasted off in a blaze of glory! Now they're all up there, totally out of reach. They beam down occasional messages and directives to us as they pass overhead but we have no way of answering them, so we tend to ignore them and just do what we know is best for our school.

Compare that commentary with survey evidence from two other school districts in which school leaders almost unanimously reported exceedingly high levels of trust and respect for their superintendents. Why the difference? How does that happen?

We have observed that it begins with a certainty in the minds of superintendents that they, alone, cannot possibly cause schools to improve, but they, alone, can certainly cause schools to perform less well. Therefore, they must lead the way in strengthening relationships and building partnerships. This means building strong teams, starting with the district leadership teams.

> Take a few minutes to consider the role you think system leaders should play in helping schools meet goals for student learning. Should they set the stage and get out of the way? Should they actively participate in the process?

In successful leadership growth and school improvement initiatives, it is less likely that effective school leadership teams will thrive if the district leadership team cannot. Put another way, strong district leadership teams are able to help foster the growth of strong school leadership teams. In turn, if school leadership teams are strong, there is a much greater likelihood that norms of distributed leadership will take root in the culture of those schools, and more numerous and **effective teams** of teachers will be able to take on an increasingly shared responsibility for the leadership of learning. To extend this idea even further, if schools are not able to support the growth of effective teams of teachers, it is less likely that those schools will show significant improvement over time.

We have concluded that the leadership of learning in any district begins with a strong commitment to high quality relationships, modelled first and frequently by district leadership. However, such relationships should not exist in isolation or devoid of context. Accordingly, in more successful organizations, collaboration is the means by which strong relationships are given greater purpose. Through collaboration, educators build trust and mutual respect. We propose that staff members don't have to love each other—they don't necessarily have to like each other very much!—but they have to be able to respect the work, and the sincerity of purpose, of their leaders and their colleagues. Otherwise, effectiveness suffers. As Goleman, Boyatzis, and McKee (2002) note,

"Climate—how people feel about working in an organization—can account for 20–30% of performance" (p. 18).

Yet relationships and collaboration alone do not make great organizations. Some form of creative tension is necessary in the daily lives of educators to bring focus to critical elements of professional practice that they want to improve or refine.

CREATING A CULTURE OF LEARNING

Barth (2002), a long-acknowledged expert in the area of school culture, defined the elusive construct as "a complex pattern of norms, attitudes, beliefs, behaviors, values, ceremonies, traditions, and myths that are deeply ingrained in the very core of the organization" (p. 6). Furthermore, Barth goes on to say that "it is the historically transmitted pattern of meaning that wields astonishing power in shaping what people think and how they act" (p. 6). Principals, both those who are new to the school and those with years of tenure, must quickly come to terms with the existing culture of the school and take the lead on reshaping it—or become a victim to its power.

Before a principal can come to terms with school culture, the construct must first be recognized. An inventory of existing ceremonies, traditions, and artifacts often forms the initial steps in culture identification. Coming to know the norms, attitudes, beliefs, and values takes much patience and ongoing watching, listening to, and dialoguing with staff, students, and parents. In time, however, a skillful leader will parse out the deeply held beliefs and make moves to fashion improved behaviours from all members of the organization. Efforts to improve culture will move the school toward achieving the agreed-upon vision, mission, and goals (Balkar, 2015; Deal & Peterson, 2009; Fullan, 2016).

To create a school culture where student learning can be at the forefront of all that is done in the building often requires that careful and dexterous attention be given to 12 seemingly common sense, yet rather elusive, norms. These norms are:

- Collegiality—Sharing of ideas, experiences, and expertise in a manner that is based on a genuine desire to see student learning increase. Being open to the suggestions of others and having a willingness to try new ideas gleaned from the shared experiences of colleagues working together.
- Experimentation—Trying new ways to improve student learning without the fear of failure lingering in the background. An openness to not only exploring new ideas but to also trying them. When the new way works, it is celebrated. When it is shown to be not really working, then blame is not assessed; it becomes a learning experience.
- High expectations—Having high expectations for self, others, and the team is the norm. There is a built-in expectation that experimentation happens, that new ideas are tried, that a push to become better is universal.

- Trust and confidence—Developing an environment where leaders trust staff, and staff trust leaders, is crucial. Trusting relationships lead directly to people being confident in each other and their abilities to try new and innovative ways to impact students' learning.
- Tangible support—"Being there" for one another and acting as champions for the growing confidence in the abilities of the team to impact student learning also, on occasion, requires supports to be put in place. These supports take on the air of commitment to ongoing professional learning and professional development. They also require financial commitments being made, even when money is tight and priorities are many.
- Reaching out to the knowledge base—An understanding has to be present that there are already existing great ways to get children to grow as students. Research, the use of data, and informed practice all culminate in a quest for better ways to maximize student learning. Embedded in this norm lies an innate curiosity that leads teachers as individuals and teams of teachers collectively to search the research literature for cutting edge, as well as long standing, practices that they can use to perform action research on and see if the "proven" works for their context.
- Appreciation and recognition—Showing respect for the good work that is occurring becomes a natural part of a school culture that is focused on the primacy of student learning. By giving appreciation and publicly acknowledging the good works that go on in the school, an atmosphere of trust, respect, and honour becomes part of the way things are done.
- Caring, celebration, and humour—"Being there" also means a physical presence where support is shown for each other, good works are celebrated, and laughter is a regular occurrence. The work of school is difficult. If it were easy, anybody could do it. With hard work also has to come a sense of play, where people on the team support each other, enjoy each other's company, and celebrate often the successes enjoyed.
- Involvement in decision making—Sharing widely the ability to influence decisions that impact student learning becomes a regular part of doing school. *Flatten the hierarchy, share the leadership, shared decision making,* and *teacher participation in decision-making processes* are all terms that become synonymous with providing a structure that allows for wide involvement in the decision-making processes of the school. The wider the involvement, the greater the likelihood of a culture that is focused on maximizing learning for all students, as the people most closely connected with doing the actual work associated with student learning are keenly involved in the decisions.
- Protection of what is important—Valuing the process of setting and living vision, mission, and goals for education. What is valued needs to be protected. When school vision, mission, and goals are clearly sighted on the primacy of

student learning, then all the ancillary things that go on in schools become just that: ancillary. The important "stuff," like teacher time with students, is protected at all costs. Principal time with teachers, in classrooms, and in teams, is also protected and honoured by central office leaders. Valuing what is important is shown when meetings just for the sake of meetings are not held, announcements during instructional time are simply not made, and being taken away from students during prime learning time does not happen.

- Traditions—Keeping in mind the great line from *Fiddler on the Roof*, tradition, in our sense of the word, "is trying to keep everyone, and everything, together." True for family and also true for school. Traditions give a sense of place and time within the context of history and a recognition of where the community has come from, yet also understanding that culture and the way of doing things will change and evolve. The tricky part is allowing for growth while also knowing what is valued and worth holding on to for the long term.

- Open, honest communication—Being able to speak one's mind while also being open to hearing, understanding, and honouring the voices of those around you keeps the organization healthy and focused on the needs of student learning.

WHAT ARE LEARNING COMMUNITIES?

As noted earlier, it is a rare organization that has not, at some point, declared itself a learning community, even in spite of evidence to the contrary. This miscalibration may be explained in several ways. On the surface, it may seem reasonable to expect that communities can create, promote, and sustain a collaborative and collegial work life based on an appreciation for learning. However, the focused effort and constant attention required to achieve such a goal has led many schools and districts to abandon the ideal and accommodate the pragmatic. They have come to think about the idea of a learning community less as a guiding structure and more as a terminal destination to be checked off an accountability list. Such relativization of the term does not acknowledge the complex processes and levels of responsibility that must accompany efforts to create and sustain those healthy elements of community that contribute most to success.

All learning communities, like all families, are not necessarily functional; the fact of their existence does not automatically imply effectiveness. Vibrant learning communities, like healthy families, can be clearly defined and identified by specific incremental rather than dichotomous criteria. Similarly, dysfunctional learning communities are characterized by particular tendencies toward such things as goal setting, decision making, problem solving, and relationships that are not absolute but that, more likely, fall along a continuum of effectiveness, depending on a host of contextual factors.

Too often, authors write extensively about the fundamental importance of learning communities to school and system effectiveness without acknowledging the reality that there are *more* and *less* effective learning communities. Readers are too often left with the impression that once the learning community designation is bestowed on an organization, that organization now possesses all the virtues that can be attached to the title.

In 2000, we began experimenting with a model that could be used by leaders to ascertain which aspects of their organization reflected characteristics of learning communities that were most essential to setting the stage for success. The model is based on critical dimensions of a learning community. For each dimension, we developed six characteristics, and for each of those, a set of key indicators. Tables 2.1 through 2.5 outline these dimensions.

Table 2.1: Dimension One—Growing Mission and Vision from Within

Characteristic	Key Question
Development	What is the process by which statements of mission and vision are created in your school?
Commitment	Do students, parents, and all staff feel ownership of the content and intent of your mission and vision statements?
Connection to Goals	Is the content and purpose of mission and vision statements reflected clearly in the goals of your school?
Connection to Principles	Do the mission and vision statements honour the guiding principles of your school?
Connection to Action	What are some activities in your school that demonstrate the purpose and goals of your mission and vision statements?
Reflection of Values	Do your mission and vision statements capture the shared values of individuals and groups in your school?

Table 2.2: Dimension Two—Building a Culture of Learning

Characteristic	Key Question or Indicator
Trust	How well do staff members depend on and share responsibility with and for each other?
Conflict Management	Are differences among members mediated in ways that enhance the achievement of goals?
Collaboration	In what ways are staff members supported in working with each other?
Teamwork	To what extent are the goals of the school achieved by members working with each other?
Sense of Belonging	What value do staff members place on membership in the school community, school identity, and loyalty?
Celebration	How do staff members show appreciation for each other? Does this affirm the work of all?

Table 2.3: Dimension Three—Examining Leadership

Characteristic	Key Question
Opportunities	How many people in your school are engaged with leadership responsibilities?
Availability	Through what means and with what frequency do your leaders make contact with staff and community members?
Modelling	What is the level of commitment of your school leaders to your teachers and their professional growth?
Risk-Taking	How would you describe the willingness of your leaders to take risks to achieve organizational goals?
Responsibility	Do your school leaders demonstrate commitment to appropriate standards of ethical and professional conduct?
Relationships	Do your school leaders engage in and promote relationships that facilitate the achievement of organizational goals?

Table 2.4: Dimension Four—Expectations to Provide Evidence

Characteristic	Key Question
Primary Focus	Is the majority of work done in your school based on and dedicated to learning?
Student Outcomes	What level of importance is accorded student learning and student achievement?
Staff Outcomes	Is the expectation of staff learning linked to school goals, mission, and vision?
Organizational Learning	How well does the school translate professional learning into enhanced effectiveness?
Opportunities for Growth	What is the quality of connections between explicit expectations for learning and structures that support professional growth?
Recognition	How do staff members show appreciation for each other? Does this affirm the work and worth of all members?

Table 2.5: Dimension Five—Organizational Processes and Structures

Characteristic	Key Question
Communication	How effective is communication among staff members and with other schools?
Policy	In what ways does policy guide practice and practice, in turn, inform policy?
Planning	Are planning activities purposeful and useful in helping the school achieve its goals?
Decision Making	Are your decision makers accessible and is the decision-making process transparent and respected by staff members?
How Work Gets Done	To what extent do staff members accept responsibility for contributing to the achievement of organizational goals?
Evaluation	How is the work and worth of all staff members assessed and valued?

Based on these criteria, we classified schools or districts into one of five different types of **communities**:

- **Withdrawn**: those least likely to consistently demonstrate the characteristics of effective organizations
- **Reactionary**: those most often exhibiting unresolved conflict, frustrated idealism, and a confrontational stance toward improvement initiatives
- **Benign**: those most often compliant and content with the status quo
- **Adaptive**: those infused with a sense of initiative-taking, productivity, and optimism
- **Generative**: those that consistently undertake actions that demonstrate enthusiastic commitment, mutual respect, and appreciation of inquiry

TYPES OF LEARNING COMMUNITIES

Through field testing and refinement, we created the rubrics found in tables 2.6–2.10 to provide a more detailed description of each characteristic of the five dimensions of the five types of learning communities.

ELABORATING UPON CHARACTERISTICS OF A GENERATIVE COMMUNITY

As mentioned earlier in this chapter, the notion of "community" has been explored over time and through many lenses, bound by disciplinary paradigms such as sociology, anthropology, business management, and psychology. Our inquiry into the nature and characteristics of education communities is often undertaken

> How does your understanding of a generative community compare with learning communities in your school? What characteristics would you add?

with feet simultaneously planted in several of these arenas, reflecting an interdisciplinary approach that crosses back and forth from the corporate world, to the academic, to the technical. In fact, some of the criteria that we use to define generative communities originated through our participation in corporate training events and transferred to our discoveries about communities in universities and public schools.

At the outset, we should be clear that generative communities are defined by "growing," rather than by "achieving." The pursuit of perfection may be alluring, and we have seen many schools and districts work frenetically over a short period of time to reach a pre-identified state of affairs that will allow everyone to breathe a collective sigh of relief that the work is finally done. They can be heard to declare, "Phew … that was a lot of extra work. I'm glad that project is over!" This is not the case in generative communities. As a matter of fact, one of the most notable characteristics of these types of

Table 2.6: Dimension One—Mission and Vision

	Withdrawn	Reactionary	Benign	Adaptive	Generative
Development	Non-participative, possibly non-existent.	Top down. In-groups and out-groups.	Statements may exist, but are rarely referred to.	Broad-based participation and recognition of statements' importance.	Inclusive, dynamic documents to which frequent reference is made.
Commitment	Few people know; few people care.	Often contrary. Often triggers argument and ill-will.	Low levels of engagement and interest.	Trying to honour the spirit of mission and vision statements.	Living out the spirit of the mission and vision, and constantly seeking refinement and improvement.
Connection to Goals	Goals are not identified and not aligned with mission and vision.	Source of conflict. Active, generalized disagreement with the relationship between goals, mission, and vision.	Little effort expended in making these connections.	Purposeful effort at alignment. Commitment to goals is explicit.	Fully engaged in goal achievement. Connections to goals are the foundation of action.
Connection to Principles	Principles are rarely mentioned. Members may not know about organizational principles.	Another source of conflict. Principles are often situational and relativized.	Members rarely engage in discussions about these connections.	Regular reference to guiding principles. Willingness to engage in productive debate over competing principles.	Principles guide action, and are constantly reviewed to test the appropriateness of connections to mission and vision.
Connection to Action	Action is idiosyncratic and rarely discussed.	Reasons for action may be highly personal, or they may serve competing political agendas.	Passive acceptance of reasons for action.	Actions are undertaken with reference to principles, goals, mission, and vision.	Action is purposeful, often collaborative, and frequently promotes reflection about goals, principles, mission, and vision.

Table 2.7: Dimension Two—A Culture of Learning

	Withdrawn	Reactionary	Benign	Adaptive	Generative
Trust	Low levels of interaction, risk-taking, and trust.	Episodic periods of intense interaction. Highly personal debate. Very low levels of trust.	Moderate levels of trust. Low levels of risk-taking.	High levels of interaction, risk-taking, and trust.	Very high levels of interaction, risk, and trust. Mutual respect is evident.
Conflict Management	Very low levels of engagement. "It's not my problem!"	Frequent engagement, open hostility, threats, subversion. "I'll get even!"	Low levels of engagement. "Let's not talk about it." "Don't rock the boat."	Moderate to high levels of engagement. "We have a problem. Let's try to solve it!"	High levels of engagement. Resolution of conflict builds organizational strength. "Never lose sight of the goal!"
Collaborative Opportunities	Rare and not welcome.	Short-term alliances for political reasons, rarely focused on learning or organizational goals.	Infrequent. Small groups may occasionally participate.	Frequent. Actively pursued. Often extended over long periods.	Very frequent, almost continuous. Engagement of all members is encouraged and rewarded.
Teamwork	Isolated events. Infrequent.	Often occurs for the wrong reasons, pitting one group against another.	Infrequent. Members do not seek opportunities.	Many different teams. Membership is fluid. Climate is supportive.	Short-term and long-term teams. Highly collaborative and inclusive of all stakeholder groups.
Sense of Belonging	Many people see themselves as outsiders. Limited sense of history.	Very low levels of loyalty. Competing claims to organizational memory. Divisive.	Low loyalty. Low levels of identification with organization.	Strong sense of identity. Agreement about collective memory. Symbols are displayed.	Highly refined sense of belonging in a climate of caring. Extensive use of symbols, icons, images, and metaphors.
Recognition and Celebration	Very low levels of interest or participation.	Individualistic. Recognition of some is often seen as the rejection of many. Dismissive.	Limited. In a good year, perhaps only half of members will attend a staff function.	Strong emphasis on awards, rewards, and symbols of success. Highly public displays.	Fully integrated into the work lives of members. Formal and informal. Frequent and varied.

Table 2.8: Dimension Three—Leadership

	Withdrawn	Reactionary	Benign	Adaptive	Generative
Opportunities	Succession planning not acknowledged; few formalized opportunities for leadership development.	Limited; the source of disputes; cliques prevail.	Leaders make few requests of members; members generally do not volunteer.	Leadership opportunities are distributed; member commitment is high.	Leadership selection is based on mission/vision, principles, and goals as well as merit and ability.
Availability	Formal leaders are inaccessible, not frequently sought out by members.	Formal leaders avoid certain members; gatekeeper function of leaders is apparent.	Formal positions, status, and lines of communication are most obvious.	Formal leaders are accessible and visible; leaders can be contacted through informal and formal channels.	Engaged in the work of the organization; decisions about availability and visibility are made purposefully.
Modelling Learning	Learning is seen as terminal and episodic, and not often relevant to all members.	Leaders' rhetoric about learning is greater than actual engagement. Efforts to model learning meet resistance.	No expectation that leaders should model learning.	Leaders are expected to be good teachers, to demonstrate their commitment to continuous learning.	Leaders are expected to be excellent teachers and life-long learners.
Risk-Taking	Risk-taking and creativity are not acknowledged as valuable.	Risk-taking is minimal and discouraged by other members.	Risk-taking is limited, not welcomed or recognized by members.	Risk-taking is encouraged and acknowledged by all members.	Key elements of organizational learning are characterized by innovation and risk-taking.
Responsibility	Behaviours are not transparent, and are not seen as contributing to organizational efficacy.	Leaders frequently take credit and assign blame. Members question leaders' motives.	Leaders emphasize accountability.	Leaders are expected to set an example. Ethical expectations are high.	Leaders model standards of ethical and professional conduct consistent with organizational mission/vision.
Relationships	Professional relationships are limited, cursory, and rarely connected to organizational goals.	Relationships are used for power and control, are situational, and are characterized by a lack of trust.	Relationships are formal and predictable.	Formal and informal relationships are encouraged. Mutual respect is promoted	Leaders excel in interpersonal relations. Mentorships flourish.

Table 2.9: Dimension Four—Evidence of Learning

	Withdrawn	Reactionary	Benign	Adaptive	Generative
Primary Focus	Greater emphasis on survival. Learning rarely discussed.	Greater emphasis on working conditions. Patterns of dispute repeat often.	Passive adherence to an emphasis on learning.	Commitment to learning is obvious.	Emphasis on learning permeates the organization.
Student Outcomes	Students appear to succeed despite the system. Students are allowed to fail.	Division between "your" students and "my" students is obvious. Results used for political reasons.	Emphasis on passing and accumulation of credits.	Students are encouraged; parents are involved. Teachers are ambitious and optimistic about student learning.	All children will learn. Learning is the primary focus.
Staff Outcomes	Rarely considered.	Great variety. Highly idiosyncratic.	Episodic attention to professional learning with low levels of staff interest.	Commitment to professional growth is high. Frequently linked to other outcomes.	Linked purposefully to goals and vision. Often collaborative.
Organizational Learning	Little interest in, or understanding of, this kind of learning.	Organizational memory often used for counter-productive purposes. Interpretations are opportunistic.	Not emphasized. Often shared by memorandum. Rarely discussed.	Openly debated. Used to inform future action. Shared with all stakeholders.	Source of motivation and pride. Broad sharing of results. Full involvement of members.
Opportunities for Growth	Not seen as important. External to the work of members.	Scattered, not focused. Individualistic.	Members may respond to annual lists of conferences. Limited initiative.	Coherence between goals, year plans and professional development. Teams are common.	Fully job embedded and focused on goals. Many opportunities for collaboration.
Recognition and Celebration	Some members don't know each other. Opportunities and events are very limited.	Some want more; some want less. Some student or community events are used for political purposes. Staff events unevenly attended.	Not frequent; rarely spontaneous. Ritualized and routinized.	Frequent and meaningful. Enjoyed by participants.	Fully integrated into the work of the organization and the lives of the members. Often spontaneous.

Table 2.10: Dimension Five—Organizational Processes and Structures

	Withdrawn	Reactionary	Benign	Adaptive	Generative
Communication Structures	Limited. Communications often ignored, or not delivered or received.	Selective, often secretive. Frequent misunderstanding and misrepresentation.	Formal, adequate, reactive.	Broad dissemination, often two-way. High expectations of involvement.	Integral to organizational success. Highly interactive.
Policy	In some cases, policy does not exist. In others, it has not been reviewed for years.	Policy handbook is continually expanding. Changes to policy are frequent and very time-consuming.	Policy documents are referred to occasionally.	Policy is seen to complement goals. Members are aware of policy and often initiate changes.	Direct and constant interplay between policy and practice that focuses on people first.
Planning	Minimal, haphazard, and rarely connected to mission/vision, goals or principles.	Often determined by default. Very uneven, reactionary, and not always purposeful. Fosters negativity.	Sufficient to meet minimal conditions of accountability.	High levels of engagement. Productive debate. Goal focused.	Very high levels of contribution by members, linked directly to mission/vision, goals and principles. Energizing.
Decision Making	Silence. Low levels of participation. Low levels of commitment.	Time for skirmishes, dragging up the past. Disputatious, acrimonious. Very uneven compliance.	Directive. Show of hands after little debate.	Informed debate, strong positions, and respectful resolutions. High commitment.	Continuous rather than episodic process. Highly integrated with communication structures. Valued.
How Work Gets Done	In isolation. Minimally. Sometimes incompetently.	Grudgingly, often on members' own terms. Separately.	Without enthusiasm, individually, but competently.	Willingly and responsibly, often with others. High levels of competence.	With enthusiasm, inspirationally, collaboratively whenever possible. Synergy results.
Evaluation	Often minimal for all members. Idiosyncratic. Often counter-productive.	Highly judgmental and destructive of trust and respect. Often avoided.	Traditional and fairly formal. Moderate levels of member engagement.	Used purposefully and comprehensively. Adds value.	Constantly evolving. Fully integrated with practice. Very high levels of member engagement.

organizations is members' high levels of tolerance for uncertainty when groups of educators engage in daily work with a publicly acknowledged comfort with messiness and fluidity. We hear them happily admit that "We started down one road together, then realized that this wasn't really the path that we should be taking and so went back to the beginning." They see the work as a sustained part of their professional lives, rather than as an add-on or a special initiative that will be finite in its timelines and responsibilities.

Furthermore, we have seen people in generative learning communities relate to, and interact with, each other in ways that are unique. Compromise occurs as a matter of course, but not to the point of abdication or apathy. Respect is evident, not as reverence, but as a sense of trust that colleagues are doing their best and are willing to set aside ego to learn and grow. Festering conflict is addressed in an empathetic but firm way that honours the individual and the collective in appropriate balance. Collaboration is an assumed norm and is seen as a synergistic strategy to enhance creativity and imaginative problem solving. Action is focused, intentional, and coherent with agreed-upon goals, yet also allows room and accommodation for individualization.

A generative learning community occurs in the presence of a generative leader who practises generative dialogue as a skill and as a sensibility. Through thousands of incidents of listening and asking authentic and timely questions, the generative leader sets the stage by undertaking often-invisible but highly impactful interactions with people and tasks. We heard one of these leaders described as "simultaneously being everywhere and nowhere." Another was described as "modelling the perfect balance between aspiration, inspiration, and perspiration!" By definition, the word *generative* means to provide impetus; in establishing the conditions of a generative learning community, these leaders set the stage by finding the context-perfect balance between tension and support. They live and model attitudes and aptitudes that provide impetus for curiosity, growth, exploration, and learning. In essence, they demonstrate the title of this book: they lead effectively by not needing to know the answers to the multitude of immensely complex questions that arise daily.

We have also observed, over many years, that leaders have a tendency to miscalibrate the nature and effectiveness of their learning communities. Some have assured us that they have a healthy organization that demonstrates all the characteristics of generativity; this, even as we have visited schools and classrooms, and observed obvious fractures in communication, trust, vision, policy enactment, and professional learning, just to name a few. What contributes to causing this to be so?

HELPFUL RESPONSES TO UNHELPFUL ASSUMPTIONS ABOUT GROWTH

In our experiences, the list of unhelpful assumptions about enhancing culture, building community, and setting the stage for a different type of leadership is unusually long. The leaders with whom we work can usually come to a fairly quick and unequivocal agreement about what *shouldn't* happen. It is far more difficult and time-consuming to examine and unravel fundamental assumptions about why we hold ideas to be true and how those ideas impact how to go about working toward a generative community. Whether due to cognitive dissonance (Festinger, 1957) or resistance to change (Kegan & Lahey, 2001; Murphy, 2016; Snyder, 2017), unhelpful assumptions by leaders are illustrative of a larger reflexive process in which beliefs and actions shape reality and vice versa. Here are some of the most frequent comments we hear about setting the stage for a generative community.

We Did a Learning Community in the Early 2000s When the Book First Came Out—We Have Moved On to Other Initiatives since Then

As difficult as it might be for current educators to imagine a time when the drive toward functioning as a professional learning community—particularly as defined and promoted by Richard DuFour—has not been in prominence, the idea has been talked about in schools for less than 20 years: a relatively short timeline for educational change. Take, for example, the educational theories and concepts forwarded by John Dewey. Some of these, such as inquiry-based learning, problem-based experiential teaching, and reflective practice are almost a century old and are just now gaining favour among a new and renewed readership.

In 2000, we were working with a number of school districts in which a majority of leaders knew virtually nothing about learning communities, their characteristics, or the type of cultural work that was necessary to successfully translate the idea into practice. Most had not yet attended their first conference, nor read their first book on the subject. From a conventional way of viewing the organization of schools, these leaders were experiencing a level of cultural shift not witnessed since the days of Sputnik. As change initiatives, such as implementation of professional learning communities, began to spread throughout educational systems around the world, the practice of school improvement also changed: the substance of schools' three-year plans began to reflect a new prominence of professional learning, collaboration, evidence-based practice, and a re-examination of education as a fundamental human right. And, almost in lock-step, formal documents about teaching and learning produced by governments began moving toward a reification of standards of practice for all those engaged in the public education enterprise.

At the turn of this century, it was not an established norm for teams of teachers to collaborate closely in their professional practice to achieve these standards, even at the behest of well-read and respected authors such as Roland Barth. Yet, in 2019, it seems more certain that the role of learning has moved to a more central position in the values and beliefs of most schools. For school leaders, the leadership of learning has taken on new meaning and helped foster a new understanding of their responsibilities. Principals are expected to model their own professional learning, even as they help lead the learning of staff and students. Teachers are encouraged to see themselves as leaders of learning in their classrooms, refining their practice through their own professional learning. Students, increasingly, have a role to play in the leadership of learning for themselves and their peers. Schools are expected to be, first, places of learning for all. We would argue that this has created the need for a framework of learning that is more inclusive than that posited by the first advocates of professional learning communities: one that includes parents, students, librarians, and bus drivers, as well as professional staff, all working together to generate the energy, knowledge, practices, and culture of collaboration that will embrace the challenges and opportunities of 21st century organizations. We would also contend that this is unique at the heart of the generative community.

My Way of Changing the Culture with My Staff Is to Clearly Tell Them What Needs to Be Done

There are still many school leaders who adhere to a chain-of-command model of school leadership, operating on a "telling curriculum" and working under the assumption that the principal knows what needs to be done and is the best person to communicate and designate responsibilities for action. Such principals may create their schools' education plans, goals, timetables, and supervision schedules with scant input from staff members. Frequently, they have minimal daily contact with individual staff members or students, they spend a disproportionate amount of time engaged in management tasks, and their professional relationships are often limited to their fellow school administrators or office support staff.

Unfortunately, giving people directions, telling them what to do, and even telling them *how* to do it can have limited utility in today's educational organizations. As we have observed in many different situations, if telling worked as well as the tellers hoped, we would not need nearly so many adults to do the work of schooling. Telling seems to contribute to a culture of compliance, inhibit innovation, interfere with commitment, and discourage collaboration. At its worst, this environment provokes reaction and limits imagination; at its best, it contributes to apathy and reverence for mediocrity. Leaders-as-tellers contribute to benign communities in which people don't rock the boat, work in relative isolation, and resent disruption. We observed a recent example of this in one system's year-long examination of student report cards, which resulted in the agreement to retain the model they had used for the previous 10 years—complete with percentages and letter grades. Since the company that had printed the report cards for the past 10 years had gone out of business, the system did commit to changing fonts and colours for the newly minted documents.

Telling implies more talking and less listening, a direct inverse of the generative dialogue that we are promoting in this book. We have found that, of all the skills of communication, listening is arguably the most powerful, and *active* listening may be the most difficult. Teachers tell us they are much more likely to commit to continuous growth in enhancing their practice when they are given time to engage in generative dialogues in which they can reflect more deeply and make more purposeful decisions about actions they will take to improve; we have observed them trying harder to incorporate new ideas into their teaching and giving greater attention to the refinement of their professional skills and strategies.

In the broader context of setting the stage for generativity, we have noted that many successful schools are guided by an ethos of shared responsibility, with adults genuinely willing and able to make a meaningful contribution to the life of the school community through sharing their time and talents in partnership with others. A leader who is more likely to tell people what to do is less likely to engage in the conversations necessary to set this stage.

My Staff Turnover Rate Is 20 percent Annually—I Don't Have Time to Change Culture

In a 2014 article in *The New Yorker*, Joshua Rothman shared some thoughts about competing meanings of the word *culture*. He wrote that while culture may be pulling itself apart from the inside, it represents, in some ways, a wish. The wish is that a group of people might discover, together, a good way of life; that their good way of life might express itself in their habits, institutions, and activities; and that individuals might flourish in their own unique ways.

The culture of a school may be understood as an aggregation of the core values, attitudes, relationships, rules, patterns of behaviour, symbols, heroes, legends, and even the taken-for-granted assumptions of all who make up the population of the community. An understanding of culture is both idiosyncratic and collective, made up in part by what its people believe about themselves and what others believe about them.

In practice, the intersection of school culture and school improvement may only bring to conscious attention those aspects of culture that lie close to the surface. As Senge (1990) noted, the deeper, more powerful elements of culture most often remain undisturbed, or unexamined, when schools embark on journeys of improvement.

In our work, we have found that staff turnover rates are not affected by just one set of variables. For example, in a school only a few hundred kilometres from Canada's Northwest Territories, a small high school has maintained very high staff retention for the last 15 years. Most of the teachers are content to stay where they are, even though the community is relatively isolated. Staff members respect each other, they appreciate most of their students, and they've had the same principal and vice-principal for the past 10 years. Factors that might make other teachers seek alternative employment—minimal parent involvement in school matters, limited contact with district office personnel, and very low expectations of academic success for students—have had the opposite effect here.

Alternately, in a large urban high school where staff retention has been a major problem since the school opened, a very different view of culture has been displayed. A majority of staff members have consistently identified their most serious concern with comments such as "No discipline!" "The inmates are running the place!" and "This school would be just fine if you'd let us get rid of about 20 students who cause 90 percent of all the problems!" Five principals have served in this school in four years. In one year, 34 of 75 teachers applied for a transfer. Sadly, the culture of the school is deeply entrenched, antagonistic, negative, divisive, and threatening. Cliques dominate interactions among staff, and students in large numbers report at every opportunity that they do not like being there. Ironically, almost everyone in the school community can see they are working in a toxic environment, yet almost no one can or will do anything about it.

The culture of schools is evolving and, in some, the emphasis on growth may cause conflicting opinions and competing attitudes. Paradoxically, standards of practice for educators seem to be mandating greater individual responsibility, yet greater collaboration; greater autonomy, yet greater compliance; greater diversity, yet greater uniformity of practice. In this culture-in-flux, educators are challenged to find their own ways, to find their places to stand, and to do it all in the face of conflicting advice, competing political agendas, and a degree of ambivalence that is probably unparalleled in the history of the teaching profession. In effect, one of the characteristics of the evolving culture of schools is a growing lack of certainty and clarity, masked by false confidence, intolerance, and stifling rectitude.

It Doesn't Do Much Good to Involve Community Members in the School—It Doesn't Lead to Any Better Outcomes and Actually Just Complicates Decision Making

As our response to this sentiment, let us provide the anecdote of Robert, a vice-principal in a large high school, at an early stage in his career. He was considered to be a good school leader, one who looked after his teachers, took care of troublesome students, and was always ready to have some fun. After a four-year principalship in a different school district, followed by two years as a curriculum director, Robert was appointed principal of his old high school. He came to his new job more skillful, more thoughtful, and more aware of his own strengths and deficiencies. In one of his first meetings with the whole staff, we observed him beginning to formulate a tentative plan for encouraging more parents to be involved in the school. Mid-sentence, he stopped and calmly stated, "I guess you can all see that I have my own ideas, but I want you to know I'm more interested in hearing from you about this topic. I'll take any ideas I can get from you, organize them into themes, and pass them back to you for your continued consideration. I am really committed to getting more parent involvement in our school, but I'm not committed to any one way of doing it. Yet."

Robert received more than the expected response from his staff, along with predictable comments about teachers being overwhelmed, as well as their need to be left alone so they could concentrate on teaching. However, it may have been an interaction in a subsequent staff meeting that turned teachers to greater support for their new principal. In that meeting, we heard a very senior teacher interrupt a discussion about school goals with the following comment: "Hey, Bob. Doesn't it seem to you that we're getting more and more of *those* kinds of students in our school?" Somewhat taken aback, Robert asked, "What kinds of students are you talking about?" The teacher replied, "Well, you know, the ones that used to be in separate classrooms." The room went quiet. Robert knew that a lot depended on how he chose his next words. He looked around the room and, with all the control he could muster, he said, "They're *all* our students, Jim. We're taking responsibility for *every* kid."

The conversations about parent involvement appeared to take a more positive turn after that encounter. A team of staff members joined with Robert in regular meetings on the subject. In a report to the school board, the high school's plan for involving parents in the school was described as *innovative*. It started small, with teams of teachers and students inviting parents who were known to be available to come to the school to participate in activities with their children. Other parents were invited to grade 10 student-led conferences, while all parents were given more frequent updates about their children's progress. At the same time, more parents were being asked to attend meetings arranged by a newly formed student services team that was taking greater responsibility for students in difficulty, and still other parents became participants in after-school activities developed by members of a student leadership group made up of students from all grades.

In Robert's own words, "We had to understand that we could not expect all parents to attend all functions. So, just sending out general invitations would not work. We decided we had to offer a variety of opportunities so that many more parents could feel part of it. In a way, we targeted groups of parents. It worked. I can't believe the number of parents I've met in the school in the last three to four months. They are doing things that contribute greatly to the spirit of the school. They're excited and happy; parent involvement has become a reality."

I Make Sure My Secretary Always Organizes a Staff Pancake Breakfast in September and a Wrap-Up Barbecue in June to Build Community

It may be a good idea to have functions such as these at the beginning and the end of each school year, but they are not guaranteed to add to or sustain a school's sense of community. Consider the monster Christmas concert (complete with live barnyard animals!) that we observed occupying nearly two months of attention by teachers and the school principal, and drawing crowds for three sittings over three school days; or the massive basketball tournament; or the huge musical spectacular that extracted enormous reserves of staff energy, time, goodwill, and sheer human resources—these kinds of events do not automatically enhance school culture. However, if they are in harmony with a school's commitment to the leadership of learning and the needs of every student, and if they also support day-to-day attention to matters of respect for all and success for all, they can certainly make a positive difference. Moreover, if they coexist with an unflinching commitment to high-quality teaching and learning in every classroom, their overall impact can be dramatic.

Regrettably, in many schools, responsibility for these types of epic events falls to a small number of dedicated staff members whose passion for their chosen activity is not shared so strongly by others. This can cause resentment for those who do the extra work and those who don't. Still, when a focus on big events is seen to be compatible with an ethos of excellence in classroom instruction and interpersonal relationships, great things can happen.

A school with which we have had contact for the last 15 years is renowned for its annual drama festival, its innovative emphasis on relationships, and its inter-school athletics program. It has always enjoyed low staff turnover and a stable student population. Staff members commonly refer to it as "a great school!" Staff are happy. Most students say they're happy. A majority of parents report that they are happy with the school. So what should be made of the fact that student academic performance in this school has been declining annually for the last five years? In fact, in a comparison of 10 similar schools, this school shows the steepest decline in critical student academic performance measures. Some teachers argue that academic results are given too much attention. They say they are more concerned about educating "the whole child." The superintendent does not agree. He replaced the school leadership team and laid down some clear expectations for student achievement over the next three years. Most staff members are not happy with many of the changes that have been put in place for the new school year: different teaching assignments, dedicated classroom instruction times for all the core subjects, and some firm limits on what can be considered acceptable co-curricular activities.

Compare this with what happened in a rural high school (650 students) over a similar time span. They started with a high school completion rate around 55 percent, a record of nearly 200 suspensions in the previous semester, a history of unresolved disputes among staff members, and only a skeleton three-year plan for school improvement. Thanks in part to the determination and skill of the school leadership team, consistent support from the central office team, courageous informal distributed leadership from an increasing number of teachers and other adults in the school, and the creation of teams of adults willing and able to take responsibility for important elements of student programs, this school completed one of the most dramatic turnarounds we have witnessed, producing significant gains on every one of 17 separate measures of school improvement. More importantly, we believe, they did so while maintaining and enhancing their emphasis on amazing musicals and concerts (for which they have become locally famous), community fairs, and fundraisers. They simply set out to involve as many people as possible in as many different ways as possible to make their school the best it could be and, collectively, they adopted the belief that *they were responsible for the success of every student.* They spoke of it frequently; they modelled it; they lived it.

SYNOPSIS: HOW DO QUESTIONING LEADERS BEGIN THE GROWTH PROCESS?

- Listen
- Build culture one relationship at a time

- Model all aspects of positive culture and community
- Become skilled at having tough conversations in difficult situations
- Take every opportunity to build trust and respect

REFLECTIONS AND WRITING PROVOCATIONS FOR LEADING GROWTH

As mentioned in chapter 1, a strategy that we often use to set the stage for reflecting about various aspects of leadership involves journal writing or free-form writing. The rules for this activity are fairly straightforward: respond to a prompt in an authentic and non-judgmental way for a set period of time; reread the reflection without evaluation or self-assessment about whether the writing meets a standard of grammar, fluency, clarity, or purpose; identify insights in the writing that are surprising or that inspire more in-depth thought; if, and not until, the culture is one of established trust, respect, and transparency, share insights with a colleague.

We have used the following provocation stems to encourage reflection around leading for growth:

- The word *community* brings to mind an image of ...
- As a leader, I encourage a learning community by ...
- The culture required to support a learning community is ...
- I model the tenets of a learning community by ...
- The link between leaders, teachers, and students in a learning community is ...

As is evident in these stems, each provocation will cause different responses across individuals and within the same individual over time. The value of reflective writing is not validity, or even consistency; rather, these stems are meant to provide one vehicle for individual learning and intentional, informed action in creating the optimal conditions for what we refer to as *leading without answers*.

SUGGESTED READINGS FOR LEADING GROWTH

Ansell, C., & Gash, A. (2008). Collaborative governance in theory and practice. *Journal of Public Administration Research and Theory, 18*(4), 543–571.
Ansell and Gash conducted a meta-analytical study for the purpose of creating a model to explain and determine various levels of effectiveness of collaborative governance. Strategies such as face-to-face dialogue and trust building are emphasized as critical components of successful collaborative models. The authors contend that an important measure of success in creating meaningful collaboration is an overall sense of trust and understanding achieved by accomplishing incremental and purposeful goals.

Beckstrom, R. A., & Brafman, O. (2006). *The starfish and the spider: The unstoppable power of leaderless organizations*. New York, NY: Portfolio Penguin.
This book explores contexts in which leadership styles are implemented. Examples are offered from an array of companies with varying levels of success based on two competing leadership forces: a top-down authoritative approach versus a collaborative, decentralized approach. These two models are represented by the analogy of the spider—which will die if its head is cut off— and the starfish—which will recreate itself if a leg is cut off. Beckstrom and Brafman equate leadership styles that are top-down with the spider, whereas the starfish represents new, innovative businesses that promote distributive leadership. As evidenced by the history of several companies, the authors posit that collaborative structures and processes are crucial for organizational success.

Carpenter, D. (2015). School culture and leadership of professional learning communities. *The International Journal of Educational Management, 29*(5), 682–694.
Carpenter investigates the culture of three schools and the state of their professional learning communities in relation to the leadership characteristics of each school. Each school shared the same leadership structure but had varying degrees of effective characteristics of school culture and professional learning communities. Carpenter found that effective professional learning was dependent upon shared leadership as a central tenet and discusses how leaders and teachers can contribute to shared leadership.

Honig, M. I. (2017). Research use as learning: The case of school district central offices. *American Educational Research Journal, 54*(5), 938–971. https://doi.org/10.3102/0002831217712466
In this research paper, Honig expands on her previous research into the purpose of central offices within school systems. Six districts were tasked with changing the culture of central services in order to increase levels of student learning. Data from 124 interviews indicated several strategies that impacted student learning: a focused, cohesive plan by central services directed at student learning, changes in practice for developing school leaders, and the use of research and data. Central office leaders who took a teaching and learning approach to their system operations experienced improvement, causing Honig to discuss the relative benefits and limitations of using outside organizations to assist with cultural change.

McLaughlin, M. W., & Talbert, J. E. (2006). *Building school-based teacher learning communities*. New York, NY: Teachers College.
McLaughlin and Talbert studied school-based teacher learning for over 15 years. In this particular book, they explore the societal pressures teachers face, including responsibility for an inequitable socioeconomic student population and preparing students with increasing complex skills. As one strategy to mitigate these pressures, McLaughlin and Talbert highlight the usefulness of school-based learning communities. McLaughlin and Talbert's book recognizes challenges associated with reculturing schools into learning communities. They contend that, because learning communities are not a common structure in many schools, school leaders must foster the notion of collective learning and build trust relationships.

Owen, S. (2016). Professional learning communities: Building skills, reinvigorating the passion, and nurturing teacher wellbeing and "flourishing" within significantly innovative school contexts. *Educational Review, 68*(4), 403–419. http://dx.doi.org/10.1080/00131911.2015.1119101

Susanne Owen employs a case study approach in this study that examines three innovative schools in order to better understand the links between the characteristics of professional learning communities and teachers' positive psychology. Her framework of positive psychology appears to closely align with elements of teacher efficacy; that is, she defines positive psychology as supporting teachers in building new skills, changing their beliefs and practices, and improving their sense of well-being. Owen makes the contention that the latter—teacher well-being—is a central outcome of "mature" professional learning communities. She found six such outcomes that were the result of effective professional learning communities, including increased levels of the following:

- Trust and meaning
- Collaborative inquiry and meaning
- Supportive leadership
- Shared vision
- Interdisciplinary sharing
- Co-design of curriculum

Philpott, C., & Oates, C. (2016). Teacher agency and professional learning communities: What can Learning Rounds in Scotland teach us? *Professional Development in Education, 43*(3) 318–333. doi:10.1080/19415257.2016.1180316

Philpott and Oates examine the impact of professional learning communities (PLCs) on teachers' learning and student achievement. They describe an approach similar to PLCs, developed and practised in Scotland, referred to as *Learning Rounds*. In studying the process of Rounds, they discuss how "problems of practice" need to be clearly articulated by teachers in order to help them identify student learning outcomes, and contend that this approach will contribute to a more effective implementation of the PLC model.

Siccone, F. (2012). *Essential skills for effective school leadership.* North York, ON: Pearson.

Frank Siccone contends that effective schools result from effective leadership, and that a minimum of five years is required to implement large-scale change. Siccone describes five sets of essential skills that effective leaders demonstrate that impact student success. These include confidence, communication, collaboration, coaching, and continuous improvement, enacted through a framework that helps manage change and foster sustainability.

REFERENCES

Balkar, B. (2015). Defining an empowering school culture: Teacher perceptions. *Issues in Educational Research, 25*(3), 205–224.

Barth, R. S. (2002). The culture builder. *Educational Leadership, 59*(8), 6–11.

Deal, T. E., & Peterson, K. D. (2009). *Shaping school culture* (2nd ed.). San Francisco, CA: Jossey-Bass.

DuFour, R. (2004). What is a professional learning community? *Educational Leadership, 61*(8), 6–11.

Festinger, L. (1957). *A theory of cognitive dissonance.* Evanston, IL: Row & Peterson.

Fullan, M. (2016). The elusive nature of whole system improvement in education. *Journal of Educational Change, 17,* 539–544. doi:10.1007/s10833-016-9289-1

Goleman, D., Boyatzis, R. E., & McKee, A. (2002). *Primal leadership: Learning to lead with emotional intelligence.* Cambridge, MA: Harvard Business School Press.

Kegan, R., & Lahey, L. L. (2001, November). The real reason people won't change. *Harvard Business Review,* 85–92.

Murphy, M. (2016). The tug of war between change and resistance. *Educational Leadership, 73*(9), 66–70.

Rothman, J. (2014, December). The meaning of culture. *New Yorker.* doi:https://www.newyorker.com/books/joshua-rothman/meaning-culture

Senge, P. (1990). *The fifth discipline: The art and practice of the learning organization.* New York, NY: Doubleday/Currency.

Snyder, R. R. (2017). Resistance to change among veteran teachers: Providing voice for more effective engagement. *International Journal of Educational Leadership Preparation, 12*(1), 152–163.

CHAPTER THREE

Generative Leadership

How Is Leading Connected to Learning?

Schools should be places where educators share a clear priority about the centrality
of learning, for their students, but also for themselves.
> —*Organisation for Economic Co-operation and Development (OECD)*

Once I got my own ego out of the way, I was much better at helping my teachers reflect
on their classroom practice through asking questions, rather than by telling.
> —*Middle school principal*

GENERATIVE LEADERSHIP

We have learned that leadership in education can be informed equally by the insights
of introverts, the craft of classroom practitioners, the risk-taking of innovators, the
thoughtfulness of philosophers, and even the guidance of bureaucrats. It is not a social
science, the stewardship of which should be left to a select few. Rather, it is a vigorous
discipline made stronger by its very inclusivity.

In our work, that statement helps describe the way
our focus on the leadership of learning has evolved over
several decades, through stages of over-confidence and
frustration, ignorance and epiphany, euphoria and humility. Even as we continue to look for "best ways" to
support and research the leadership of learning, we acknowledge that there are almost certainly more effective approaches than we will ever have the chance to explore.

> If you were to propose a
> "research" project for your school,
> how would people react? Is there
> a word or phrase that would
> better capture your intent? What
> would it be?

As a specific example, the methodology we use in many of our research and development projects has morphed quite noticeably over the decades. In the beginning, it was
full-on action research. With little variation, that model worked for us until about 1999,
when practitioners in the field challenged us to refine the method, give it a new look, and
a new name. It was at that point that we were reminded how the word *research* continues
to evoke strong reactions in educators. Some leaders and teachers told us they were experiencing initiative fatigue: a noticeable and palpable lapse of energy and willingness

to engage in implementation of yet another cycle of another action research project on another topic that was often described as the "flavour of the month." This weariness and wariness took the form of two types of responses to school improvement and pedagogy: some took the "we've already done that" approach, looking narrowly at the intervention that was the focus of their action research, rather than engaging more intentionally with the structures and processes that were part of the action research cycle. For example, one central office leader assured us that "We did the PLC thing in our last three-year cycle of action research; we've moved on from there to numeracy." Others were defensive and fearful, expressing to us that the word *research* was problematic because it was not seen to be within the skill or responsibility of educators in the field who were doing other highly complex and demanding work. Rather, they believed that it was up to those in the "ivory tower" to fulfill the research responsibility, even as they saw that as irrelevant to their instructional leadership.

Accordingly, and in short order, we adopted the term *collaborative inquiry* as a more meaningful way of explaining the emerging strategy for educator professional learning in general (DeLuca et al., 2015) and school leadership development in particular (Byrne-Jiménez, Orr, & Sobol, 2007; Cherkowski & Schnellert, 2017; Wang, 2016). The two words, in combination, seem to resonate with educators as a more accurate and less intimidating way of describing their approach to identifying and solving issues of shared curiosity. This inquiry approach seems to more effectively integrate contextual realities of schools with a scholarly approach that enables collaborative problem solving between university researchers, central office leaders, school leadership teams, and teachers (Normore, 2006; Orr & Orphanos, 2011; Pounder, 2011).

> When you read the term *collaborative inquiry,* how does it resonate with you? What thoughts does the term conjure? What does the term mean to you? What types of behaviours would you see educators engaged in this approach?

In a similar way, our greater emphasis on the power of teams, and the power of questions, grew with every new set of results our collaborative inquiries produced, as has our awareness of, for example, the role of central office leadership in promoting growth. Still, nothing quite compares with the wonderful journey of discovery that has accompanied our growing commitment to a process we have called *generative dialogue,* a concept that will be described more fully in chapter 4. In implementing the skills of generative dialogue, we have observed some impressive shifts in leaders' approaches, skills, and results in impacting teaching practices and student learning—in short, as they engage in *generative leadership.*

In this chapter, we first offer the case study of superintendent Pierre L'Ile and tell the story of his success and challenges as he applied a generative leadership approach to system growth. We then focus on instructional leadership as an essential framework through which to make a paradigmatic shift to impact professional learning and student achievement. This shift requires a re-examination of some time-honoured axioms about educational leadership underpinned by historical and sociopolitical assumptions that we will briefly address. Next, we will pose a model of generative leadership and suggest several structures and strategies that we have seen to be instrumental in leading learning through this particular model. We then expand on the foundations upon which generative leadership rests and explore some basic learning structures for effectively leading learning. Lastly, we offer a series of assumptions about generative leadership that require reconsideration or, perhaps, recommitment to a shifting paradigm of leadership.

Case Study: Superintendent L'Ile Sits in a Fishbowl

At a school district retreat in September, an event designed to kick off a three-year initiative devoted to leadership growth, district superintendent Dr. Pierre L'Ile volunteered for the first activity: a fishbowl where he was observed answering questions about his commitment to his own professional learning. As he explained on his way to the middle of the room, he did not expect any other members of his leadership team to do anything he was not prepared to do first. Surrounded by 11 central office leaders, 25 school principals, and 34 vice-principals, and sitting side-by-side with the retreat presenters, Pierre quickly identified "capacity building" as one of his key priorities for the current school year. More specifically, in response to probing questions, he set out his intentions in the following way:

> Our district has gone through quite a lot of change in the last two years, but I believe that's only the beginning. We can expect about a 40 percent turnover in our school leadership in the next three years, and something similar at the district office level. As I look around the system, I am concerned that I have not been doing enough to ensure that current and future vice-principals have the skill and confidence they need to move into principal positions when the time comes. That's my biggest worry. So, as one of my goals for this year, I am going to devote a considerable amount of my leadership time to the professional learning of vice-principals. That's going to be my number one goal.

When asked what particular strategies he would employ to accomplish his goal, Pierre seemed hesitant. He spoke generally about the kinds of conversations he hoped to have, and about the professional learning opportunities he expected vice-principals to access. At one point he worried that he was just rambling too much, not being specific enough about what he would do. Then he stopped talking, emitted a long "Aaahhh," laughed at himself, and asked, "Can we go over this again?"

Later, he would tell everyone that, at that point, his mind went blank. He realized he had not thought his ideas through and, even as he was talking, he was becoming acutely aware that what he was about to commit to in front of every other leader in the district could not be taken lightly. In short, he was experiencing a moment of **reflection-in-action**.

continued

As the dialogue resumed, Pierre outlined possible strategies, analyzed their implications for his workload, dropped some and added others, until he was confident that he had chosen a course of action he would be able to follow. He committed to setting up a schedule of one-on-one meetings at school sites so he could engage his less-experienced leaders in regular discussions about their aspirations, philosophies, vision for the district, and any other matters relevant to their growth. He reiterated his hope that he would be able to concentrate on building their leadership capacity, even as he attended to all the other demands of his position. Then he mused, almost rhetorically, "Where am I going to find the extra time to do this?" At that very moment, he began to outline a plan to examine his own use of time. He decided he would enlist the help of his administrative assistant to track, precisely every half hour, how he spent his time over the course of one full workweek so he could see more clearly where time might be saved to undertake the strategies to which he had committed.

Pierre's reflections led him to a conclusion that this was one important way for him to assume greater responsibility for the leadership of learning within his district, concentrating particularly on the knowledge and skills of his cadre of vice-principals. When asked if he had considered formulating a question to guide his efforts, Pierre responded promptly, "Yes, I've got lots of questions. I'm wondering if the strategies I've chosen will really help me accomplish my goal. I wonder if I can find the time to do it properly. I'm also thinking about what evidence I'll have to produce to show that my efforts have made any difference."

When the retreat was over, Pierre immersed himself in his work. During the third week of the year, he and his assistant completed the time-task audit and arrived at some valuable findings. They concluded that an unbalanced amount of Pierre's time was consumed by informal and unscheduled conversations within the district office. Consequently, Pierre arranged regular individual meetings throughout this year (and subsequent years) with all of his school leaders, sometimes meeting them for lunch or for coffee at the school site.

In addition, external teams composed of a university researcher, central office leader, and district principal made monthly visits to schools; part of the monthly administrators' meeting was focused on matters of leadership capacity and growth; and, over time, all leaders in the district came to a deeper understanding of the power of inquiry and the value of evidence in identifying elements of professional practice more likely to influence growth.

For his part, Pierre evolved his inquiry to the following question: In what ways and to what extent can my relentless focus on critical aspects of the professional growth of vice-principals contribute to enhanced leadership capacity in our district?

He was able to sustain his commitment to the growth of less-experienced leaders for three years. Moreover, by the end of three years, his predictions of change and staff turnover in this district of 25 schools were proven to be most conservative. For example, of the 14 educators who held leadership positions in the central office at the beginning of Pierre's tenure, 11 held new or different positions after three years. Some went to other districts. Some went back into schools. Some were promoted. In addition, 12 schools had different principals, while 17 schools had new vice-principals. Upon his promotion to the superintendency of a larger and highly complex international school system, Pierre solicited responses from all leaders in his district regarding his leadership. The respondents noted the value and the impact of Pierre's leadership in helping them perform their leadership tasks, pursue their leadership growth, and generate within them their capacity, curiosity, and efficacy in their roles as future school or district leaders.

Case Study Reflections: The Art of Generative Leadership

- Which, if any, of Pierre's strategies are atypical at the level of school or system leadership?
- What reasons might Pierre have had, other than those he expressed during the retreat, for focusing on vice-principals?
- Analyze the structure and content of Pierre's inquiry question. Identify ways that it differs in substance and approach from other goals or educational plans.
- In addition to time limitations, what other challenges might Pierre have faced in implementing his plan?
- What are examples of the ways that Pierre's actions reflect his leadership approach?
- How might Pierre's leadership choices described in this case study contribute to organizational growth?

WHAT SHOULD BE THE ROLE OF THE PRINCIPAL?

School principals have been, and continue to be, the most influential leaders in a system, even as the vision of what constitutes effectiveness in the principalship has undergone many shifts over the years. Early literature on educational leadership suggested that an ideal principal be hands-on and directly involved with curriculum and classroom practice, as well as with teacher mentoring (Hallinger & Murphy, 1985). Such persons would apply their leadership expertise to the classroom to improve teaching. However, a dramatic increase in the size and complexity of schools, and the breadth of curriculum, relegated leadership to management through much of the 1980s and 1990s.

Yet, in spite of continued trends toward larger schools and expanded curriculum, it has become widely accepted that effective principals should avoid myopic managerialism. A case study by Fletcher-Sodat (2010) described the positive effects that an organizationally oriented, non-managerial principal can have. In the study, a rural Virginia elementary principal with a history of especially successful leadership was interviewed. This principal had transformed a below-average school to one that substantially exceeded district and state norms. He summarized his leadership work as a combination of nurturing his staff, protecting them from external pressures, providing them with rich professional development opportunities, and making room for teachers to assume leadership roles. That is, he viewed his job primarily as leading rather than managing.

Similarly, researchers from Korea (Park & Jeong, 2013) explored qualities of effective leaders by analyzing how a principal's behaviour, as defined by the Change Facilitator Style Questionnaire (Hall & George, 1999), impacts teacher resistance to change or reform. They concluded that government-driven reform elicited high levels of teacher resistance, but that effective principal leadership was the lynchpin for reducing negative teacher behaviour and emotional resistance. They referred to the leadership styles of these effective principals as *initiative-oriented*, which include forward-thinking competencies away from managerialism.

In Canada, Newton and Wallin (2013) conducted semi-structured interviews with 12 principals in rural communities across Alberta and Manitoba. They found that traditional models of principal leadership (Leithwood, Seashore Louis, Anderson, & Wahlstrom, 2004) did not apply; rather, the principals in their study reported feeling discomfort with formal supervision. This conclusion is particularly relevant to the present trend toward instructional leadership in which, as reported by the Organisation for Economic Co-operation and Development (OECD, 2016), "a vast majority of principals act as instructional leaders, but about one-third still rarely engage in instructional leadership actions" (p. 28).

> With all we know about teacher supervision, why is there still hesitancy when it comes to actually doing this work? Where do you, as an educational leader, see teacher supervision fitting into your practice? What does the term *supervision* mean to you?

EARLY DAYS OF THE 21ST CENTURY: WHERE DID INSTRUCTIONAL LEADERSHIP ORIGINATE?

The Institute for Instructional Leadership (now the Institute for Educational Leadership) in Washington, DC, defined *instructional leadership* as "those actions that a principal takes, or delegates to others, to promote growth in student learning" (De Bevoise, 1984). Yet, over the past 30 years, a number of descriptions of instructional leadership have been posited. For example, Hallinger and Murphy (1985) contended that instructional leadership refers only to three dimensions of responsibility, including defining the school's mission, managing the instructional program, and promoting a positive school learning-climate. They viewed the overall orientation of instructional leadership to be managerial in nature (Townsend, Acker-Hoover, Ballenger, & Place, 2013). Based on our experiences, such a definition may require a 21st century update.

The US Department of Education Journal *Reading First* (US Department of Education, 1998) recently extended the instructional leadership role beyond the scope of the school principal to include central office personnel—superintendents and curriculum consultants—as well as assistant principals and instructional coaches. Other authors (Barth, 1990, 2001; Crowther, Ferguson, & Hann, 2009; Harris, Muijs, Chapman, Stoll, & Russ, 2003; Hauserman & Stick, 2013; Lambert, 2003; MacDonald & Weller, 2017; Marks & Printy, 2003; Riveros, Newton, & da Costa, 2013) include classroom teachers as instructional leaders, especially if they are working as members of collaborative inquiry teams.

Still, for the most part, school principals have been the primary focus of research on instructional leadership. An investigation by Neumerski (2013) found that peer-reviewed publications tend to divide instructional leadership research into three categories, distinguished by principals, teachers, and coaches. According to Neumerski, this division is problematic because instructional leadership practices occur within a rich context that involves all types of leaders. Rather than focusing on *who* the leaders should be, Neumerski argues that more attention needs to shift onto *how* the leaders lead, interpersonally and systemically.

Instructional Leadership as a Framework

Many conventional leadership models place principals in the role of *fixing* ineffective instructional practices, fighting against resistant teachers, and hoping that *telling* will inspire change. Alternately, Sergiovanni is frequently cited as one of the first authors to suggest that the work of school principals should focus primarily on instructional leadership. This idea was promoted in the text he co-authored with Robert Starratt on the subject of instructional supervision (Sergiovanni & Starratt, 1971), which has survived through five decades and seven editions. Sergiovanni's (1985) early conceptualization of instructional leadership was based on five elements: technical, human, educational, symbolic, and cultural. He explained that technical forces included planning, leadership theory, time management, and organizational development. Human forces were the interpersonal components aligned with communicating, motivating, and facilitating. Teaching, learning, and implementing curricula made up the educational forces. The symbolic and cultural forces, according to Sergiovanni, were closely aligned, combining the leader's ability to become the symbol of what is important, while consistently articulating beliefs and values. Subsequent models of instructional leadership focused on attributes, personality, and style, while encouraging school leaders to direct their attention first to leading teachers. At the same time, Acheson (1985) created a stir when he argued that it would be more effective to leave the instructional leadership roles to educators other than the principal. Like Acheson, Glickman, Gordon, and Ross-Gordon (2017) envisioned a system in which "clinical supervisors" would fulfill much of the instructional leadership role. Yet, Lashway (1995) observed that by the middle of the 1980s the idea that school principals should first be instructional leaders had gained broad acceptance.

Townsend et al. (2013) analyzed data collected under the No Child Left Behind Act that contained interviews with school principals and superintendents regarding their perspectives on school improvement. The authors found that traditional top-down decision-making models often used in schools contribute to a negative and punitive environment that impedes change, stunts growth, and creates fear. Townsend et al. concluded that these types of problems result from the narrow focus of traditional instructional leadership and suggest consideration of other paradigms.

One such paradigm has been widely referred to as "leading for learning," intended to weaken hierarchical power structures. For example, Day and Sammons (2013) identified two types of leadership: instructional and transformational. Sun and Leithwood (2012) described a similar *integrated transformational school leadership* model.

> When you hear the term *transformational leadership,* what image does it conjure up for you? What does it have to do with your practice of educational leadership?

Siccone (2012) noted a renewed interest in models of instructional leadership advocated by the American National Association of Elementary School Principals. The following are their six standards for the knowledge and skills of principals:

- Standard 1: Lead student and **adult learning**
- Standard 2: Lead diverse communities
- Standard 3: Lead 21st-century learning
- Standard 4: Lead continuous improvement
- Standard 5: Lead using knowledge and data
- Standard 6: Lead parent, family, and community engagement

> How do these six standards compare with the leadership standards applicable to your school system?

Throughout Canada, legislated standards for school leaders frequently include a component of instructional leadership. As examples, a selection of provincial standards is included in table 3.1.

It appears, then, that descriptions of effective instructional leadership vary from a focus on supervision and evaluation to a focus on collaboration and community (Blase & Blase, 2002; Glickman et al., 2017).

Who Does Instructional Leadership?

Marzano, Waters, and McNulty (2005) are three authors among several who identify a growing need for collaboration among teachers, administrators, superintendents, and

Table 3.1: A Comparison of Selected Canadian Leadership Standards

	Ontario	Alberta	British Columbia
Legislated Document	Ontario Leadership Framework	Leadership Quality Standard	Leadership Standard for Principals and Vice-Principals
Components	• Setting Direction • Building relationships and people • Developing the organization • **Leading the instructional program** • Securing accountability • School improvement • Fostering a culture of professionalism • Leadership development • Administrative structures • Parent and community supports • Succession planning	• Fostering effective relationships • Modelling commitment to professional learning • Embodying visionary leadership • Leading a learning community • Supporting the application of foundational knowledge about First Nations, Metis and Inuit • **Providing instructional leadership** • Developing leadership capacity • Managing school operations and resources • Understanding and responding to the larger societal context	• Moral leadership • **Instructional Leadership** • Organizational leadership • Relational leadership
Role of Instructional Leadership	The [leader] sets high expectations for learning outcomes and monitors and evaluates the effectiveness of instructional leadership. The supervisory officer manages the system effectively so that everyone can focus on teaching and learning.	A leader ensures that every student has access to quality teaching and optimum learning experiences.	Principals and vice-principals engage in effective supervision that focuses on instructional and assessment practices that maximize student development, engagement, and learning. Principals and vice-principals are knowledgeable and provide guidance regarding curricula, instructional and assessment practices, and their impact on student development, engagement, and learning.

Note: Text in italics indicates provinces that include instructional leadership as a competency.

the community in the process of instructional leadership. In particular, they firmly advocate for system leaders to become more active members in instructional leadership because their research findings show a direct and positive correlation between effective system leadership and student achievement. Similar results have been published by Adams (2016), Robinson (2011), and Timperley (2011a).

District leaders that model and support sustainable instructional leadership can ensure that gains in student learning will be more likely. Leithwood (2010b) asserted that district leaders must begin with a legislated vision for student learning; this vision and direction will guide and foster an instructional climate that promotes high standards and achievement, and will support the effective application of instructional leadership at the school level. District culture and climate must also establish and communicate shared norms and values to support collaboration in teacher learning (Fullan, 2001; Heinrich & Good, 2018).

Can Instructional Leadership Be Distributed?

Traditionally, *school leadership*, as a noun rather than a verb, described one person. Now, it is unrealistic to believe that schools can effectively function under singular leadership (Spillane & Orina, 2005). As Leithwood (2010a) noted, school leaders cannot possibly attend to all responsibilities and requests on their own, so successful leadership must recognize others' strengths and knowledge, and utilize the help of others where needed. Research confirms that school leadership has a more significant impact on teaching and learning when it is broadly and strategically shared (Black, 1998; Harris, 2013; Kitchen, Gray, & Jeurissen, 2016: Leithwood, Harris, & Hopkins, 2008). Moreover, the sense of ownership that can result from effective structures of distributed leadership helps set the direction for a collective commitment to improved teaching and learning at all levels (Hallinger & Heck, 2010a). It could be argued that distributed leadership is more common in more schools and districts, in part because it is an expectation of new competencies for school leaders that the principal will not be the sole leader. Furthermore, in the current context, one fair measure of a principal's effectiveness is an ability to generate collaboration and teamwork among staff members (Spillane, Healey, Parise, & Kenney, 2011).

How Are Coaching and Instructional Leadership Similar?

Unlike clinical supervision, with its built-in expectations of hierarchy and its allusions to sterility and white coats, coaching models have enjoyed a friendlier relationship with instructional leadership. Arthur Costa and Robert Garmston (2002) may have been two of the first authors to introduce the concept of cognitive coaching and link it to instructional leadership. Several years later, Bruce Joyce and Beverly Showers brought forward their concept of peer coaching, first widely articulated in a series of articles on the theme of transfer of training for teachers (Joyce & Showers, 1981, 1982, 1987;

Showers & Joyce, 1996). Their research contended that 90 percent of teachers would transfer a new skill into their practice as a result of theory, demonstration, practice, and corrective feedback during training, when followed up with job-embedded coaching.[1]

In the late 1980s, Joyce and Showers transitioned to the term *instructional coaching* to describe their work. For much of the next 20 years, they identified peer coaching teams as an important component of their model. Then, almost 40 years later, the concept was given new life, purpose, and meaning through the work of authors such as Knight (2009), Knight and van Nieuwerburgh (2012), and Grenny (2002, 2009). Their ideas are helping new generations of educators become more skillful in strategies for instructional leadership to enhance teaching.

> From your readings thus far, in what ways do you think cognitive coaching/instructional coaching is related to generative leadership? Where do the two approaches to instructional leadership converge and diverge?

What Is the End Goal?

On one point, there does not appear to be much disagreement. The role of the school leader continues to expand in complexity (Alberta Teachers' Association, 2014), making the balance between manager and leader ever more demanding (Seashore Louis, Leithwood, Wahlstrom, & Anderson, 2010; Slater, Garduno, & Mentz, 2018). For example, in the Alberta context, school leaders are being challenged to build a culture and climate of trust, collaboration, professional learning, and distributed leadership, while acting in a pedagogically sound, research-informed manner (Alberta Education, 2009). Nor can there be any doubt that the primary focus of school leadership is to improve student learning (Government of Alberta, 2018; Hallinger & Heck, 2010b; Leithwood, Patten, & Jantzi, 2010; Marzano et al., 2005; Seashore Louis et al., 2010). A variety of leadership styles has been identified, analyzed, researched, and applied to help school leaders sustain a focus on learning. Yet, great difficulty still lies in determining the most effective leadership competencies, given all the contextual variables of schools, staffs, students, parents, and communities.

> Think about the contextual variables at play in your school. What are they? How do they influence your leadership? What can you do to use these variables to support your leadership of learning?

SYNOPSIS

Instructional leadership as a concept continues to be characterized in the literature by a plethora of elements. On one extreme, it is the sum total of everything that happens in a school and its classrooms that contributes to student learning. On the other, it is a very carefully described, limited number of actions that have been found through research to be the primary responsibilities of school principals.

The term *instructional leadership* came to the forefront in the 1980s, faded in usage and application during the 1990s, and has now regained a position of eminence in public school systems in the second decade of the 21st century. It is arguably the most comprehensive term available to describe the work of school leaders. As that work is more clearly understood, more broadly shared, and more thoroughly integrated with norms of professional practice, it is reasonable to expect that increasing numbers of school leaders will be able to work together and learn from each other as they pursue the most important goal of public education: ensuring that all students receive the quality of educational service to which they are entitled.

There is general agreement that effective instructional leadership starts at the district level, with the certain commitment of educators and others who have positional and political authority within the jurisdiction. Their leadership can help school leaders feel more supported, more responsible, more passionate about their work, more willing to take up a district's mission, vision, and goals. Once a certain standard of district-level instructional leadership has been established, schools are more likely to become places in which the creation of a culture of trust, and the development of a shared set of norms and values that focus on high standards for teaching and learning, can be a fair and reasonable expectation. In such a community of learning, collaboration can thrive, and teachers, students, and parents alike can recognize, honour, and use to their greatest advantage the knowledge, skills, and strengths of others.

THE GENERATIVE LEADERSHIP MODEL

Generative leadership has, as its primary focal point, optimizing student learning (Townsend & Adams, 2009). This is best achieved by leaders at all levels of the organization—formal and informal—who consistently and frequently communicate expectations of and establish conditions for purposeful, focused, learner-centric teaching supported by elbow-to-elbow instructional leadership.

Generative leadership necessitates the interactivity of seven key fundamentals:

- Teachers and school leaders use inquiry-informed professional growth plans.
- Classroom observations are frequent, purposeful, focused, and aligned with the professional growth planning process.
- Regular reflective conversations (we will refer to these in a later chapter as *generative dialogues*) contribute to a process of instructional leadership that integrates evidence-based questions into daily interactions between system leader and principal; principal and teacher; teacher and teacher; and teacher and student.
- School and system leaders model the generative dialogue process.
- The central office leadership teams (COLT) make monthly visits to school sites, school leaders have monthly visits with teachers and school staff, and teachers use generative dialogue with students as an informal assessment strategy.

- Teams of various compositions of teachers and leaders are clearly sighted on the optimization of student learning and monthly team meetings during which everyone shares responsibility for reflection-in-action.
- Evidence and data are generated in order to build upon or contribute to existing knowledge as well as to integrate recent research findings into the practices of the school.

Figure 3.1 represents the fundamental elements of the generative leadership model.

Inquiry-Guided Professional Growth Plans

Leaders are living in an era of great opportunity and challenge regarding their own professional learning. Tremendous knowledge development and growth opportunities are available now more than ever to all who serve in the education system. Educational policy is evolving to provide clear support and expectations for educators in all roles

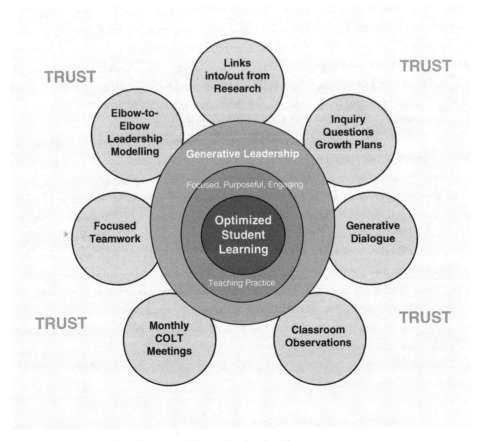

Figure 3.1: The Seven Key Elements of Generative Leadership

to assume active responsibility for their professional learning. Such policies are intended to encourage self-assessment, broad choice, self-directed personal growth, and learning. Yet, it is not always evident that educators are willing to engage in a sustained process of professional learning that encourages them to deeply assess, understand, and improve their practice. Our research has brought us to the conclusion that stagnation may be due to a number of factors that mitigate full implementation of policy and best practice. The factors include lack of opportunity for authentic self-assessment; reduced occurrence of focused conversations between leaders and teachers about professional practice; ineffective leadership of learning; an over-reliance on old models of professional development; and intermittent use of professional learning as a driving force behind optimizing student learning.

> Reflect on these factors for a few minutes. First of all, do you agree or disagree with what we are saying? If so, what evidence from your practice, or the practice of others, supports your agreement? If not, what evidence from your practice, or the practice of others, supports your disagreement?

First, self-assessment and reflection serve a critical role during the process of professional growth. While some reflection-on-practice is informal and necessarily independent, we contend that an over-privatization of self-evaluation may not always contribute to fulsome professional growth and learning. Multiple forms of collaboration that externalize and synergize self-assessment and reflective activities are key to promoting and realizing professional growth (Darling-Hammond, Wei, Andree, Richardson, & Orphanos, 2009; Jamison & Clayton, 2016; Jao & McDougall, 2016). We will explore the concept of reflective practice in greater detail in chapter 5 and will offer some strategies and templates to help support leaders' skills in this area.

In addition, educators (including, and perhaps especially, leaders) crave opportunities to speak about their professional practice. These conversations can happen with colleagues in a one-on-one format, within professional learning groups where the focus is on improved practice leading to improved student learning, and/or with school leaders as an outgrowth of conversations centred on the professional growth planning process (Darling-Hammond et al., 2009; Tichnor-Wagner, Harrison, & Cohen-Vogel, 2016).

Next, effective leadership at the system and school levels plays an essential role in teacher growth and the teacher growth planning processes that is sometimes overlooked and often minimized. Similarly, effective leaders are active participants in professional growth, not just observers. Instructional leaders play a substantive role in helping teachers develop and improve through such growth (Adams & Miskell, 2016; Butler, Schnellert, & Macneil, 2015; Timperley, 2011b).

Lastly, the nature of contemporary professional learning may be defined by several guideposts. These include the following:

- A meaningful investment of time
- Teachers engaged in active learning, rather than a "sit and get" format

- A strong focus on all aspects of pedagogy
- Collective participation through coaching, modelling, observation, and feedback
- Explicit links to, and alignment with, the school's curriculum and organizational priorities
- Integration of **collaborative inquiry** forms of learning

While Fenwick (2004) found that many of these guideposts are more of an aspiration than a reality in schools, we have found that in schools that have moved from underperforming to exceeding performance expectations, these aspirations have become a reality. Through the adoption of a generative leadership model, school leaders do initiate ongoing and frequent conversations between members of the school leadership team, members of school-based communities of learning, and teachers, either individually or collectively, around professional growth plan questions, strategies, measures, evidence, and reflections.

Classroom Observations

In this generative leadership model vice-principals, associate principals, assistant principals, department heads, lead teachers work with the principal to make frequent, purposeful, and focused classroom visits. These are not social calls to say "good morning" to the boys and girls (although those visits are important and serve a purpose as well). These are not visits with a clipboard in hand and checklists to complete. These are not visits meant to leave the teacher with a little congratulatory note about some aspect of the lesson. Rather, these visits are aligned with, and are an extension of, the professional growth planning process.

Once teachers put together a rough draft of their inquiry-guided professional growth plan, they meet with a school leader. It is at this point that these plans take on a serious professional upgrade, changing from a compliance document to an authentic plan for growth. The school leader enters into the first steps associated with the generative dialogue through a process of simply asking questions of the teacher. The questions can take different forms and serve different purposes. Some areas and sample questions include the following:

- Clarification questions (What do you mean by …?)
- Questions about the question (Why is this question important to you?)
- Assumption probes (What led you to that conclusion?)
- Reason and evidence probes (Why this course of action now?)
- Origin or source questions (Where did you get this idea?)
- Implications and consequences (What would be the most desirable outcome?)
- Viewpoint questions (How have other people responded to what you are proposing?)

In many cases, teachers use this conversation to solidify their thinking around their goals and resulting inquiry question. Once the conversation is complete, teachers will finalize their growth plans and begin implementing those strategies that will lead to an answer to their question. Simultaneously, school leaders are meeting with school district leaders to share,

> Now that you have some preliminary information about generative dialogue, how do you see it as being similar to models of coaching? Different from models of coaching?

clarify, and then finalize their own growth plans. School district leaders are doing the same with the superintendent. And ... superintendents don't get away lightly! They meet with a university researcher or a colleague to practise and experience the same process as teachers, school leaders, and school district leaders; their meetings are often held with all school and school district leaders watching, listening, and providing feedback through questions to the superintendent.

Classroom visits become a focal point for pre-observation, observation, and post-observation conversations. One important characteristic of these visits is the negotiation of purpose and data to be collected by the school leader. This begins with a pre-observation that involves a review of growth plan goals and inquiry question(s) in order that the school leader can identify what the teacher would like to focus on during the visit. During the class observation, the school leader is noting and recording how the teacher is approaching the negotiated work. In the post-observation, the school leader does not make judgmental or evaluative statements, but rather asks the teacher questions to clarify what was observed, learn more about the assumptions that underpin the particular approaches used by the teacher, check to ensure that reason and evidence are clearly understood, and explore how the teacher perceived the lesson to be impacting student learning. In the end, the conversation is all about the teacher's learning and growth, not about what the school leader thinks, assumes, or even knows. A successful generative dialogue causes multiple types and levels of teacher reflection on, and for, practice. Most often, when generative dialogue happens, the teacher is the one who does most of the talking while the school leader listens, probes, clarifies, looks for evidence, and is present as a facilitator of teacher reflection-in-action.

Evidence-Based Questions

Generative leadership emphasizes the need for inquiry questions to grow from goals. The development and use of goal statements alone can be insufficient if professional growth plans are to actually impact teaching practice in ways that lead to optimized learning for all students. Goals, by themselves, can be a limiting agent rather than a growth promoter; in many cases, we have noted that goals can become part of lengthy to-do lists that are created out of compliance or, worse, competition for *busy-ness*.

Since the early days of our work in schools when we first became curious about the use of professional growth plans, we became aware that goal statements referred to episodic projects, or the latest trending author's book, or fields of practice so broad as to be unmanageable. Often, they gave no hint of aspects of the teacher's classroom teaching, assessment practices, management, or professional growth that would be affected by their implementation. Consider the following list of goals, all of which we have encountered in recent years:

- "I plan on implementing Daily 5 into my math program this year."
- "This year I would like to introduce the Leader in Me program to my students."
- "I am going to use PBL (problem-based learning) to change my social studies program."
- "My goal is literacy."
- "I'm using a behaviour matrix this year."

In some cases, we observed confusion between goals and strategies. For instance, some teachers identified their goal as taking a course at a local university or completing a program sponsored by the local professional development consortium.

School leaders, too, offered similar examples. Many did not write a growth plan of their own, and those who did were focused on projects and initiatives: starting professional learning communities; introducing student round tables to integrate student voice in policy development; starting a book club; or being more visible in the hallways. As for district leaders, we rarely saw their professional growth plans in the early days.

In addition, goal statements that explicitly included improved student learning measures were rare. In fact, goal statements frequently caused *decreased responsibility* for student learning. However, after districts adopted the generative leadership model and the use of inquiry questions to guide the work of professional growth plans, we began to observe goals morphing into aspirational and actionable statements with a direct link to student learning. Goal statements became more connected to professional inquiry, and a change in language marked a clear integration of goals, guiding questions, strategies, and evidence.

For example, one teacher developed a goal associated with the introduction of a change to the numeracy program. This goal was converted into an inquiry by the teacher asking "In what ways and to what extent will the introduction of Daily 5 impact my weakest students' skills of problem solving?" With only a goal of introducing a numeracy program, the teacher may very well be able to report at the end of the year that indeed the program was started, that a little more was known about the program, or that the program was introduced and a few students were participating. None of these provides any indication that the teacher grew in pedagogy or enhanced student learning. In fact, almost anything goes when a simple goal statement is accepted as growth. Evidence of practice, evidence of impact on student learning, evidence of any kind might be implied, but not necessarily acted upon, with the goal of introducing the numeracy program. In earlier inquiries we conducted, we found it rare that an explicit connection was made between teacher goals and evidence of student learning.

Conversely, when school leaders guide teachers to use an inquiry approach to professional growth, many questions start with phrases such as "in what ways and to what extent." The "what ways" section gets teachers to think about qualitative indicators of their inquiry. The words help them focus on the ways in which their teaching is actually impacting student learning. From the aforementioned example, the teacher may reconsider the goal of introducing Daily 5 into teaching mathematics by inquiring into the ways in which students are now using problem-solving strategies in a more focused and purposeful manner, the ways in which numeracy skill is being demonstrated in their daily tasks, and ways in which the least confident students are benefitting from small-group collaboration. When it comes to the "what extent" section of the question, the teacher in this example would be encouraged to explore just how much of a quantitative impact the Daily 5 program is having on students. The teacher may use either their own impact assessments or standardized assessments. In our observations, teachers will often develop their own valid and reliable indicators that allow them to dig deep into their own instructional practice.

School and district leaders also design questions that begin with the words "in what ways and to what extent" in relationship to some element of their practice. Their questions often explore the impact of their practice on teaching and learning in the school or school district.

With inquiry questions in place, district leaders can now ask generative questions of school leaders, school leaders can ask teachers, and, when the system is really working as it should, teachers can ask each other and their students. Each time these respective groups get together, they begin their conversations with the same four questions. These questions set the stage to delve into reflection on practice:

- "What did you do since the last time we met?" This question is predicated on the practice of ensuring that each time the groups meet, it ends with a notification about what will be attempted in the next seven days, 30 days, or whenever the next meeting is to occur.
- "What did you learn?" This question creates a space for sharing insights and best practices, and prompting self-assessment in a nonthreatening way.
- "What evidence do you have to show that impact is occurring?"
- "What will you do between now and the next time we meet?" This question is important in reinforcing an ethos of shared responsibility. It ensures that when a commitment to action is made, colleagues can trust that it will be acted upon.

The third question, the one that deals with evidence of impact, is meant to cause deep thinking about actions, impacts, and next steps, and can lead to adoption of a research frame of mind. This promotes a reflection on what is working, what is not working, and why.

In schools where generative leadership has become the norm, we see the use of evidence on a more sustained and widespread basis. Principals use data and other forms of evidence when they work with the school staff to think about, implement, and evaluate programs that help drive improved teaching and learning within the school. Teachers are readier to accept the idea that, before a new program is implemented, it must be accompanied by rigorous indicators of improved student learning. What we see in these schools is that using a question to contextualize strategies and measures is critical for the evolution toward evidence-based decision making.

Leaders Who Model

Researchers Helen Timperley (Timperley, 2011b), Viviane Robinson (Robinson, 2010), and Carol Campbell (Campbell, 2017) espouse the necessity of school leaders working alongside teachers to implement new programs around teaching and learning. They have been able to show that when principals are engaged as learners alongside their teachers, and when they participate in every aspect of an initiative, more teachers will actually improve their practice, and student achievement will increase. Yet, for a principal to find the time to participate in all elements of teacher learning, as well as lead the plethora of initiatives that schools are undertaking, can be a very daunting task.

In many schools, leader succession planning entails a fairly predictable series of processes: a highly proficient classroom teacher gets tapped on the shoulder and goes from being one of the many to being a vice-principal and, eventually, a principal. As this happens, the newly ordained school leader is somehow supposed to have all the answers: to be the one that other teachers can turn to for the magic pill, the panacea, the silver bullet that will somehow cause more and better learning to happen in a more efficacious way. This fallacy of expertise, however, is just that. New leaders don't come with all the answers (Germain, 2012). Many come with nervousness and fear of failure, albeit with a sincere hope that they might be able to help children through more focused work with teachers. In the generative leadership process, these new leaders truly appreciate the liberating experience of being able to ask their colleagues questions, rather than always having to provide an answer.

As new district programs and initiatives are adopted by these schools and districts, leaders model learning by participating in it, thereby presenting a different perspective on succession planning. They come to know what each initiative is about and how to potentially impact the children of the school. They help identify possible sources of evidence they will accept as indicators of impact on student learning. Then, they work closely with teachers to ask the questions necessary to cause reflection; in doing so, they are freed from the necessity of being the expert; instead, they are encouraged to *learn alongside*.

This process certainly does not excuse leaders from learning nor from being at the forefront of proven practices that enhance student learning. It actually encourages such endeavours because, as more and more teachers explore ways in which they can answer their own questions about student learning, leaders are required to know what teachers are doing so they, in turn, can ask the most effective questions. As leaders become more active learners and more effective questioners, they elevate their credibility and explicit skill in *leading learning*.

One example of the transition from knowing the answers to asking the right questions occurred in a school trying to implement generative leadership. This school was seeking to increase grade one reading levels. The principal had identified that, even though the school was well into the use of guided reading, students were not attaining the desired results as determined by Fountas and Pinnell benchmarking. Benchmarking results indicated that over half the students fell well below the acceptable level and most of the remaining students were just above the level that indicated average results. Almost none were in the exceeding level. Prior to our working with the school, the leadership team had taken a very directive approach to getting teachers to better utilize the guided reading process. The poor results continued.

Once generative leadership was implemented, a change in process ensued. School leaders now spent time in the grade one classrooms working alongside teachers; all teachers and leaders debriefed regularly by asking and answering questions about guided reading and, particularly, how it was being employed in daily interactions with the children. Questions were asked, answers were given, evidence was presented, small improvements were noted, and change started to happen. As an environment of inspection changed to one of collaboration centred on an inquiry process, teachers noted small gains in student literacy when they completed their quarterly benchmarking. Leaders asked deep questions about why the improvements were happening. Teachers took increased ownership of changes and bigger improvements were noted at the next quarter. Midway through the following year, 75 percent of the students met or exceeded the acceptable level and the remaining 25 percent were just under the acceptable level. The leaders certainly understood what guided reading looked like, felt like, was like, but to do so with conviction, they had to stop being the experts and start being inquirers. They assumed a learning role. Moreover, they modelled the process of inquiry by asking questions and searching for evidence of impact.

Central Office Leadership

To this point in the chapter, we have only alluded to the role that central office leaders play in generative leadership; now, we become explicit about this important element. Before the principals and vice-principals in our projects start to function as generative leaders, they undergo a year-long awareness and readiness program, during which they experience what it entails to be participants in the process. They write an inquiry-based professional growth plan (after reviewing the professional standards for school leaders), reflect on where their growth could best help the school reach its desired goals, craft an inquiry question or questions to guide their work, and identify areas of evidence that could be used to answer their question. Approximately every 30 days, members of the Central Office Leadership Team (COLT) visit school sites. During each visit, a COLT leader will ask the questions introduced earlier in this chapter: What did you do since our last visit (professional growth plan–related)? What did you learn? What evidence do you have to support the learning? What are you going to do in the next 7 days or 30 days?

In the beginning, the COLT leaders may have to ask more probing questions to get school leaders to think more deeply, make connections between beliefs and practices, explore possible sources of evidence (and what counts as valid pieces of evidence), and examine how they are making progress in answering their question. Quickly, however, as the process becomes routine, the school leaders are doing more of the talking and only occasionally do district leaders have to ask so many probing questions.

When interviewed about the process of being involved in generative leadership, school leaders have described how much they valued the visits by members of the COLT. They claim that this process has helped them to do the following:

- Develop valuable new knowledge and skills
- Form greater appreciation of and respect for their COLT colleagues
- Expand their professional networks throughout the district
- Engage in more purposeful conversations with more teachers
- Experience an increased commitment to leadership
- Extend the impact of collaboration within their schools

These school leaders also expressed their belief that participation in generative leadership through COLT visits challenged them to focus on aspects of school leadership that, heretofore, had not always been accorded such high priority. There was a generalized agreement on the value of regular monthly visits by external teams, the questioning process that was at the heart of collaborative inquiry, the emphasis placed on growth rather than evaluation, and the active pursuit of agreed-upon goals. These school leaders saw themselves as becoming more accountable, more responsible, and more effective in their leadership practices.

In survey results from several districts, school leaders also painted a very positive picture about the organizational culture that resulted from the COLT visits. There was definitely a stronger sense of efficacy being expressed and demonstrated by educational leaders in the schools and throughout the district. In addition, data derived from field notes pointed to other areas of obvious success and growth that deserve to be mentioned. These included enhanced collaboration, professional learning, confidence, and trust among school leaders; the development of more effective teams of leaders and teachers and, with that, a noteworthy increase in levels of mutual respect and thoughtfulness; much greater attention to the quality of teaching and learning happening in schools; a strong and emerging focus on evidence of goal achievement (through the answering of their own inquiry questions); clear indications of capacity building among the school leadership groups; and increased attention to the needs of all students in the schools.

The Value of Teams

One perceptive vice-principal from a generative leadership school expressed the sentiment that "My participation in this process has led me to believe that as teachers we must collaborate, collaborate, collaborate, and when we think we have collaborated enough, collaborate some more." This participant also noted that the whole idea of *team* took on a much clearer meaning when squarely sighted on the primacy of the work leading to improved student learning because of the "famous four" questions: What did you do? What did you learn? What evidence do you have? What will you do between now and when we next meet? She indicated that the often-talked-about ideal of teachers being responsible for the learning of all students was closer to being a reality in her school.

Generative leadership requires that school leadership teams (principals, vice-principals, lead teachers) become highly focused on purposeful work that leads directly to student learning. When the process is working best, the school leadership team shares a guiding question, the answers to which provide evidence of the extent to which the team is able to achieve an agreed-upon goal. In the case of teachers, they meet in teams, with a meeting schedule embedded in the timetable as a regular part of the school day. Certainly, team meetings may happen after school, but for the most part, school leaders find the time for this important work to happen when teachers are fresh, not rushed, and when they are actually paid to be in the building. How school leaders make this embedded time happen is as diverse as the schools themselves. Some school leaders take entire grades of students for team-building exercises while their teachers meet. Others organize a series of guest speakers to come into the school while freeing teachers from the necessity of supervision and, by so doing, provide time for team meetings to happen. One very focused school leader built a rotating schedule for multi-grade reading buddies to occur, thus allowing teacher teams to meet regularly. Another promoted forms of team-teaching that freed teacher teams to concentrate on their growth plans. In all instances, students were kept engaged in the process of learning while their teachers met to plan for further learning to occur.

When teachers meet, they are guided by their own collaborative inquiry question. Their question is mutually agreed upon and, in most cases, aligned in some way with the school plan. Teachers hold each other accountable and responsible for the work of the team by proceeding through the famous four questions. Leaders are either appointed by the principal or naturally arise, based on the type of work being undertaken. Leaders report on the work of the team to the principal and share the team's discoveries at regular full meetings of the staff. The obligatory monthly staff meetings take on an inquiry focus. Teachers are able to share pieces of evidence they have been using to answer their inquiry question, demonstrate their growth, and show impact on student learning.

HELPFUL RESPONSES TO UNHELPFUL ASSUMPTIONS ABOUT GENERATIVE LEADERSHIP

As might be anticipated, many elements of the generative leadership model that we posit have come under scrutiny and criticism. Most often, these have come to us in a form that requires that we check or recalibrate our commitment to some fundamental assumptions. Taken as a whole, these assumptions represent a paradigmatic shift in leading learning; however, as we often see, system and school leaders rarely consistently enact statements that appear at first to be innocuous or self-evident. Sometimes, quite the opposite! Well-intentioned, hard-working, and dedicated educators, when challenged to identify specific examples in response to the question "What does this look like?" often realize that they may not truly believe some of their cherished, taken-for-granted assumptions after all.

We offer several here for your consideration. We challenge you to identify your demonstrable leadership behaviours that represent the extent to which you believe these assumptions are central to your practice.

Learning Is Possible in a Single Event or Episode—Educators Are Professional and They Will Immediately Implement What They Are Told

Most effective leaders we observe were also effective teachers. Most believe, as a matter of theory and practice, that each of their students was unique, with learning needs, strengths, and weaknesses; they will recall fondly their success in "reaching every student" or their highlights in helping students achieve. They will also acknowledge that doing so requires patience, sustained persistence, and dedication to a long-term process of uneven progress.

Yet, few consistently apply those same criteria when leading learning. Accordingly, it is not uncommon to observe "sit and get" events characterized by one-time, transmissional models of professional learning: the system administrator meetings during which a superintendent proselytizes for hours, handing out volumes of paper or referencing multiple online documents, before asking "Does anyone have any questions?"; the school professional development days when a principal brings in an external guru to speak on a topic unrelated to the learning curiosities or goals of the staff; a curriculum development and assessment "workshop" for staff in which the goal is to rewrite a unit test; or a ministry presentation comprising 134 slides outlining new directions for education.

All these cases, and many more that we have observed over the years, assume that professional learners are pedagogically tabula rasa. Although seemingly efficient, these types of processes remove the locus of control for learning to an external source, usually a perceived expert, and limit the likelihood that observable changes in practice will occur.

Leading Professional Learning through a Collaborative Process Is Just Too Time-Consuming

We will spend additional time in chapter 6 discussing the power and limitations of collaboration and, in particular, how collaborative learning processes are grounded in postmodern, constructivist ontologies that can support effective leadership. We are also aware of learning theories that advocate the balanced use of interdependent and independent learning experiences. In a measured and reasoned approach to leading learning, there is a place for learning through, with, and in the presence of colleagues as much as there is a place for learning through individual reflection and contemplation. Rather than excluding one in favour of the other, we draw leaders' attention to the necessity of using a wide variety of strategies that will support and accommodate the unique learning needs of those for whom they are leading learning. Some of the most effective examples of leading learning that we have witnessed have included, in a short two-hour session, strategies such as turn and talk, jigsaw readings, journal reflections, guided table discussion, individual case study analysis, and small group brainstorming. And yet leaders who struggle to enact this assumption often lament the time it takes to organize this type of learning and explain how it is more efficient to *tell* rather than teach.

Professional Practice Is about Complying with the Expectations Told to Me by My Superiors

We often ask leaders to reflect on the question stems "I wonder who/when/why …?" "What keeps you up at night?" or "Who do you think about on your drive home from work?" "What are the persistent questions that keep frustrating you and limiting your effectiveness?" and "What gets in the way of you doing what you hope for in your work?"

We contend that the answers to any of these questions should be strongly reflected in the goals and learning plans of leaders. In turn, effective leaders should see in others their attempts to address the relentless curiosities about their lived professional practices. In doing so, levels of professional autonomy and responsibility increase and, paradoxically, professional collaboration is pursued, maximized, and appreciated. In fact, authentic curiosity enhances professional practice and growth.

Yet many educators are familiar with the more sanitized version of setting goals for professional practice: "I will complete my masters' degree"; "I will read a book about literacy"; "I will spend more time in teachers' classrooms." Or, even more obtuse to professional practice: "I will do more yoga to decrease stress"; "I will learn how to use a Chromebook"; "I will not take as much marking home with me." The next chapter will address the contrast in theory and practice between professional development and professional learning; however, for the purposes of examining assumptions, it is instructive to reflect on the extent to which organizational and individual goals encompass the daily, job-embedded curiosities of leaders and teachers. If they do not, why not?

There Are Definite Categories of Effectiveness

A leader's responsibility is to identify where everyone fits along a continuum. This is a tough one for leaders to consistently overcome without falter. To do so requires a deep commitment to moving away from judgment and toward a genuine curiosity in the skills and "wonderings" of others as they grow and improve their professional practice. We also believe that many leaders habitually and unconsciously work backwards from a deficit model that presumes "fixing," not because they are incompetent, ineffective, or just plain mean, but because they have become so wrapped up in the frenetic pace that is school and system leadership that they find it difficult to move out of crisis problem-solving mode.

Another factor that often causes a checklist or fix-it approach to the notion of presumed competence is reflected in policies around leaders' responsibility to supervise and evaluate. In a recent study (Brandon et al., 2018), there was found to be a general uncertainty and inconsistent interpretation among teachers, school principals, and central office leaders about the approaches and activities that supervision and evaluation comprise. In some cases, evaluation and supervision were seen to be synonymous; in these cases, it should not be surprising for us to observe those in positions of leadership making elaborate, sometimes unfounded, judgments that result in erosion of trust, lack of communication, disengagement, and even opposition toward professional growth and improving practice.

Leaders Just Know When They Are Effective; They Don't Need to Be Able to Explain How or Why

Abraham Maslow (1943) is often attributed with developing the four-stage learning theory of progressive competence. We present an adaptation of these stages as follows:

Unconscious incompetence. An educator may not understand or know how to do something and may not necessarily recognize the deficit; in fact, they may deny the usefulness of the skill or the extent to which learning the skill will positively impact practice.

↓

Conscious incompetence. An educator may not understand or know how to do something, but they recognize the deficit, as well as the value of a new skill in addressing the deficit. Making mistakes through supported risk-taking can be integral to the learning process at this stage.

↓

Unconscious competence. An educator performs a skill well; however, it may be difficult to articulate what the skill or competency actually is or why choices were made about the use of the skill. When identified, there is heavy conscious involvement in executing the new skill.

↓

Conscious competence. An educator has had so much practice with a skill that it has become "second nature" and can be performed easily. Decisions about the skill are made purposefully, with a full understanding of and ability to articulate the rationale and impact of the skill. The individual may be able to teach it to others, depending upon how and when it was learned.

When integrated with the previous assumption about **assumed competence**, it is the responsibility of leaders to create the conditions, provide the opportunities, and facilitate the learning process that will cause teachers and colleagues to reflect upon their areas of unexamined competence and help them grow in areas of unconscious competence. A true culture of learning is most evident when all members of the organization are at high, sophisticated levels of conscious competence and are able to make highly informed commitments to a progressive career of sustained growth for themselves and others.

Leading Learning Is at the Bottom of My Long To-Do List
We believe that leading learning is analogous to teaching. For principals or vice-principals who no longer have direct instructional roles with students, we view staff members as their class: professional learning sessions are their lessons, professional growth is the curriculum, and enhanced pedagogy is the learning outcome. Similarly, for system leaders, their students are their directors, coordinators, principals, and vice-principals. In this context, when we ask the question "How do you teach them to ensure that they learn?" we are not being cheeky or judgmental. Rather, we are hoping to trigger a moment of recognition that shifts the nature of their approach to leading learning from one of manager to one of educator.

An effective teacher would not presume to "wing it" for a lesson. The best teachers are conscientious about planning learning outcomes, instructional strategies, assessment methods, and self-evaluation. Similarly, an effective leader is rigorous about prioritizing, planning, and assessing the effectiveness of all professional days, individual learning opportunities, and instructional leadership interactions: they are purposeful, aware, strategic, and visibly committed to being lead learners, and the leaders of learners.

REFLECTIONS AND WRITING PROVOCATIONS FOR ADOPTING GENERATIVE LEADERSHIP

As we have mentioned in the first two chapters, we often use a strategy of reflective writing to encourage leaders to think more deeply about assumptions and world views that may hinder their growth or their authentic engagement in generative leadership. In this regard, free-form writing has been particularly helpful. As we use it, free-form writing requires leaders to make only two commitments to thinking about their leadership experiences: don't stop writing until an agreed-upon time limit is reached, and don't correct, censor, judge, or otherwise evaluate the thoughts that are being written.

We start the free-form writing protocol with a fairly short period of writing time: five to eight minutes is often enough to inspire reflection. However, by the third or fourth time, most leaders can endure the required physical and attentional rigour, and are able to write uninterrupted for over 20 minutes.

We have used the following stems to provoke reflections around the concept of generative leadership:

- From the list of assumptions presented in this chapter, the one that I grapple with the most is …
- When I think about discussing my professional goals in front of colleagues, I feel …
- If the school principal can have the single greatest impact on teachers' effectiveness, then …
- Yeah, but what about …
- To me, the word *generate* in generative leadership means that …
- The conditions I think are most necessary for effective instructional leadership are …

CONCLUSION

Generative leadership has, at its core, improved student learning. This is achieved by leaders who establish the conditions and expectations for purposeful, focused, learner-centric teaching that is supported by elbow-to-elbow instructional leadership practices. Generative leadership entails the interactivity of six key elements:

- Inquiry-based professional growth for and by everyone in the organization
- Classroom observations that are frequent, purposeful, focused, and aligned with the professional growth planning process
- Generative dialogue that integrates evidence-based questions
- Leaders who model the generative dialogue process
- Monthly visits to school sites by system leaders, monthly visits by school leaders with teachers and school staff, and teachers using generative dialogue with students as an informal assessment strategy
- Teams that are clearly sighted on the optimization of student learning and use monthly team meetings to answer four key questions: What have you done to move your professional practice forward? What have you learned? What evidence have you collected? What will you commit to in the next 30 days?

As we will discuss in the next chapter, these generative leaders also possess some habits of mind and specific skills that allow them to achieve their responsibilities by *leading with powerful questions*. They demonstrate an amazing capacity to be curious about the work of others and to ask those well-placed and well-crafted questions that will cause reflection and growth-oriented action.

SUGGESTED READINGS FOR GENERATIVE LEADERSHIP

Brandon, J., Saar, C., Friesen, S., Brown, B., & Yee, D. (2016). Pedagogical leadership teams: Magnifying and spreading impact. In M. A. Takeuchi, A. P. Preciado Babb, & J. Lock (Eds.), *Proceedings of the ideas: Designing for innovation* (pp. 152–161). Calgary, AB: University of Calgary.

This paper contributes to the emergence of the conceptualization of pedagogical leadership teaming. Pedagogical leadership teaming is rooted in five strands of research: (1) effective teaching; (2) shared instructional leadership; (3) professional learning; (4) evidence, **relational trust**, and reflective discourse; and (5) learning-focused district leadership. In their further inquiry, the authors sought to illustrate various ways that pedagogical leadership teams magnify and spread the impact of teachers and leader learning on student success.

Fullan, M. (2016). The elusive nature of whole system improvement in education. *Journal of Educational Change, 17*(4), 539–544. doi:10.1007/s10833-016-9289-1

In this article, Fullan provides an analysis of the impact of his earlier work on whole-system reform. Central to his work are four educational drivers: capacity building, collaboration, pedagogy, and systemic policies. He examines six case studies where these drivers were applied with varying degrees of impact. Although Fullan acknowledges the progress that has been made, he contends that the changes seen were not deep enough to produce fundamental whole-system change. To address this, he recommends a deep change in learning culture, local ownership of the learning agenda, and a system of continuous improvement that is simultaneously bottom-up, top-down, and horizontal. He concludes with a call to develop networks that capitalize on humans' natural drive to connect and help others.

Hopkins, M., & Woulfin, S. (2015). School system (re)design: Developing educational infrastructures to support school leadership and teaching practice. *Journal of Educational Change, 16*(4), 371–377. doi:10.1007/s10833-015-9260-6

In this work, Hopkins and Woulfin examine a series of articles that address the impact of infrastructure on educational change. They define infrastructure as the "scaffolds and networks that facilitate function" (p. 372) that need to be maintained and supported. They contend that to properly understand educational infrastructure one must consider both the structures and how they are built. Hopkins and Woulfin explore the connection between infrastructure and practice and, based on the studies they examined, conclude that what constitutes educational infrastructure is determined by how a given object or structure is used. Finally, in their conclusion, Hopkins and Woulfin suggest that the process of developing educational infrastructure should be shared by educational stakeholders at all levels.

Kirtman, L., & Fullan, M. (2016). *Leadership: Key competencies for whole-system change.* Bloomington, IN: Solution Tree Press.

In this collaborative work, Kirtman's ideas about leadership competencies are synthesized with Fullan's analysis of system-wide change. Addressing an education system that is increasingly complex and over-regulated, Kirtman and Fullan encourage the development of a simple and focused leadership practice that moves beyond initiative fatigue. Their theoretical work is regularly supported with examples from the field as they lay out seven core competencies: challenging the status quo, building trust, creating a common success plan, focusing on teams, urgency for sustainable change, continuous improvement of self and system, and developing external support networks. Building on this foundation, they outline how these core competencies allow leaders to move beyond the educational drivers that stifle initiative to those that increase instructional capacity throughout an entire educational system.

Klimek, K. J., Ritzenhein, E., & Sullivan, K. D. (2008). *Generative leadership: Shaping new futures for today's schools.* Thousand Oaks, CA: Corwin Press.

Generative Leadership: Shaping New Futures for Today's Schools by Klimek, Ritzenhein, and Sullivan defines their model of generative leadership as built on a foundation of generativity, living-system principles, and brain/mind science. Generativity, as discussed by Klimek et al., includes the ability to challenge assumptions, question what has been taken for granted, and seek creative solutions. A living-system principle in this context includes the idea that schools are systems rather than structures and that the models we use to consider them are generally too simplistic. Using this knowledge, a generative leader can work with a school's identity, flow of information, and relationships to strengthen it. Brain/mind science is applied by Klimek et al. to three interactive elements: relaxed alertness, orchestrated immersion, and active processing. Using this basis, the generative leader is encouraged to build on the existing capacity in the school by using generative questions to challenge hidden assumptions. Finally, a series of resources for applying this theory are provided.

Kouzes, J., & Posner, B. (2012). *The leadership challenge: How to make extraordinary things happen in organizations* (5th ed.). San Francisco, CA: Leadership Challenge.

Kouzes and Posner, in their fifth edition, maintain that leadership is everyone's business and that accepting the leadership challenge is the only antidote to chaos, stagnation, and disintegration. Rising to the leadership challenge can be accomplished by following the Five Practices of Exemplary Leadership: model the way, inspire a shared vision, challenge the process, enable others to act, and encourage the heart. The authors outline the Ten Commitments of Leadership and the essential behaviours that leaders employ to make extraordinary things happen. They persist in asking the same question from their initial undertaking of this research in 1982: "What did you do when you were at your personal best as a leader?" This question is fundamental to their belief that mastery of the art of leadership comes from mastery of self.

Penuel, W. R., Briggs, D. C., Davidson, K. L., Herlihy, C., Sherer, D., Hill, H. C., … Allen, A. R. (2017). How school and district leaders access, perceive, and use research. *AERA Open, 3*(2), 1–17. doi:10.1177/2332858417705370

In the first national survey of its kind to shed light on research use among local education leaders, a representative sample of 733 school and district leaders across the United States was surveyed to develop an understanding of the prevalence of research use, the nature of leaders' attitudes toward research, and individual and organizational correlates of research use. In the study, leaders reported high levels of research use to make decisions, expand their thinking about issues, and persuade others of other points of view. Additionally, research was used to choose curricula, justify programs, and fulfill grant requirements. Overall, the study finds that leaders have a strong appetite for research and find it valuable in their decision making.

NOTE

1. On a related point, Hargreaves, Shirley, Harris, and Boyle (2010) note that while teacher collaboration is on the rise, principal collaboration is not. They contend that it is important for the superintendent and other system personnel to facilitate principal collaboration and instructional leadership development.

REFERENCES

Acheson, K. (1985). The principal's role in instructional leadership. *OSSC Bulletin, 28*(8), 31–34.

Adams, C. M., & Miskell, R. C. (2016). Teacher trust in district administration: A promising line of inquiry. *Educational Administration Quarterly, 52*(4), 675–706. doi:10.1177/0013161X16652202

Adams, P. (2012). *Framework for professional learning: Implementing a collaborative inquiry model to personalize professional learning for educators.* Edmonton, AB: Alberta Education Workforce Planning Branch.

Adams, P. (2016). A noticeable impact: Perceptions of how system leaders can affect leading and learning. *Journal of Educational Administration and Foundations, 25*(3), 39–55.

Alberta Education. (2009). *The principal quality practice guideline: Promoting successful school leadership in Alberta.* Edmonton, AB: Alberta Education. Retrieved from http://education.alberta.ca/admin/resources.aspx

Alberta Teachers' Association. (2014). *The future of the principalship in Canada: A national research study.* Edmonton, AB: Alberta Teachers' Association.

Barth, R. S. (1990). *Improving schools from within: Teachers, parents, and principals can make the difference.* San Francisco, CA: Jossey-Bass.

Barth, R. S. (2001). Teacher leader. *Phi Delta Kappan, 82*(6), 443–447.

Black, S. (1998). A different kind of leader. *American School Board Journal, 185*(6), 32–35.

Blase, J., & Blase, J. (2002). The micropolitics of instructional supervision: A call for research. *Educational Administration Quarterly, 38*(1), 6–44. doi:10.1177/0013161x02381002

Brandon, J., Friesen, S., Koh, K., Parsons, D., Adams, P., Mombourquette, C., … Hunter, D. (2018). *Building, supporting, and assuring quality professional practice: A research study of teacher growth, supervision, and evaluation in Alberta.* Edmonton, AB: Alberta Education.

Butler, D. L., Schnellert, L., & Macneil, K. (2015). Collaborative inquiry and distributed agency in educational change: A case study of a multi-level community of inquiry. *Journal of Educational Change, 16*(1), 1–26. doi:http://dx.doi.org/10.1007/s10833-014-9227-z

Byrne-Jiménez, M., Orr, M. T., & Sobol, T. (2007). *Developing effective principals through collaborative inquiry.* New York, NY: Teachers College Press.

Cacari-Stone, L., Wallerstein, N., Garcia, A. P., & Minkler, M. (2014). The promise of community-based participatory research for health equity: A conceptual model for bridging evidence with policy. *American Journal of Public Health, 104*(9), 1615–1623.

Campbell, C. (2017). Developing teachers' professional learning: Canadian evidence and experiences in a world of educational improvement. *Canadian Journal of Education, 40*(2), 1–33.

Campbell, C., Zeichner, K. M., Lieberman, A., & Osmond-Johnson, P. (2017). *Empowered educators in Canada: How high-performing systems shape teaching quality.* San Francisco, CA: Jossey-Bass.

Cherkowski, S., & Schnellert, L. (2017). Exploring teacher leadership in a rural, secondary school: Reciprocal learning teams as a catalyst for emergent leadership. *International Journal of Teacher Leadership, 8*(1), 6–25.

Costa, A. L., & Garmston, R. J. (1994). *Cognitive coaching: A foundation for renaissance schools.* Norwood, MA: Christopher-Gordon.

Costa, A. L., & Garmston, R. J. (2002). *Cognitive coaching: A foundation for renaissance schools* (2nd ed.). Kanham, MA: Rowman & Littlefield.

Crowther, F., Ferguson, M., & Hann, L. (2009). *Developing teacher leaders: How teacher leadership enhances school success.* Thousand Oaks, CA: Corwin Press.

Darling-Hammond, L., Wei, R., Andree, A., Richardson, N., & Orphanos, S. (2009). *Professional learning in the learning profession: A status report on teacher development in the United States and abroad.* Palo Alto, CA: National Staff Development Council.

Day, C., & Sammons, P. (2013). *Successful leadership: A review of the international literature.* University of Oxford: CfBT Education Trust.

De Bevoise, W. (1984). Synthesis of research on the principal as instructional leader. *Educational Leadership, 41*(5), 14–20.

DeLuca, C., Shulha, J., Luhanga, U., Shulha, L., Christou, T. M., & Klinger, D. (2015). Collaborative inquiry as a professional learning structure for educators: A scoping review. *Professional Development in Education, 41*(4), 640–670.

DuFour, R., & Marzano, R. (2011). Leaders of learning: How district, school, and classroom leaders improve student achievement. Bloomington, IN: Solution Tree Press.

Emihovich, C., & Battaglia, C. (2000). Creating cultures for collaborative inquiry: New challenges for school leaders. *International Journal of Leadership in Education, 3*(3), 225–238. doi:10.1080/13603120050083918

Fenwick, T. (2004). Teacher learning and professional growth plans: Implementation of a provincial policy. *Journal of Curriculum and Supervision, 19*(3), 259–282.

Fletcher-Sodat, C. L. (2010). *One principal's educational leadership in a rural and low-performing middle school in Virginia: A case study* (Doctoral dissertation). Virginia Commonwealth University, Richmond, VA. Retrieved from https://scholarscompass.vcu.edu/cgi/viewcontent.cgi?article=3335&context=etd

Fullan, M. (2001). *Leading in a culture of change.* San Francisco, CA: Jossey-Bass.

Germain, M.-L. (2012). Traits and skills theories as the nexus between leadership and expertise: Reality or fallacy? *Performance Improvement, 51*(5), 32–39. doi:10.1002/pfi.21265

Glickman, C., Gordon, S., & Ross-Gordon, J. (2017). *Supervision and instructional leadership* (10th ed.). New York, NY: Pearson.

Government of Alberta. (2018). School leadership standard. Edmonton, AB: Government of Alberta. Retrieved from https://education.alberta.ca/media/3739621/standardsdoc-lqs-_fa-web-2018-01-17.pdf

Grenny, J. (2002). Crucial conversations. *Executive Excellence, 19*(9), 10–20.

Grenny, J. (2009). Crucial conversations: The most potent force for eliminating disruptive behavior. *The Health Care Manager, 28*(3), 240–250.

Hall, G., & George, A. (1999). The impact of principal change facilitator style on school and classroom culture. In J. H. Freiberg (Ed.), *School climate: Measuring, improving, and sustaining healthy learning evironments.* Philadelphia, PA: Falmer Press.

Hallinger, P., & Heck, R. (2010a). Collaborative leadership and school improvement: Understanding the impact on school capacity and student learning. *School Leadership & Management, 30*(2), 95–110. doi:10.1080/13632431003663214

Hallinger, P., & Heck, R. (2010b). Leadership for learning: Does collaborative leadership make a difference in school improvement? *Educational Management Administration & Leadership, 38*(6), 654–678. doi:10.1177/1741143210379060

Hallinger, P., & Murphy, J. (1985). Assessing the instructional management behaviour of principals. *The Elementary School Journal, 86*(2), 217–247.

Hargreaves, A., Shirley, D., Harris, A., & Boyle, A. (2010). Collaborative edge: How helping others helps you. *Principal, 89*(4), 16–20.

Harris, A. (2013). Distributed leadership: Friend or foe? *Educational Management Administration & Leadership, 41*(5), 545–554. doi:10.1177/1741143213497635

Harris, A., Muijs, D., Chapman, C., Stoll, L., & Russ, J. (2003). *Raising attainment in the former coalfield areas.* London, UK: Department for Education and Skills, Moorfoot.

Hauserman, C. P., & Stick, S. L. (2013). The leadership teachers want from principals: Transformational. *Canadian Journal of Education, 36*(3), 184–203.

Heinrich, C. J., & Good, A. (2018). Research-informed practice improvements: Exploring linkages between school district use of research evidence and educational outcomes over time. *School Effectiveness and School Improvement, 29*(3), 418–445. doi:10.1080/09243453.2018.1445116

Jamison, K., & Clayton, J. (2016). Exploring the experiences of administrative interns. *Journal of Educational Administration, 54*(5), 514–536.

Jao, L., & McDougall, D. (2016). Moving beyond the barriers: Supporting meaningful teacher collaboration to improve secondary school mathematics. *Teacher Development, 20*(4), 557–573. doi:10.1080/13664530.2016.1164747

Joyce, B., & Showers, B. (1981). Transfer of training: The contribution of coaching. *The Journal of Education, 163*(2), 163–172.

Joyce, B., & Showers, B. (1982). The coaching of teaching. *Educational Leadership, 1*(10), 4–9.

Joyce, B., & Showers, B. (1987). Low-cost arrangements for peer-coaching. *Journal of Staff Development, 8*(1), 22–28.

Kitchen, M., Gray, S., & Jeurissen, M. (2016). Principals' collaborative roles as leaders for learning. *Leadership and Policy in Schools, 15*(2), 168–191. doi:10.1080/15700763.2015.1031255

Knight, J. (2009). Coaching: The key to translating research into practice lies in continuous, job-embedded learning with ongoing support. *Journal of Staff Development, 30*(1), 18–24.

Knight, J., & van Nieuwerburgh, C. (2012). Instructional coaching: A focus on practice. *Coaching: An International Journal of Theory, Research and Practice, 5*(2), 100–112. doi:10.108 0/17521882.2012.707668

Lambert, L. (2003). Leadership redefined: An evocative context for teacher leadership. *School Leadership & Management, 23*(4), 421–430. doi:10.1080/1363243032000150953

Lashway, L. (1995). Facilitative leadership. *ERIC Digest, 1*(96), 1–6.

Leithwood, K. (2010a). Characteristics of school districts that are exceptionally effective in closing the achievement gap. *Leadership and Policy in Schools, 9*(1), 245–291. doi:10.1080/15700761003731500

Leithwood, K. (2010b). *Turning around underperforming school systems: Guidelines for district leaders.* Edmonton, AB: College of Alberta School Superintendents.

Leithwood, K., Harris, A., & Hopkins, D. (2008). Seven strong claims about successful school leadership. *School Leadership and Management, 28*(1), 27–42. doi:10.1080/13632430701800060

Leithwood, K., Patten, S., & Jantzi, D. (2010). Testing a conception of how school leadership influences student learning. *Educational Administration Quarterly, 46*(5), 671–706. doi:10.1177/0013161x10377347

Leithwood, K., Seashore Louis, K., Anderson, S., & Wahlstrom, K. (2004). *How leadership influences student learning.* Minneapolis, MN: University of Minnesota.

MacDonald, M., & Weller, K. (2017). Redefining our roles as teachers, learners, and leaders through continuous cycles of practitioner inquiry. *The New Educator, 13*(2), 137–147. doi: 10.1080/1547688X.2016.1144121

Marks, H. M., & Printy, S. M. (2003). Principal leadership and school performance: An integration of transformational and instructional leadership. *Educational Administration Quarterly, 39*(3), 370–397. doi:10.1177/0013161x03253412

Marzano, R., Waters, T., & McNulty, B. (2005). *School leadership that works: From research to results.* Alexandria, VA: Association for Supervision and Curriculum Development.

Maslow, A. (1943). A theory of human motivation. *Psychological Review, 50*(4), 370–396.

Neumerski, C. M. (2013). Rethinking instructional leadership, a review: What do we know about principal, teacher, and coach instructional leadership, and where should we go from here? *Educational Administration Quarterly, 49*(2), 310–347. doi:10.1177/0013161x12456700

Newton, P., & Wallin, D. (2013). The teaching principal: An untenable position or a promising model? *Alberta Journal of Educational Research, 59*(1), 55–71.

Normore, A. H. (2006). A new agenda for research in educational leadership. *Journal of Educational Administration, 44*(5), 520–522. doi:10.1108/09578230610683796

Organisation for Economic Co-operation and Development. (2016). *School leadership for learning: Insights from TALIS 2013*. Paris, France: OECD. Retrieved from http://dx.doi.org/10.1787/9789264258341-en

Orr, M. T., & Orphanos, S. (2011). How graduate-level preparation influences the effectiveness of school leaders: A comparison of the outcomes of exemplary and conventional leadership preparation programs for principals. *Educational Administration Quarterly, 47*(1), 18–70. doi:10.1177/0011000010378610

Park, J.-H., & Jeong, D. W. (2013). School reforms, principal leadership, and teacher resistance: Evidence from Korea. *Asia Pacific Journal of Education, 33*(1), 34–52. doi:10.1080/02188791.2012.756392

Pounder, D. (2011). Leader preparation special issue: Implications for policy, practice, and research. *Educational Administration Quarterly, 47*(1), 258–267. doi:10.1177/0011000010378615

Riveros, A., Newton, P., & da Costa, J. (2013). From teachers to teacher-leaders: A case study. *International Journal of Teacher Leadership, 4*(1), 1–15.

Robinson, V. (2010). From instructional leadership to leadership capabilities: Empirical findings and methodological challenges. *Leadership and Policy in Schools, 9*(1), 1–26. doi:10.1080/15700760903026748

Robinson, V. (2011). *Student-centered leadership*. San Francisco, CA: Jossey-Bass.

Seashore Louis, K., Leithwood, K., Wahlstrom, K., & Anderson, S. (2010). Investigating the links to improved student learning. Minneapolis, MN: University of Minnesota.

Sergiovanni, T. J. (1985). Landscapes, mindscapes, and reflective practice in supervision. *Journal of Curriculum & Supervision, 1*(1), 5–17.

Sergiovanni, T. J., & Starratt, R. J. (1971). *Emerging patterns of supervision: Human perspectives*. New York, NY: McGraw-Hill.

Showers, B., & Joyce, B. (1996). The evolution of peer coaching. *Educational Leadership, 53*(6), 12–17.

Siccone, F. (2012). *Essential skills for effective school leadership*. Boston, MA: Pearson Education.

Slater, C., Garduno, J. M. G., & Mentz, K. (2018). Frameworks for principal preparation and leadership development: Contributions of the International Study of Principal Preparation. *Management in Education, 32*(3), 126–134. doi:10.1177/0892020617747611

Spillane, J. P., & Orina, E. (2005). Investigating leadership practice: Exploring the entailments of taking a distributed perspective. *Leadership & Policy in Schools, 4*(3), 157–176. doi:10.1080/15700760500244728

Spillane, J. P., Healey, K., Parise, L. M., & Kenney, A. (2011). A distributed perspective on learning leadership. In J. Robertson & H. Timperley (Eds.), *Leadership and learning* (pp. 159–171). London, UK: Sage.

Sun, J., & Leithwood, K. (2012). Transformational school leadership effects on student achievement. *Leadership and Policy in Schools, 11*(4), 418–451. doi:10.1080/15700763.2012.681001

Tichnor-Wagner, A., Harrison, C., & Cohen-Vogel, L. (2016). Cultures of learning in effective high schools. *Educational Administration Quarterly, 52*(4), 602–642. doi:10.1177/0013161X16644957

Timperley, H. (2011a). Knowledge and the leadership of learning. *Leadership and Policy in Schools, 10*, 145–170. doi:10.1080/15700763.2011.557519

Timperley, H. (2011b). *Realizing the power of professional learning.* Maidenhead, UK: Open University Press.

Townsend, D., & Adams, P. (2009). *The essential equation: A handbook for school improvement.* Calgary, AB: Detselig.

Townsend, T., Acker-Hoover, M., Ballenger, J., & Place, A. (2013). Voices from the field: What have we learned about instructional leadership? *Leadership and Policy in Schools, 12*(1), 12–40. doi:10.1080/15700763.2013.766349

US Department of Education. (1998). *Turning around low-performing schools: A guide for state and local leaders.* Washington, DC: US Department of Education.

Wang, T. (2016). School leadership and professional learning community: Case study of two senior high schools in Northeast China. *Asia Pacific Journal of Education, 36*(2), 202–216. doi:10.1080/02188791.2016.1148849

CHAPTER FOUR

Generative Dialogue

How Do You Lead without Having All the Answers?

It is not the answer that enlightens, but the question.
— *Eugène Ionesco, Découvertes*

After a year of practising, I finally get the difference between this and cognitive coaching; it has to do with why I am asking the question, the purpose behind it, the reason for the question. It all has to do with curiosity and wonder.
— *Associate superintendent*

LEADING WITHOUT ANSWERS

We are nearing the end of the second decade of a not-so-new millennium, and public education systems around the world continue to struggle with solving some of their most pressing problems. Despite the time and effort expended on professional development, policy development, and research, many educational leaders remain uncertain about how to lead the learning of students and teachers, and, indeed, how to engage in meaningful learning for themselves.

An historical précis demonstrates the ongoing gap between what is hoped for in the name of educational leadership and what happens in the sociopolitical context in which leadership is lived out. For example, in the 1980s, many educators were trained as instructional leaders, following approaches such as servant leadership (Greenleaf, 1977), principle-based leadership (Covey, 1989), or distributed leadership (Spillane, 1999). These educators took up their leadership roles just in time to oversee the restructuring of schools and systems that required them to behave more like mid-level business managers than leaders of learning. In the 1990s, leadership authors were presenting models of moral leadership (Sergiovanni, 1994), transformational leadership (Leithwood & Jantzi, 1990), and systems-thinking leadership (Senge, 1990). Simultaneously, educational leaders almost everywhere were facing large budget cuts and demands for increased accountability that constantly drew energy and commitment away from innovative instructional leadership practices. Unsurprisingly, by the end of the 1990s, many system and school leaders had come to realize that mandated restructuring had not fundamentally impacted student learning. By 2000, Richard Elmore was prompted to state the following:

> Whatever problems of leadership might lie in the administration of schools and school systems, these problems are reflected and amplified in policy leadership. Administrative and policy leaders are joined in a codependent, largely dysfunctional relationship and, as in most relationships, the bond is strengthened by its pathology. (p. 19)

It would be naive of us to advocate that the success or failure of leaders is not a complex phenomenon. Timing is an influential variable, as are craft knowledge, staff morale, cultural history, social capital, and trust. However, the critical role that leaders play in leading the learning of teachers and impacting the learning of students is too often minimized or overlooked altogether. Furthermore, we believe that the skills associated with "how to" lead learning are deceptively simple, but require a persistent mindset and daily practice, undertaken by generative leaders. We refer to this process of deliberate conversations among leaders and teachers, focusing on learning and leadership growth, as *generative dialogue*. In practice, our form of generative dialogue pays homage to the work of authors as diverse as Alfred Adler, Lev Vygotsky, Donald Schön, Kurt Lewin, and Daniel Goleman. In addition, many of the communication skills we employ to help superintendents and principals engage in more meaningful educational conversations have been thoroughly analyzed and explained in the writings of Carl Rogers, Thomas Gordon, and John Wallen (whose Method of Joint Inquiry was first postulated in 1967).

In this chapter, you will read about Eric Middleton's leadership experiences in his early attempts to use generative dialogue. We then present a description of the conceptual evolution of the fundamentals of generative dialogue and outline the skills of a questioning approach to leadership. We describe ways in which feedback can be incorporated into generative dialogue without assumptions of judgment or emulation, and then "go live" by presenting a recent case study of what a systemic approach to generative dialogue might look like.

Case Study: Principal Eric Middleton's Journey toward Questioning

When first invited to participate in his district's collaborative inquiry/generative dialogue initiative, middle school principal Eric Middleton was skeptical. In fact, he was positively resistant. In the parking lot following the administrator meeting at which he heard what his superintendent was proposing, Eric let his fellow principals know, in no uncertain terms, just what he thought about this next great plan for professional learning for school leaders.

To be fair to Eric, he had a pretty good relationship with most of his 35 teachers. Over his four years as principal, he had found many effective ways to keep his teachers happy: no big shocks; don't bug them; give them lots of freedom to handle any problems that came their way; and always support them. What could he learn from this new process that would make his work easier or better than it was already?

Despite the opposition of Eric and a few of his colleagues, the superintendent decided to move forward with a three-year generative leadership project, the primary aim of which was to ensure that all leaders in the district met or exceeded the standards of practice recently brought into law by the ministry. Eric's reaction was one of compliance, usually displayed passive-aggressively. He attended scheduled meetings, though often wearing a frown of disapproval. He welcomed an external team of educators into his building every month but, on every occasion during the first year, he raised objections about such matters as classroom visits, conversations with teachers about their professional growth plans, lack of time, and expectations of alignment between school and district goals. He suggested to the superintendent that he really didn't believe it was his job to help his teachers become more effective and that there was no literature around that pointed to any evidence that this was even possible! Eric was especially vocal about the notion that he or his vice-principals might ever use video as part of their professional practice. On this point he proclaimed, frequently, that he had never seen himself on video, and he never wanted to!

As might have been anticipated, Eric and his school leadership team went through most of the first year doing things their way. Their conversations with teachers about yearly plans, data, the achievement of individual students, staff collaboration—in short, almost anything to do with critical measures of school improvement and student learning—were limited, disjointed, and perfunctory.

What happened over the summer holidays was never fully disclosed, but one thing is certain: Eric welcomed the new school year with renewed energy and a greatly enhanced willingness to develop new leadership skills. He admitted he had done some professional reading over the holidays. He added that he was not totally satisfied with the way some staff members had dealt with students in the previous year, particularly students who were experiencing academic and personal difficulties. And above all, he confessed, he was not very happy with the way he was doing his job. He wanted to do more to build capacity in his staff. He wanted to have more conversations with staff members who had different views to his, and he wanted to help make his school the best it could be. So much change of attitude. So much renewed professional vigour. How would his staff react?

One of the first big steps he and his vice-principals took was to meet with all staff members to ask questions about professional growth plans. In advance of these meetings, Eric and his team met with their associate superintendent, agreed on a team goal for themselves, divided up the responsibility for staff interviews,

continued

and negotiated a procedure for helping all staff get ready for their growth plan conversations. Outside school, Eric and his partners connected with three other teams of principals and vice-principals in what was to become a weekly breakfast meeting at which they could all share ideas and experiences about how to lead the learning of all teachers and support staff.

During successive visits to his school, Eric's team seemed to be more willing to share evidence of their progress and more willing to ask and answer questions. Above all, they showed a growing confidence in their ability to engage in more meaningful conversations with staff members. Halfway through the year, they came up with an idea that really showed they were getting more serious about leadership and learning: they decided to have all three of them take part in all their conversations with teachers. That was a dramatic change for all involved. At first, several of the teachers did not take kindly to the new process. Yet, as Eric and his team continued to build trust, they could see themselves developing valuable skills and greater confidence in having difficult conversations with staff members. In short order, most teachers bought into the process. Eric commented that he had seen how the use of generative dialogue had impacted his team, and he was sure they could have a similar effect on teacher teams. The tone and focus of generative conversations also changed, as the school leaders were more willing and able to share evidence of their growing effectiveness, evidence of teacher resistance and how they had handled it, and evidence of more purposeful uses of data to inform their deliberations.

Near the end of the second year, Eric arranged for a team of teachers to meet with him and the associate superintendent of learning services. Most of the teachers responded with enthusiasm and openness to the opportunity to talk about their practice. They spoke about their efforts at collaboration that were producing better results, their extra attention to the needs of all students, and their plans for next year. They shared evidence of their impact on student achievement.

Still, a couple of teachers did not appreciate the process, and one made a point of disengaging from the conversation in a fairly dramatic way. Eric reported that before he came to see his principal role as one of contributing to the leadership of learning he would have just let that incident pass. This time, he used it as an opportunity to spend more time with the reluctant teachers, seeking to discover what caused them to disengage and asking what he could do to help them stay more involved. There was no perfect resolution, Eric noted, but he did find ways of causing teachers to reflect.

The following year, Eric told the external team members that he wanted to do something in his leadership work that he had never done before. His associate superintendent asked, "Would you be willing to video yourself engaged in a conversation with one of your teachers?" At first, Eric was silent. Then, calmly, he replied, "Why not? What have I got to lose? I'll finally get to see myself on TV."

At the next district principals' meeting, Eric shared an excerpted 15-minute video with all his leadership colleagues. In it, he interviewed one of his math teachers, a person with 24 years of teaching experience. As he explained in his introduction, Eric tried to show how his questioning skills had improved, how he really could listen attentively, and how he could help teachers reflect on their practice. It was nowhere near a perfect demonstration, but it drew long and loud affirmation from all in attendance as it came to an end. A highlight of the interview was the following comment by the teacher, who said, "I don't know how long I've been waiting for the chance to have a real conversation about why I teach the way I do, and how my teaching works for kids. Thanks."

Eric has continued to develop his leadership skills, sharing his growing expertise with colleagues, and working even more closely with his staff members. He is a trusted senior member of the district's group of school leaders, humble, focused, and unashamedly committed to lifelong learning. When he mentors upcoming school leaders, Eric reiterates his belief that he was able to change his practice because of the expectation and support to engage in the monthly generative dialogue. He needed time to work out new ways of leading, and the process gave him that time. He needed encouragement to take risks and try new things, and the regular generative dialogues offered that encouragement. He needed new skills to work differently with colleagues and staff, and, over time, through sharing and reflection, he came to trust that he had the necessary skills to deal with increasingly complex aspects of school leadership, manage conflict, and help more staff members gain greater confidence in the quality of their own professional practice.

Case Study Reflections: Leading without Answers

- If you could ask Eric only one more question about leadership, what would it be?
- What critical elements of the generative dialogue process are revealed in the case study?
- How would you rate this case study as an example of generative dialogue? Why?
- Which aspects of this case study are demonstrably *generative*? In what ways?

GENERATIVE DIALOGUE: A THEORETICAL FRAMEWORK

Our histories in the use of generative dialogue began decades before the term was ever formally applied to conversations between educators discussing their professional practice. As early as the 1980s, we attempted to introduce a similar clinical supervision model (Gall & Acheson, 1980) into a rural school district that favoured less direction on the part of supervisors, more active listening, and greater teacher reflection. We had hoped to persuade school leaders that they could better promote teacher growth if they could hold back on their own opinions, suspend judgment, avoid criticism, and listen as much as they talked: the results at that time were not encouraging.

Our team formally adopted the use of the term *generative dialogue* in 2009. Since then, our interpretation of the term *generative dialogue* has evolved to refer to *the adoption of a specific, rigorous set of skills that shifts how we converse with each other about professional practice for the purpose of clarifying and bringing into existence new ideas and thoughts that lead to more purposeful action.*

What Is Generative Dialogue?

At its most essential, generative dialogue is interaction between individuals that has the power to cause or give rise to productive, creative, and unique understandings. From the French *génératif*, originally used to describe the physiological function of reproduction (Generative, n.d.), when conceptually aligned with dialogue, its meaning focuses directly on the ability of conversation to generate deep and original thought. In the context of professional learning and growth, generative dialogue invites teachers and leaders into an environment of empathy and trust, to critically reflect upon assumptions and discern unique insights related to their professional selves with the explicit purpose of setting learning goals to improve instructional and leadership practice (Isaac, 1999).

Conceptually, generative dialogue lies at the nexus of four complementary sets of understandings: the sociocultural construction of the person within **communities of practice** (Vygotsky, 1978; Lave & Wenger, 1991); transformative adult learning (Mezirow, 1991, 1997) and critically reflective practice (Brookfield, 1995, 2017); essential principles embedded in the person-centred perspectives of Adler (1956) and Rogers (1961, 1980); and Socratic questioning as a way of inviting deep reflection (Barnes & Payette, 2017; Paul & Elder, 2007). Taken together, these understandings offer a robust conceptual framework and a compelling rationale for the use of generative dialogue as a means of prompting **critical reflection** and clarifying professional learning goals.

Sociocultural Understandings: Construction of the Person within Communities of Practice

Generative dialogue emerges from sociocultural understandings of the construction of the person: a human being is shaped, essentially, by culture (Vygotsky, 1978; Rogoff,

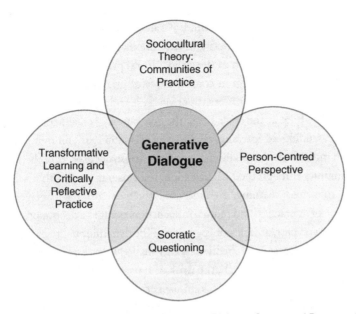

Figure 4.1: The Key Elements Comprising the Generative Dialogue Conceptual Framework

1990); dynamically, over time (Vygotsky & Luria, 1993; Rogoff, 2003); and, specifically, within communities of practice (Lave & Wenger, 1991). Forming the theoretical bedrock of our work, these three sets of understandings influence the ways in which we interact with teachers and leaders.

Vygotsky identified the social and cultural origins of complex forms of human behaviour and unique psychological processes; this is referred to interchangeably as the sociocultural, sociohistorical, or cultural-historical theory of human development (John-Steiner & Mahn, 1996; Rogoff, 2003). Departing from the prevailing view that human beings develop according to innate psychological structures, he argued that culture and social environment make a person, not just by providing knowledge but, more fundamentally, by transforming the very structure of psychological processes and, thus, prompting the development of specific, culturally driven techniques within each person for using his or her abilities. Explicating this relationship between human cognition and action and culture, Rogoff (1990) posited, "I regard context as inseparable from human actions in cognitive events or activities. I regard all human activity as embedded in context; there are neither context-free situations nor de-contextualized skills" (p. 27). It follows, then, that individuals, embedded within social and cultural contexts, will be shaped and reshaped over time as their circumstances change (Bruner, 1986, 2004), while at the same time contributing to changes in their cultural communities (Rogoff, 2003). It is a dynamic process of *becoming* for both individuals and their cultural contexts.

With an explicit focus on learning, Lave and Wenger (1991) identified the process of knowing, not as transmission and cerebral assimilation but as an integral and inseparable aspect of social practice. Based on the understanding that learning involves the whole person, acting on and in the world, Lave and Wenger argued that learners participate in "communities of practitioners and that the mastery of skill requires newcomers to move toward full participation in the sociocultural practices of a community" (p. 29). Moreover, through participation in communities of practice, the individual is shaped: "Learning implies becoming a different person … learning involves the construction of identities" (p. 53) while, at the same time, the community is itself transformed.

This understanding of learning as active participation in communities of practice, through which individuals, gradually and over time, construct aspects of their identities and alter the community through their participation, informs our work with teachers and leaders and their professional learning. To understand the relationship between culture and the individual as one of interaction and mutual influence encourages a deep appreciation for context, both current and past, as well as recognition of the dynamic quality of professional lives.

We believe educators are embedded in and shaped by culture. For us, as facilitators of professional learning and growth, the work of Lave and Wenger (1991) is particularly instructive. By positioning learning as an aspect of social participation in communities of practice, educators are prompted to think about their influence and impact on those communities. Sociocultural understandings require educators to view professional learning, ultimately, as change in who they are and who they are becoming as teachers and leaders.

Engaging Adult Learners: Transformative Learning and Reflective Practice

The second set of understandings shaping generative dialogue complements the first by focusing directly on the nature of the adult learner and the role of critical reflection. While numerous scholars and practitioners over the past century have explored adult learning as distinct from pedagogy (see Merriam, 2001), the work of Mezirow (1991) and transformative learning most directly informs our practice. In addition, we rely on Brookfield's notion of critical reflection as underpinning the process of professional learning for teacher and leaders (Brookfield, 1995, 2017).

Recognizing that meaning exists within ourselves and is acquired and validated through human interaction and communication, Mezirow (1991) observed, "Our need to understand our experiences is perhaps our most distinctively human attribute. We *have* to understand them in order to know how to act effectively" (p. 10, emphasis in original). To accomplish this, we develop frames of reference that come to define our lives: intentionally and unintentionally, over the decades of our lives, we construct and **reconstruct understandings** of our experience in the form of "meaning schemes" (p. 11), which, when clustered together, result in more complex "meaning perspectives" (p. 44). Described by Mezirow (1991) as "boundary structures" (p. 4), these schemes and perspectives become our frames of reference: the structures of assumptions through experiences are understood. In addition, these assumptions guide expectations, perceptions, cognition, and feelings; ultimately, they influence decisions and actions (Mezirow, 1997).

Transformative learning is, then, the process of altering established frames of reference through a critical interrogation of the assumptions and premises underlying constructed meanings of experience with the goal of acting on these transformed understandings:

> Perspective transformation is the process of becoming critically aware of how and why our assumptions have come to constrain the way we perceive, understand, and feel about the world; changing these structures of habitual expectation to make possible a more inclusive, discriminating, and integrative perspective; and finally, making choices or otherwise acting upon these new understandings. (Mezirow, 1991, p. 167)

The responsibility of the leader in this transformative learning process is threefold: to help the learner focus on and examine the assumptions that underlie beliefs, feelings, and actions; to identify and explore alternative sets of assumptions; and to test the validity of assumptions through effective participation in reflective dialogue (Mezirow, 1991; see also Mezirow, 1997).

As with Mezirow, Brookfield (1995, 2017) recognized the role of critical reflection in the interrogation of assumptions specifically related to instructional and leadership practice. Explicating the notion of the critically reflective teacher, Brookfield (2017) wrote that reflection is a "process of intentional and continual scrutiny of assumptions that inform your teaching practice. These assumptions are scrutinized by viewing them through the four lenses available to any teacher: students' eyes, colleagues' perceptions, personal experience, and theory" (p. 19). Describing critical reflection as sustained and disciplined practice, Brookfield argued student learning is enhanced through this process of identifying and checking both the explicit and implicit assumptions informing our decisions as teachers and leaders.

Understanding adult learning as the transformation of frames of reference through critical professional reflection focused on assumptions about learning, teaching, and leading has shaped generative dialogue, conceptually and practically. Instructional and leadership frames of reference are constructed and reconstructed over time. Developed through experiences of childhood schooling and later as teachers with students, these structures and perspectives rest on assumptions and beliefs often unrecognized and unacknowledged; nonetheless, they shape and direct practice. Our responsibility, as facilitators of generative dialogue, is to support adult learners as they engage in critical reflection, invite alternate understandings of professional experience, transform frames of reference, and act on these new understandings related to instructional and leadership practice.

Person-Centred Perspective: Essential Principles Guiding Interaction

Taken together, the work of Adler and Rogers has significantly shaped the conceptual development of generative dialogue by offering guiding principles for engagement.

Writing in the early decades of the 1900s, Adler is credited with anticipating and outlining a number of the central tenets that would later characterize the Rogerian therapeutic model (see Ansbacher & Ansbacher, 1956; Watts, 1996, 1998; Lemberger, 2017). Labelling it the "person-centred approach," Rogers (1961) came to view these principles as enhancing not only therapeutic relationships, but relationships of all kinds: with students, with staff members, with family, and with children. He wrote, "This approach offers exciting possibilities for the development of creative, adaptive, autonomous persons" (p. 38).

Three specific aspects of their work have shaped our theoretical framework and guide our interaction with teachers and leaders. First and foremost, individuals have within themselves both the desire and the capability to become a whole or complete person explained by Adler (1956) as "striving for perfection" (p. 103). Similarly, Rogers based his person-centred approach on the essential understanding that "persons have a basically positive direction" (1961, p. 26) toward self-actualization that takes place through a process of personal growth and development. Within every person, he maintained, there are vast resources for self-understanding and for altering self-concepts, basic attitudes, and self-directed behaviour that can be tapped if a climate for growth is facilitated. Rogers (1961) wrote:

> My experience has forced me to conclude that [individuals have within themselves] the capacity and the tendency, latent if not evident, to move forward toward maturity. In a suitable psychological climate this tendency is released, and becomes actual rather than potential. (p. 35)

Second, Adler and Rogers recognized that individuals could not be understood apart from their social context. Adler stated, "Individual Psychology regards and examines the individual as socially embedded. We refuse to recognize and examine an isolated human being" (as cited in Ansbacher & Ansbacher, 1956, p. 2). Rogers echoed the importance of recognizing the social and personal context in his outline of the conditions necessary to create a climate for self-reflection and, ultimately, growth. Identifying *genuineness* as the first condition, he highlights the need for facilitators to acknowledge their own context. Describing this variously as realness, congruence, and transparency, he maintained that the more facilitators *are* themselves, recognizing their own understandings and emotions, the more likely others will change and grow in a constructive manner: "It is only by providing the genuine reality that is in me, that the other person can successfully seek for the reality that is in him" (Rogers, 1961, p. 33). The next condition informing the foundation of the person-centred approach is *acceptance*, or "unconditional positive regard" (Rogers, 1980, p. 116). Rogers observed that acceptance of the circumstances and attitudes of another, unconditional regard for who that person *is*, in all their complexities, nurtures a relationship of trust, which, in turn, is more likely to invite self-reflection and prompt movement toward maturity. For both Adler and Rogers, recognizing social and personal contexts is an essential condition for working constructively with others.

The third aspect of their work that informs our interaction with teachers and leaders is reflected in what both Adler and Rogers refer to as *empathy*. Labelling it "intuitive empathy," Adler (1956) wrote: "By making comparisons between oneself and the patient, between different attitudes of the same patient, or between similar attitudes of different patients, one acquires insight into the essential nature of the other" (p. 329). Rogers described the condition necessary for creating a climate suitable for supporting growth toward maturity, "empathetic understanding," as the ability to sense the feelings and personal meanings others are experiencing for the purpose of communicating these understandings to facilitate self-reflection. At its most effective, empathetic understanding draws the listener inside the private world of others to help clarify not only meanings of which others are aware, but even those just below the level of awareness (Rogers, 1980, p. 116). Being an empathetic listener, drawn into the life world of others, is for Rogers an essential aspect of his approach.

Generative dialogue has been influenced, essentially, by these understandings posited by Adler and Rogers. In our work with teachers and leaders, we believe, first and foremost, that each individual is competent and capable, and has within themselves the tendency and the ability to engage in professional learning and growth. In other words, the autonomous and professionally responsible nature of the individual is a core assumption of our interaction with others. Second, as facilitators of professional growth, we acknowledge our own contexts and are genuinely and authentically engaged in supporting the development of the other within the context of their own circumstances. This commitment prompts shared learning and mutual respect for the contributions of others. Finally, through empathetic listening we are drawn into the professional world of others. By listening more and talking less, by describing and clarifying, we come to recognize their values, beliefs, opinions, and experiences and offer support for reflection and, ultimately, professional learning and growth.

Asking Socratic Questions: A Means of Encouraging Professional Reflection

Socratic questioning has its beginnings in a style of discourse originating with the ancient Greek philosopher Socrates, who hoped to encourage insights and provoke understandings by posing open-ended questions. The Socratic method is distinguished from other types of questioning in that it is systematic, disciplined, and most often focused on foundational concepts, principles, theories, issues, or problems (see Barnes & Payette, 2017; Paul & Elder, 2007; Elder & Paul, 1998). As an entry point for divergent and nuanced thinking, **Socratic questions** invite reflection on assumptions, goals and purposes, implications and consequences, as well as viewpoints and perspectives.

Designed to incite discovery and provoke unique understandings, Socratic questioning has been defined as *maieutic*: that is, this method of interaction has the power to reach below the surface and draw forth ideas latent in the mind (Maieutic, n.d.). Through conversation focused on deep and purposeful reflection, previously unarticulated understandings and cognitive associations can be born (Carson, 1986). So it is with generative dialogue: the intentional use of the Socratic method offers the opportunity not only for the consolidation of existing perceptions, but for critical consideration of assumptions about learning, teaching, and leading; for the transformation of frames of reference; and for decisions and actions emerging from new understandings. Open-ended and stimulating, Socratic questions are powerful prompts for considering our professional learning and practice.

HIGH-QUALITY COMMUNICATION: THE GENERATIVE DIALOGUE

Generative dialogue is a process that is disarmingly simple, yet frustratingly complex. In broad strokes, this dialogue is manifested through frequent and focused conversations, initiated and sustained by effective leaders, about shared goals, guiding questions, strategies, and evidence of growth.

Elements of the Generative Dialogue

Through years of engagement with and observations of school and district leaders, we have been able to identify patterns of communication that affirm mutual respect, build trust, stimulate reflection, strengthen professional partnerships, and facilitate learning. Alternately, we have identified other strategies that are more likely to inhibit reflection, trigger defensiveness, or promote disengagement. Some of our contentions are at odds with conventional wisdom and some may appear counterintuitive; nonetheless, we present them here for consideration.

Praise Reconsidered

In our analysis of hundreds of video recordings of episodes where feedback was given to and by leaders, we have seen how the use of praise is equally likely to result in negative rather than positive outcomes. We have consistently noted that one common response to praise is denial. For example, a principal might say to one of her exemplary teachers, "You certainly had all of your students fully engaged today. Your classroom management was excellent!" Teachers will often respond with "I have a really good group of students this year" or "I guess I was just lucky today when you came to observe." Another common response is uncomfortable silence: a teacher may be embarrassed or simply uncertain about what to say next.

We have also seen the misuse of praise under the guise of "the baloney sandwich." This form of praise is often used to make people amenable to subsequent judgment or criticism. A typical interaction might sound like this:

Vice-principal: It seemed to work very well when you had students answering on their own personalized whiteboards.

Teacher: Yes, this class really enjoys that type of activity.

Vice-principal: Most students got the answers correct the first time. Did you notice the three students at the back of the room drawing cartoon characters on their boards? Do you usually allow them to be doodling?

Teacher: Oh … I didn't notice them.

Vice-principal: Don't worry. It probably doesn't happen all the time!

Another common pattern of communication sounds like this: "I really liked the way you got students ready for the video clip and how you elicited answers to your questions from many students. However, you weren't clear enough about your expectations for the writing activity that followed the video. I don't think the students got it. I've got some ideas for how you might improve that; just drop by anytime and we can talk more!" Only the most resilient teacher would be likely to take up such an invitation. More often, even when offered in a kindly way, this approach induces defensiveness, uncertainty, fear, or decreased efficacy.

There are some important differences between praise and the type of feedback that causes authentic reflection as employed in the generative dialogue. Praise often originates in a value system, potentially independent of or incongruent with the value system of the person receiving the praise. Statements such as "I really liked how you referenced the weekend's football game to get the students to settle in" or "You did an excellent job of getting the boys to read out loud during literacy circle" or "It was so lovely and quiet when I walked in the room!" clearly reflect a set of values of the person making the statements. The list could go on, but you get the idea: although subtle, this kind of praise seeks to align the behaviour of the observed with that of the observer.

Generative dialogue, on the other hand, is based on descriptions of behaviour, the specifics of which are both known and agreed upon by both parties. For example, "As we agreed, I have completed a proximity movement map of the first 20 minutes of your lesson. You've had an opportunity to look at it. What are your impressions?"

The Impact of Judgment and Criticism

Judgment and criticism, even more dramatically than misapplied praise, can undermine efficacy, reduce autonomy, and induce defensiveness or resentment. While some educators become anxious when receiving feedback, we have observed quite the opposite: when conversations about their practice are handled skillfully, most have little difficulty identifying aspects that are effective or not so effective; methods they would use again, modify, or put aside; or different strategies they would like to use in future. In short, it is our experience that the vast majority of teachers, school leaders, and central office personnel are quite adept at determining areas in which they are confident, other areas about which they are curious, and yet others in which they would like to improve and grow.

Unfortunately, conversations that include perceived judgment or criticism have potential to create misunderstandings and hurt feelings that can endure, possibly for an entire career. Teachers have reported extensively and personally on the negative effects of what they consider to be examples of unwarranted or unappreciated judgment or criticism by supervisors. Often, this judgment is referred to in a well-intentioned way as feedback or constructive criticism. Yet, over the decades, educators with whom we have worked to improve their generative dialogue skills have reflected upon, and written about, the impact of judgment and criticism on their sense of self-worth, their beliefs about their own professional effectiveness, their morale, and even their desire to stay in the profession. We are not talking about a mere handful of young, unconfident, or ineffective teachers; literally hundreds of educators with whom we have worked over the years have in common a pronounced distaste for the kind of professional judgment and criticism that causes them to feel less valued as educators and as competent human beings.

As a sidebar note to the effectiveness of constructive criticism, we offer you the following challenge:

> Before you go home this evening, compile a list of the top 10 things about your best friend that, with the right kind of constructive criticism, could be improved. When you next meet, pour both of you a nice beverage and invite your friend to relax while you share your list. What might be some of the more obvious outcomes of this exercise in arrogance and foolhardiness? What is the likelihood that your suggestions will change the behaviours or traits that you identified?

If constructive criticism does not work very well with someone with whom you share a close and valuable relationship, what chance does it have with people to whom you are not emotionally invested, with people you know only on a professional level, or with people with whom you may actually disagree?

The Limited Value of Personal Anecdote: Sharing War Stories

In a great majority of discussions between leaders and teachers or colleagues, we have observed that a single event or even a brief comment by one often triggers an extensive, emotional, exuberant, or highly personal response from the other. For example, in a conversation with her principal about her students' learning, we observed a high school mathematics teacher offer her opinion that one grade 12 student "seems to be trying to fail every part of this course." Immediately, her principal launched into a long and very personal history of his own son's high school experiences with math. Similarly, a vice-principal trying to mentor a beginner teacher who was having difficulties managing a grade eight physical education class began to share a lengthy story of what he did when he was faced with a similar set of circumstances 20 years before. We watched 10 minutes of talking by the vice-principal, with virtually no input from the teacher! In yet another session, a principal expressed to her superintendent some concerns about a teacher whose students had not done well on a standardized exam. The superintendent then spent the rest of the meeting sharing one story after another about the high school he turned around in another district.

These are but a few of multiple examples of how colonizing a conversation with personal war stories, although well intentioned, will result in unproductive outcomes, very little growth, and almost no personal reflection (except on the part of the story-teller!). Virtually all educators have a supply of personal anecdotes to fit most occasions. However, using those stories to promote reflection and to enhance practice in colleagues is mostly ineffectual. Worse, when leaders intervene in others' reflection, the message is clear that the only stories that matter are those that mirror the values, perspectives, and problem-solving strategies highlighted in the story. Not only can this result in compliance, it is almost certain to limit creative and critical thinking. In promoting the benefits of generative dialogue, we observe that very effective leaders harness their egos, and the need to share their stories, in favour of finding numerous ways to ask questions that result in a transfer of responsibility and problem solving.

Who Gets to Talk?

We have noted that some leaders who are engaged in professional conversations about learning and growth talk for up to 90 percent of the available time. Without practice in generative dialogue, many educators approach conversations with their colleagues as an opportunity to share what they know, how they feel, what they want to see, and their overall perceptions of how well the others are doing. As they come to realize the nuanced elements of the generative dialogue, leaders frequently reduce the amount of time they talk, exchanging it with more intensive listening, more thoughtful questions, and more specific observations about agreed-upon topics and outcomes.

In a recent three-year project focusing on leadership growth, 82 percent of school leaders (principals and vice-principals responsible for over 600 teachers) reported their greatest area of improvement to be either "listening skills" or "questioning skills." Not surprisingly, one clear indicator of the usefulness of the generative dialogue is the amount of time that leaders are *not* talking but, instead, are listening in an intense way as a first step, to promote deep reflection. We refer to this as having *authentic curiosity* about the thoughts, ideas, insights, and conundrums of teachers and colleagues that provide an environment of acceptance, trust, and failing forward.

SELECTED TECHNIQUES OF GENERATIVE DIALOGUE

A small caveat should be offered before we embark on specific skills and questions that a generative dialogue comprises. Situated as it is in a larger model of generative leadership, the generative dialogue draws its power from the willingness of educators, regardless of positional authority, to work with each other in a spirit of mutual respect and a climate of trust. In the absence of essential levels of respect and trust, educators are much less likely to take the risks necessary to pursue a commitment to continuous professional growth over the life-span of their careers. Moreover, without trust and respect, neither teachers nor leaders will enter into the kinds of collaborations most likely to enhance professional practice and contribute most to learning. Compliance will overtake initiative, and the need for certainty (not to be seen to be "wrong") will overwhelm a willingness to explore.

Requisite Habits of Mind

Effective use of the generative dialogue can begin with the acquisition and practice of some basic habits of mind.

- *Convey positive regard.* In your interactions with professional colleagues you convey, verbally and non-verbally, respect for the values, beliefs, opinions, and experiences of others.
- *Encourage responsibility.* Through thoughtful conversation, you try to sustain in your colleagues their commitment to learning and action. You engage with them, with the assumption that the learning and action resulting from your conversations will be primarily their responsibility.
- *Suspend judgment.* Your comments, questions, and responses demonstrate that you will not be a source of judgmental comments, statements of evaluation, disparaging non-verbal responses, or inappropriate humour.
- *Limit reinforcing responses.* You demonstrate care and caution in the use of praise or blame, realizing that either may damage your colleagues' responsibility and self-accountability.
- *Practise effective listening.* You talk less and listen more and, in doing so, cultivate a healthy sense of humility that accompanies active listening and authentic curiosity. You convey to your colleagues that you are curious and are processing what you are hearing.
- *Presume professional competence.* You assume your colleagues are competent. You expect that they are as committed to their work as you are. You are careful not to try to rescue or "save" those with whom you are engaged in conversation, nor do you excessively explain, on their behalf, reasons (you think) events or circumstances unfolded as they did.

Asking the Questions

Reflective questioning, when applied in conversations between professional partners, can help ensure that participants are more aware of false assumptions, contradictions, origins, implications, and consequences of their thinking. While there are no prescribed responses or questions that make up a more or less effective generative dialogue, we have found that questions often fall roughly into the following categories.

Clarification Questions

- What do you mean by …?
- What is your main point?
- What is your definition of …?
- Could you say that another way?
- Can you give me an example?
- How does _____ relate to _____?
- Talk more about …
- What would that look like?

Origin or Source Questions

- Where did you get this idea?
- Who do you know who does this very well?
- Can you think of some alternatives?
- What effect do you want this action to have?
- Can you explain the history of this process?
- Which authors or researchers are guiding your work?

Viewpoint Questions

- Is this idea or action consistent with your professional view?
- What concerns you about this plan?
- How have other people responded?
- What would you say to someone who totally disagrees with you?
- What elements of that idea are most or least appealing to you?
- How are you feeling about this matter?
- What other strategies have you already tried?

Reason and Evidence Questions

- How do you know?
- How can you be so sure?
- What led you to that conclusion?
- Why this course of action now?
- What key words come to mind as you are thinking about this problem?
- What did you do the last time you handled a problem like this one?
- What will you accept as evidence that you're being successful?

Implication and Consequence Questions

- What would be the most desirable outcome?
- Can you see any difficulties arising from that course of action?
- Is that what you intended?
- What if that assumption is false?
- What do you stand to gain or lose if you go with that decision?
- Is this action consistent with school or district policy?
- What additional knowledge or skills do you need in order to do what you're planning to accomplish?

Questions about the Question

- Is my question clear?
- Why is this question important?
- Does that question trigger more than one answer for you?
- Should I have asked that question in a different way?

The Role of Feedback in Generative Dialogue

Much has been written about leaders providing feedback as constructive information that can help teachers and colleagues become aware of their behaviours or performance (Donaldson, 2013; Goff, Guthrie, Goldring, & Bickman, 2014; Joyce & Showers, 1981; Kraft & Gilmour, 2016; Rigby et al., 2017; Scheeler, Ruhl, & McAfee, 2004). We often hear this referred to as the role of critical friend. While we have observed some cases of very skilled leaders who were able to reconcile the apparent tension between *critical* and *friendship*, the judgmental and evaluative undertones in feedback can be detected more often than not, causing it to become corrective, strongly suggestive, or even punitive.

Within a larger context of the generative dialogue, feedback is frequently offered as a prelude to questioning. We contend that feedback must be based on a mutual agreement about what information will be offered and how this information will be translated into questions that will contribute to—rather than abbreviate—reflection and growth. In most circumstances, it is important to give feedback in a way that is not threatening and will not cause defensiveness: the more defensive they are, the less open colleagues will be to hearing, understanding, and assimilating feedback.

Leaders can provide helpful, nonthreatening, effective feedback to teachers and colleagues within a generative dialogue by focusing on some key strategies.

Focus Feedback on Actions Rather Than People

It is important that leaders refer to observed behaviours rather than imagined or extrapolated intentions. Focusing on actions includes using adverbs (which relate to actions) rather than adjectives (which relate to qualities).

Focus Feedback on Observations Rather Than Inferences

Observations refer to that which can be seen or heard, while inferences refer to interpretations and conclusions from what is seen or heard. In a sense, inferences or conclusions by a leader can contaminate observations and cloud the intentions of providing feedback. When inferences are made, it is important that they be so identified.

Focus Feedback on Description Rather Than Judgment

The effort to describe represents a process of reporting what occurred; judgment refers to an evaluation of good or bad, right or wrong, nice or not nice. As noted earlier, judgments arise out of a personal frame of reference or value system, whereas description represents as neutral a reporting as possible.

Focus Feedback on Descriptors of Behaviour in Terms of More or Less Rather Than in Terms of Either/Or

More-or-less vocabulary views action along a continuum that, in some ways, offers a richer description. Either/or vocabulary sends a message of subjectivity based on judgment, evaluation, and right or wrong. The paradox with this focus is that providing feedback based on a continuous scale of measurement may cause educators to formulate sub-categories that, taken to the extreme, reinforce a good/bad, right/wrong paradigm.

Focus Feedback on Behaviour Specific to a Situation, Preferably in the "Here and Now," Rather Than on an Abstract Recollection of "If and When"

Leaders can help teachers and colleagues "fence in" their reflections and actions by giving feedback that is tied to time, place, and purpose. Initially, in the feedback stage

---

Curriculum Director Max Smiley might be tempted to intimate "Lissa, you seem to be quite unhappy with how you are differentiating reading for your grade three English language learners." Instead, Lissa's reflections are more likely to be authentic with a question such as "I am sensing by the tone of your voice that you are frustrated about that lesson. What is the source of that?"

Faculty Supervisor Janine Baldry tells a practising student teacher, "You are having a lot of difficulty getting your lessons started on time. You need to get this on track immediately." To describe rather than judge, Janine might say, "Nineteen minutes after the bell rang, you began taking attendance and loading the PowerPoint slides for the lesson."

Principal Sarah George is evaluating a second-year teacher for contract certification purposes. She suggests, "You either need to get all students in this class engaged or start keeping them in at recess." Instead, she might have asked, "What are some strategies that you have tried to keep all your students engaged with the material?"

Superintendent Ramona Boulet may say to a principal, "We have spent this year examining the impact of your community-building efforts. With one-quarter of your staff retiring over the next year, how do you predict you might sustain your gains in this area?"

of generative dialogue, immediacy is important. Later, leaders may begin asking questions that cause colleagues to predict or envisage future actions or expectations.

Focus Feedback on Sharing Ideas and Data Rather Than on Giving Advice

When leaders share ideas and information in response to an invitation to do so, they open the space for colleagues to decide for themselves how they will use this data—in the light of their own goals in a particular situation at a particular time. Most advice is given with goodwill; however, doing so often limits ownership, autonomy, and responsibility.

Focus Feedback on Exploration of Alternatives Rather Than Answers or Solutions

The more leaders can focus on a variety of procedures and means for accomplishing a particular goal, the less likely premature answers or superficial solutions will be implemented. Most of us have a collection of answers and solutions that we think of as our treasury of advice; unfortunately, these are usually general responses for no immediate, relevant problem.

Focus Feedback on Its Value to Others, Not on the "Release" It Provides the Person Giving the Feedback

The beneficiary of the feedback should be the receiver. Often leaders give feedback to serve their own multiplicity of needs, both professional and personal. Support and feedback need to be given and heard as an offer, not as something forced upon colleagues; to do otherwise erodes trust.

Focus Feedback through a Finite, Usable Amount of Information Rather Than on the Total Amount You Might Wish to Give

If colleagues are overloaded with feedback, their effective use and integration of the information is reduced. When leaders give additional, supplementary, or tangential information, they may be satisfying some need for themselves rather than supporting a colleague's practice.

Vice-Principal Susan Daley might say "John, in our grade-level collaboration meeting you expressed three concerns about the new curriculum." This observation is more likely to cause reflection within the generative dialogue framework than "John, in meetings with your teaching team you are always so negative in expressing your opinions."

A ministry official is speaking with Deputy Superintendent Roselia Gonsalis about budget cuts to the equity education program and advises, "When I faced a similar situation back in the 90s, I found that I just had to keep my head down and do what was necessary to cause the least friction. It worked for me; maybe it will work for you?" Roselia may better grow as a leader with the question "What are the two best options that you can brainstorm for dealing with this challenge?"

During a lesson evaluation, Principal Brad Singer whispers to a first-year teacher on his way out of the classroom, "Joel, as soon as this lesson is over, please get your teaching partner to cover your next class and come down to my office to discuss my observations." Alternately, at the end of the lesson, the principal might say, "Joel, please email me at the end of the day with a time in the next week when you and I can discuss your lesson. Where would you like to meet?"

Focus Feedback on Time and Place so That Personal Data Can Be Shared at Appropriate Times

Because receiving feedback involves many possible emotional reactions, it is important that leaders are savvy and sensitive about the appropriate time to give feedback. Excellent feedback presented at an inappropriate time may do more harm than good. In short, giving and receiving feedback requires courage, skill, understanding, and respect for self and others.

Focus Feedback on **What** *Is Said Rather Than* **Why It** *Is Said*

When leaders relate feedback to *why* things are said, the conversation takes a shift from the observable to the assumed, bringing up questions of motive or intent.

During a system discussion comparing student achievement among six large high schools, one principal says to a colleague, "I see that your school's scores are at the bottom of the achievement list. I have some suggestions for your own good so that you can get your students up to par for this standardized test. I'm not a big fan of what the superintendent believes about these tests, but I know how to get your teachers to ace them!"

"GOING LIVE" WITH GENERATIVE DIALOGUE: WHAT MIGHT IT LOOK LIKE?

Generative dialogue by leaders who strive to model exemplary listening skills, an avoidance of criticism and praise, and an absence of judgment is closely linked to a spirit of inquiry that is extant throughout a school, system, or organization. Everyone, but especially leaders, is curious about their colleagues' work, full of expectation that their colleagues are competent and trying to do their best, and ready to offer support whenever necessary.

When embedded in the model of generative leadership, described in chapter 3, site visits by central office leaders result in school leadership teams assuming shared responsibility for their practice. Trusted district office leaders commit to a regular schedule of meetings with school-based leadership teams, with a focus on goals and growth. Ideally, such site-visit meetings take place once per month. In turn, those meetings promote the need for further meetings between school leadership teams and other teams that have formed in individual schools, consistent with the concept of distributed leadership. Each team comprises men and women of goodwill working together toward the achievement of agreed-upon goals. Everyone involved in the process is committed to using their emerging skills with generative dialogue to support collective efficacy and individual effectiveness.

The monthly meeting structure has been shown to contribute to task completion, higher levels of trust, and greater confidence. Initially, many school leaders do not believe that the regularly scheduled monthly meetings can offer them much help in their work. To many, such meetings smack of micromanagement, excessive accountability, or an infringement of autonomy. That changes as external team leaders and school-based leaders learn to work together in the pursuit of important goals, in support of all staff, and in service to all students. In the great majority of schools that have participated in the projects reported in this text, monthly visits have been identified as a critical, positive factor in nurturing leadership growth and contributing to goal achievement.

Initially, we focus on building the skills and knowledge of the district leadership team and school leadership teams (principals and vice-principals). In conjunction with workshops and readings, we schedule monthly meetings between an external team and every school leadership team. An external team might be made up of a university researcher, a central office leader, and a volunteer school leader seconded to that task for one day per year. In most districts, external teams are able to visit three to four school sites per day. A district of 40 schools might have three or four external teams making site visits according to a carefully planned schedule.

In schools and districts where leadership growth has been championed and a commitment to continuous growth for teachers has become an embedded expectation, evidence shows increased effectiveness in the achievement of goals on a wide variety of measures. One district of 11,000 students reported five years of sustained growth on most of 16 measures of school effectiveness. A second large district recorded 17-year highs on 12 out of 16 measures of school improvement after three years of project participation. A single high school of 600 students has provided evidence of dramatic improvements, over six years, in attendance rates, high school completion rates, parent satisfaction, and student morale. A different high school in a small town showed growth in high school student success that can be directly attributed to strong, consistent, generative leadership over more than 15 years. In 2001, the high school completion rate for this school was approximately 65 percent. While the demographics of the student population have not changed very much, in 2017, just over 92 percent of students completed high school, and the school itself was recognized as one of the most outstanding, among schools of all sizes, for its ability to put students first. Yet another district, already considered to be successful, implemented a model of collaborative inquiry/generative dialogue that has been embraced by almost all school leaders. They have adopted these practices as a form of adult learning that has, quite literally, moved them to greater levels of effectiveness and satisfaction in their leadership work.

Finally, when schools and districts commit to the leadership of learning, benefits can flow to all parts of the system. A strong and purposeful district office team can make powerful contributions to the work of school leadership teams through modelling, expectation, and support. In turn, school leadership teams with clear focus and purpose can better foster the emergence of teams of staff members who are ready and able to share responsibility for the achievement of agreed-upon goals and, since those goals are so often aimed at indicators of student success, they help spread the leadership of learning to all classrooms. So many schools in these projects have, embedded in their goals, the aim of growth for *all* educators and success for *all* students. As one outstanding superintendent told us, "In this work, we are focused on every child."

JOURNAL REFLECTIONS AND WRITING PROVOCATIONS AS YOU EMBARK ON GENERATIVE DIALOGUE

The reflective writing provocations in this chapter are designed to reveal areas of un-easiness in using a model of questions. As a basic level of skill, generative questions are meant to do the following:

- Cause reflection
- Encourage conscious competence
- Promote intentional action
- Inspire professional learning

Don't forget that free-form writing requires leaders to make only two commitments to thinking about their leadership experiences: don't stop writing until an agreed-upon time limit is reached, and don't correct, sensor, judge, or otherwise evaluate the thoughts that are being written.

We have used the following provocation stems to encourage reflections around the concept of generative dialogue:

- The single most impactful question that someone could ask about my professional practice would be …
- When I think about "asking" rather than "telling," I am worried that …
- To me, facilitating reflection in others looks like …
- One obstacle that might prevent me from engaging in generative dialogue is …
- The idea of assuming competence during generative dialogue seems …
- The one habit of mind that would be most difficult for me is …

CONCLUSION

The skills of generative dialogue are essential to effective instructional leadership and to the generative leadership model presented in chapter 3. Although mentoring, coaching, and crit-ical conversations may appear comparable to generative dialogue, we cannot emphasize the fundamental importance of asking questions with a spirit of authentic curiosity as the core mindset of generative dialogue that differentiates it from many other approaches that we have observed and used. These questions are not designed to manipulate people into answering in a particular way; they are not structured to make people feel dependent on or in awe of the expertise of the questioner; they are not Pavlovian, nor are they meant to cause actions that have been predetermined. One district principal in Western Canada described it this way:

In the midst of very busy jobs, where it is easy to get caught up in the day-to-day, generative dialogue helps us concentrate and reflect on our bigger picture goals.

It helps maintain clarity and focus on our leadership growth, making goals more attainable through specific actions. Through questioning and genuine curiosity, a colleague acts as a reflective sounding board and helps focus your expertise and energy. The process can help you recognize all the things you do and achieve, at the same time as it empowers and encourages continuous growth. Generative dialogue is intentional and focused time set aside for *you*, as a leader and a reflective professional.

SUGGESTED READINGS FOR GENERATIVE DIALOGUE

Bungay Stanier, M. (2016). *The coaching habit: Say less, ask more & change the way you lead forever.* Toronto, ON: Box of Crayons Press.
Stanier notes that coaching is relatively simple and can be done in 10 minutes; however, to be effective, it should be done informally and daily as part of a coaching habit. He writes about breaking free from three vicious cycles: creating over-dependence through coaching, getting overwhelmed by over-coaching, and becoming disconnected as a result of ineffective coaching. To break free, the author present the following seven strategies in a question format: Kickstart, Awe, Focus, Foundation, Lazy, Strategic, and Learning. The Kickstart Question and the Learning Question are Coaching Bookends that ensure that everyone finds their interactions with leaders more useful.

Costa, A. L., Garmston, R. J., Hayes, C., & Ellison, H. (2016). *Cognitive coaching: Developing self-directed leaders and learners* (3rd ed.). Lanham, MD: Rowman & Littlefield.
Costa, Garmston, Hayes, and Ellison, in their third book on cognitive coaching, update and expand on their previous work. Cognitive coaching is an approach that focuses on improved decision making and self-directed learning. In this work, Costa et al. share the components of cognitive coaching: skills, capabilities, mental maps, beliefs, values, and commitments. They also are very clear about how cognitive coaching is not evaluation. It includes elements of effective consultation and genuine collaboration, but cognitive coaching goes further and allows the learner to provide the impetus for growth and development. One of the key elements of their work is the role of the coach as a mediator of thinking who is concerned not just with behaviour but also with the thought process behind it, as they engage in very intentional dialogue with a learner. One notable feature of this work is its thorough analysis and extensive connections to the fields of psychology, brain research, and constructivist learning theory.

Knight, J. (2016). *Better conversations: Coaching ourselves and each other to be more credible, caring, and connected.* Thousand Oaks, CA: Corwin.
Knight's work on better conversations is centred around the belief that conversation is the lifeblood of any school. He posits that people need to listen, pay attention, care, seek out the things we hold in common with others, demonstrate empathy, and be a witness to what is good. Through these actions, Knight believes people can begin to coach themselves to improve their communication

skills. He outlines Better Conversation Habits and Beliefs as a mode of developing the trust necessary to have better conversations. Knight presents Better Conversation Beliefs that focus on the ideas of seeing conversation partners as equals, believing people should have a lot of autonomy, not judging others, and conversation being a back-and-forth, life-giving practice.

Stoltzfus, T. (2008). *Coaching questions: A coach's guide to powerful asking skills*. Virginia Beach, VA: Tony Stoltzfus.

This is a practical guide to using questioning techniques in a life-coaching context. In it, Stoltzfus lays out questioning techniques as applied to the coaching process in general, the work of developing one's purpose in life, and the improvement of one's current state. This resource is based on the premise that questions level the power structures in relationships and promote good listening skills. Additionally, Stoltzfus maintains that coaching questions foster affirmation, buy-in, empowerment, leadership skills, and authenticity. Much of this work is focused on sample questions, but the intent is that readers use them to prime their memory rather than memorizing them verbatim.

Vogt, E., Brown, J., & Isaac, D. (2003). *The art of powerful questions*. Mill Valley, CA: Whole Systems.

Written from a human resource perspective, Vogt et al. offer a through and compelling argument for the use of powerful questions to inspire creative action. The book offers a diagnostic set of criteria to determine the extent to which leaders may be fostering an inquiry system. Importantly, the authors describe a glimpse into the evolution of generative dialogue as it has unfolded in corporate communities.

Walsh, J. A., & Sattes, B. D. (2010). Leading through quality questioning: Creating capacity, commitment, and community. *Reference and Research Book News, 25*(2).

Walsh and Sattes build on their earlier work and expand the application of quality questions to school leadership in this book. Built around a four-by-four matrix, the authors connect the four elements of quality questions—crafting questions, question presentation, extending thinking, and fostering inquiry—with four key leadership functions—maximizing capacity, mobilizing people, mediating conflicts, and monitoring progress. Of note in this work is the presence of embedded coaching, regular inclusion of sample questions, and practical resource sections.

Zepeda, S. J., Parylo, O., & Klar, H. W. (2017). Educational leadership for teaching and learning. In D. Waite & I. Bogotch (Eds.), *The Wiley international handbook of educational leadership* (pp. 227–252). Hoboken, NJ: John Wiley & Sons.

This chapter by Zepeda, Parylo, and Klar examines the state of educational leadership in relation to teaching and learning in the context of the fluid educational milieu that has developed since the 1980s. They touch on the trends in learning-centred leadership, instructional leadership, and distributed leadership. Additionally, Zepeda et al. consider the shifting role of the principal, the effect that central office inaction has on sustainable learning, and the possible future direction of leadership for teaching and learning.

REFERENCES

Adler, A. (1956). *The individual psychology of Alfred Adler: A systematic presentation in selections from his writings.* H. L. Ansbacher & R. R. Ansbacher (Eds.). New York, NY: Basic Books.

Ansbacher, H., & Ansbacher, R. (1956). Individual psychology in its larger setting. In H. L. Ansbacher & R. R. Ansbacher (Eds.), *The individual psychology of Alfred Adler* (pp. 1–18). New York, NY: Basic Books.

Barnes, B., & Payette, P. (2017). Socratic questioning. *The National Teaching & Learning Forum, 26*(6), 6–8.

Brookfield, S. (1995). *Becoming a critically reflective teacher.* San Francisco, CA: Jossey-Bass.

Brookfield, S. (2017). *Becoming a critically reflective teacher* (2nd ed.). San Francisco, CA: John Wiley & Sons.

Bruner, J. (1986). *Actual minds, possible worlds.* Cambridge, MA: Harvard University Press.

Bruner, J. (2004). Life as narrative. *Social Research, 71*(3), 691–710.

Carson, T. (1986). Closing the gap between research and practice: Conversation as a mode of doing research. *Phenomenology + Pedagogy, 4*(2), 73–85.

Covey, S. (1989). *The seven habits of highly effective people.* New York, NY: Free Press.

Donaldson, M. L. (2013). Principals' approaches to cultivating teacher effectiveness: Constraints and opportunities in hiring, assigning, evaluating, and developing teachers. *Educational Administration Quarterly, 49*(5), 838–882. doi:10.1177/0013161x13485961

Elder, L., & Paul, R. (1998). The role of Socratic questioning in thinking, teaching, and learning. *The Clearing House, 71*(5), 297–301. doi:10.1080/00098659809602729

Elmore, R. (2000). *Building a new structure for school leadership.* Washington, DC: The Albert Shanker Institute.

Gall, M. D., & Acheson, K. A. (1980). *Techniques in the clinical supervision of teachers: Preservice and inservice applications.* New York, NY: Longman.

Generative. (n.d.). In *OED online.* Retrieved from http://www.oed.com/view/Entry/77523?redirectedFrom=generative

Goff, P., Guthrie, E. J., Goldring, E., & Bickman, L. (2014). Changing principals' leadership through feedback and coaching. *Journal of Educational Administration, 52*(5), 682–704.

Greenleaf, R. (1977). *Servant leadership: A journey into the nature of legitimate power and greatness.* Mahwah, NJ: Paulist Press.

Isaac, I. (1999). A generative approach to psychological and educational measurement. *Journal of Educational Measurement, 36*(2), 158–184.

John-Steiner, V., & Mahn, H. (1996). Sociocultural approaches to learning and development: A Vygotskian framework. *Educational Psychologist, 31*(3/4), 191–206.

Joyce, B., & Showers, B. (1981). Transfer of training: The contribution of coaching. *The Journal of Education, 163*(2), 163–172.

Kraft, M. A., & Gilmour, A. F. (2016). Can principals promote teacher development as evaluators? A case study of principals' views and experiences. *Educational Administration Quarterly, 52*(5), 711–753. doi:10.1177/0013161X16653445

Lave, J., & Wenger, E. (1991). *Situated learning: Legitimate peripheral participation.* Cambridge, UK: Cambridge University Press.

Leithwood, K., & Jantzi, D. (1990). Transformational leadership: How principals can help reform school culture. *School Effectiveness & School Improvement, 1*(4), 249–280.

Lemberger, M. (2017). Adler as a preceptor of humanistic psychotherapy. *The Journal of Individual Psychology, 73*(2), 124–138.

Maieutic. (n.d.). In *OED online.* Retrieved from http://www.oed.com/view/Entry/112474?redir ectedFrom=maieutic&

Merriam, S. (2001). Andragogy and self-directed learning: Pillars of adult learning theory. *New Directions for Adult and Continuing Education, 89*, 3–13.

Mezirow, J. (1991). Transformative dimension of adult learning. San Francisco, CA: John Wiley & Sons.

Mezirow, J. (1997). Transformative learning: Theory to practice. *New Directions for Adult and Continuing Education, 74*, 5–12.

Paul, R., & Elder, L. (2007). Critical thinking: The art of Socratic questioning. *Journal of Developmental Education, 31*(1), 36–37.

Rigby, J. G., Larbi-Cherif, A., Rosenquist, B. A., Sharpe, C. J., Cobb, P., & Smith, T. (2017). Administrator observation and feedback: Does it lead toward improvement in inquiry-oriented math instruction? *Educational Administration Quarterly, 53*(3), 475–516. doi:10.1177/0013161X16687006

Rogers, C. (1961). *On becoming a person.* New York, NY: Houghton Mifflin Harcourt.

Rogers, C. (1980). *A way of being.* New York, NY: Houghton Mifflin Harcourt.

Rogoff, B. (1990). *Apprenticeship in thinking: Cognitive development in social context.* New York, NY: Oxford University Press.

Rogoff, B. (2003). *The cultural nature of human development.* New York, NY: Oxford University Press.

Scheeler, M. C., Ruhl, K. L., & McAfee, J. K. (2004). Providing performance feedback to teachers: A review. *Teacher Education and Special Education, 27*(4), 396–407. doi:10.1177/088840640402700407

Senge, P. (1990). *The fifth discipline: The art and practice of the learning organization.* New York, NY: Random House.

Sergiovanni. T. (1994). *Building community in schools.* New York, NY: Wiley.

Spillane, J. P., Halverson, R., & Diamond, J. B. (1999). *Distributed leadership: Toward a theory of school leadership practice.* Evanston, IL: Institute for Policy Research, Northwestern University.

Vygotsky, L. S. (1978). *Mind in society: The development of higher psychological processes* (A. R. Luria, M. Cole, M. Lopez-Morillas, & J. Wertsch, Trans.). Cambridge, MA: Harvard University Press.

Vygotsky, L. S., & Luria, A. R. (1993). The child and its behavior. In V. I. Golod and J. E. Knox (Eds. and Trans.), *Studies on the history of behavior: Ape, primitive, child* (pp. 140–231). Hillsdale, NJ: Lawrence Erlbaum Associates.

Watts, R. E. (1996). Social interest and the core conditions: Could it be that Adler influenced Rogers? *Journal of Humanistic Education and Development, 34*(4), 165–170. doi:10.1002/j.2164-4683.1996.tb00342.x

Watts, R. E. (1998). The remarkable parallel between Rogers's core conditions and Adler's social interest. *The Journal of Individual Psychology, 54*(1), 4–9.

CHAPTER FIVE

The Power of Reflection

I Wonder Why We Have to Reflect So Much?

By three methods we may learn wisdom: First, by reflection, which is the noblest; second, by imitation, which is the easiest; and third, by experience, which is the bitterest.
   —*Confucius*

I had anticipated, rather naively, that most leaders and teachers would welcome an opportunity to talk more about, and take greater responsibility for, their professional practice. I discovered that, in the absence of my effectiveness to create trust and facilitate reflection, most educators just don't have the time or inclination to think deeply about improving. They are reluctant to reflect on their practice, and hesitant to take too much ownership. But mostly, they are just too busy!
   —*Former deputy superintendent*

What I consistently tell my school leaders is that it is non-negotiable for you to be involved in professional learning. That's non-negotiable. You can join us in this work that we are doing or you can come up with something else and tell me the alternative—and I am genuinely happy and interested if there is something that will work better for you—but what's non-negotiable is that you are all here to improve.
   —*Retired superintendent*

THE LINK BETWEEN REFLECTION AND PROFESSIONAL LEARNING

In their most recent[1] analysis (2013) of the Teaching and Learning Inter vey (TALIS) results, the Organisation for Economic Co-operation and (OECD) reported the following:

Most teachers are still teaching largely in isolation, as over half of very rarely or never team-teaching with colleagues, and two-thir rates for observing their colleagues teach. Some 46% of teach ceiving feedback on their teaching from their school leader received feedback from other members of the school management. Only slightly more than a third of teachers in TALIS countries report that the feedback they receive on their teaching leads to a moderate or large positive change in the likelihood of career advancement. (OECD, 2014, p. 19)

As disheartening as the 2013 report may be in signalling that educators are not engaging more often and purposefully in reflection-for-practice, almost 60 percent of teachers indicated that they would appreciate more feedback, or performance appraisals that caused them to think about and improve their practice. Similarly, in Alberta, Canada, Brandon et al. (2018) reported that teachers and leaders are yearning for, and appreciative of, opportunities to reflect on and collaborate about their professional learning goals with other teachers and school leaders. They long for timely, useful, and **generative feedback** within collective and supportive learning cultures. They want more opportunities and time to reflect, deconstruct their practice, and grow as professionals.

Yet many system and school leaders seem to be spending more and more time attending off-site meetings, and less time in classrooms or in conversations with teachers that contribute to reflection, professional learning, and enhanced practice (Jones & Thessin, 2015; Townsend & Adams, 2009). In the early days of the 21st century, Roland Barth (2001) posited that all educators, both teachers and leaders, should be considering some fundamental questions, including the following:

- To what extent am I identifying and acting on what it is that I am passionate about learning? In what ways am I enabling others to do the same?
- Who are those that model voracious, sustained reflection and learning? To what extent am I such a role model?
- In what ways am I contributing to or detracting from those conditions that support reflection and that help others construct their own knowledge?
- To what extent would I consider my system, school, or classroom to be a culture that fosters a sense of wonder?
- Are the relationships that characterize the community that I lead ones of collegiality? Isolation? Competitiveness? Adversarialism? Is the culture conducive to vulnerability and learning? Supportive of reflection?

We encourage you to refer to these questions as you proceed through this chapter.

The question that heads this chapter was asked of one of us in a graduate class, and we could not help but be amused by the *double entendre*! Throughout this chapter, we will focus on the importance of professional reflection and its place in the larger scheme of generative leadership. You will read about a group of vice-principals and principals who were so eager for sustained professional reflective opportunities that they formed their own Leaders of Learning Network.[2] Three years later, the network is thriving and offers others a venue for authentic reflection and growth. Next, we will differentiate between the semantics of professional learning and professional development, and present some elements that flag whether professional conditions are fertile for reflection. One of the key ways we have been successful in promoting reflective practice is a very practical one: by ensuring that all members of the organization set yearly growth plans based on inquiry questions. We will illustrate several of these templates as exemplars and describe how a culture of collaborative inquiry is an important strategy to move a school or system toward large-scale improvement. And, as with past chapters, there will be helpful responses to unhelpful assumptions and writing provocations to enable your own and others' reflection.

Case Study: The Leaders of Learning Network Reflects

There is an old proverb that states we do not have eyes in the back of our head because we are meant to move forward; it is an educator's sole purpose to foster growth and progress. What if looking back is a crucial component to moving forward? What would happen if improvement requires a backwards examination? The following voices highlight the work of participants in our Leaders of Learning Network and, in particular, how the role of an assistant principal can be positively influenced by generative dialogue and reflection. Assistant principals need to be mentored and coached, but our network found this to be most valuable by developing a supportive, collaborative professional group that asks questions, listens with purpose, and provokes a self-awareness of leadership efficacy. The questions that guided all our meetings, "What have you learned about your leadership journey today?" "What actions/steps will you commit to before we next meet?" and "How will you know you have met your goal?" required us to constantly rewind and replay decisions, conversations, and actions. The Leaders of Learning Network supported our forward movement through a backwards look and reflection on our leadership practices so we were able to grow as school leaders. In the reflections that follow, five leaders from the network speak to the relationship they have with the network, their professional colleagues, and the role that reflection now plays in their professional lives.

Bonnie: It's All about the *Relationships*

I was an assistant principal with a large urban school board and on the verge of completing my Master of Education in Educational Leadership. I had network of professional colleagues and was a voracious reader of all thi to leadership. But even with what I knew, had learned, and had e' wanted more. I was surprised at how much I enjoyed my gradu perience and realized it was because of the camaraderie I develo' hort. I wanted to continue learning with others, so I connecte professors, who had the expertise to influence growing leadership capacities in ways that extended and complemented the leadership qualities that were being implemented in our province. At her suggestion, I organized a Leaders of Learning Network and invited a few of my leadership colleagues to participate in a grass-roots, organic venture of professional growth.

Our first meeting was a "get-to-know" each other conversation about what the network would be all about. Our common goal was growing our leadership capacity. We decided our work would be centred around learning the skills of generative dialogue combined with sustained reflection on practice. What began as a collaborative growth opportunity grew into a highly effective leadership practice.

One thing that I appreciated early on in our Leaders of Learning Network collaboration was that we were able to easily integrate our work with the larger system's work, and with the demands and expectations of the jurisdiction. For me, it was of great value to take what we were practising and having conversations about in the Network, and then use these skills as a school leader. Heaven knows, I didn't need extra work added to my plate! I needed a different tool to support my work. Learning how to leverage growth through dialogue, rather than trying to be a leader with all the answers, was both freeing and transformational. During our network meetings, our conversations would be informal and organic, but our genuine curiosity for what each of us was struggling with gave me the foundation for my professional growth. We held each other accountable for our actions and I was asked questions that provoked me to recognize, acknowledge, and address areas of my leadership. In reflecting, I also was able to identify my strengths, which was important to increasing my self-efficacy and confidence. A consistent through-line during my reflections was my prioritization of the people I work with. Leadership is people-centred, and I realized through the network experience how important those relationships were to my leadership style. I accepted that belief as a strength and used it to facilitate the professional growth of those around me.

Maria: It's All about *Consistency*

Before I even stepped into my assistant principal role, I knew the learning curve would be steep. My principal was a veteran administrator who had come to know the staff, community, and building under his leadership for well over a decade. The two of us were just in the early stages of getting to know each other and design our professional alliance when he needed to step away from the building to attend to an emergent family matter. This initial interruption turned into a leave and, ultimately, his early retirement. I was lucky to have another veteran principal temporarily step in to finish the year, but knew that I could expect a fresh start with someone else the following year.

In September, I started with another veteran principal, recently returned from a secondment, who was looking to take the next steps in his career from school leadership to a more senior system role. Because he had his sights elsewhere, opportunities for professional growth afforded by the close mentor I had hoped for were far too few during this time. Although all the principals I worked with certainly had a wealth of knowledge and experience to share, there were extenuating circumstances that seemed to get in the way of me accessing their expertise and professional knowledge. I had the clear realization that even though I was learning, I wasn't growing. So I eagerly accepted the invitation to join the Leaders of Learning Network.

Our initial meeting opened the door to a conversation about our shared roles, experiences, and challenges, and what we hoped could be the potential focus of our fledgling professional development network. Since most attendees were relatively new to the assistant principal role and the school district had been making significant changes to how they selected and developed potential administrators, the network decided to make use of generative dialogue in our regular meetings so we could unpack our shared experiences and support one another as we collaboratively honed our leadership competencies.

The meetings that followed varied in the order of the agenda, but our core purpose always included time to share experiences, ask questions to dig deeper, challenge assumptions, reflect on professional practice, engage in collaborative problem solving, and establish accountability for the next meeting. The reflection that occurred during the generative dialogue was particularly helpful when discussing challenging situations. It opened a safe space to explore any given scenario through multiple perspectives; I found these opportunities for personal and collaborative reflection particularly beneficial since the pace of a typical workday made such a luxury virtually impossible! The accountability piece was also critical to keeping our professional growth on track. Being able to leave each meeting with a plan, knowing that I would report to my peers about my success or learning, was a powerful motivator.

In the end, it was the consistency of our focus and processes that kept me coming back to meet time and time again. As a relatively new assistant principal, I craved the opportunity to build on my professional growth with a group of like-minded individuals. The Leaders of Learning Network provided me with a consistent professional-competency development focus and peer support during a time that I couldn't reasonably expect to find it in my own building.

Theresa: It's All about *Believing*

As a leader, I try to live by these words: "The way to keep yourself from making assumptions is to ask questions. Make sure that the communication is clear. If you don't understand, ask."

continued

The work of school leadership is demanding; rich, exciting, varied, but always demanding. In the speed of a day, I can proceed through multiple meetings, deal with student disputes, respond to a dozen parents, and then move to "clean-up in aisle three" when the facility operator is out on lunch! This pace and increasing demands for results and accountability can distract from our core work: providing assistance and ongoing feedback in support of teaching and learning.

When I joined the Leaders of Learning Network, I accepted the invitation because I wanted to surround myself with smart people and wanted more time with my colleagues. I went without expectation, not knowing what the process would be. From my first meeting, I was hooked. I loved the dedicated time to reflect, not just to consider what I could have done differently in a specific situation or encounter, but time to reflect on my core beliefs in relation to my practice. Through the writing prompts, I was able to liberate my mind from the to-do lists and focus on why I became a teacher and what drew me to leadership.

During this time, I was engaged in our jurisdictional process for becoming an aspiring principal. This was a cumbersome process, filled with matrixes and interviews. Of greatest importance, I needed to clearly articulate my beliefs and practice within the leadership competencies. Through my writing, our discussion as a group, and through our guide's modelling of the generative dialogue process, I was taken on a journey of self-evaluation and goal-setting like I had never experienced. This was focused, targeted work that pushed me to wrestle with my beliefs and my desire to meet leadership competencies, and to honestly examine who I wanted to be as a leader.

What did I learn about myself? I found my voice in this process; I was able to step out of the shadow of my mentors and previous leaders, refining my vision of who I am. I realized my core beliefs about teachers and their desire to serve students was the starting point for all my work. I realized I didn't need to be "perfect" (if perfect leadership even exists), but needed to be good enough in difficult moments and to reflect on a continuous basis. Most importantly, I learned to ask questions, in support of understanding and honouring the relationship, rather than making assumptions.

The generative dialogue process forced me to look at my own personal strengths and weaknesses, trying to set aside bias to learn about the people doing the work. The components of the process I found most impactful were the times spent with my colleagues, having a focused conversation related to a specific problem or struggle. Through experiencing someone challenging me to think about my practice, examining how I came to this need for growth or change, and pushing me to be clear around my action steps, I was able to let go of the story and the details, focusing on my role in seeking forward movement. The group challenged me to commit to action steps and what I needed to do before we next met. This experience enabled me to apply these strategies in supporting other colleagues and staff at different points in their own professional journey. I also embraced the leadership journey as an ever-evolving experience, far more coloured and expansive than a checklist of qualities or competencies.

Carissa: It's All about *Preparing for the Future*

Nine years after completing my Master of Education in Educational Leadership, I felt a strong pull to take the risk and enter a leadership role in my school district. I was fortunate to quickly move into an assistant principal role, and I embraced the experience with all its gifts and challenges. It was a steep learning curve and I truly felt I was moving my career forward and supporting learning and teaching in a rich and active way.

After my fifth year as an assistant principal, I started to become more confident with my new position and more curious of other leadership opportunities, not only in my jurisdictional professional learning leadership program but also in other places such as Australia and New Zealand. The first time I was invited to participate in a Leaders of Learning Network dialogue, I became alive and energized with the possibilities and the humbling knowledge that I could begin to assimilate my own visions of educational leadership that I had been withholding. It had been so long since I was able to expand on questions of my leadership without the immediate demands of the work infiltrating my reflections.

Improvement has always been my personal passion, particularly in a professional learning capacity. Yet, up to the point when I joined the Leaders of Learning Network, I am not sure I ever allowed critical friends to see this level of vulnerability. When the facilitator began a session with 10 minutes for reflective writing and then asked questions using the generative dialogue process to reveal the true meaning of my thoughts, I realized I was ready to embrace improvement through empowerment. My own curiosity and willingness to fully let go of my inhibitions and worries of judgment allowed me to discover my personal vision of leadership, as well as to identify what I believed to be my next steps in my improvement. Sharing my own goals and actionable steps in leadership in the presence of other respected leaders was inspirational. I was able to make this statement after an hour-long generative dialogue session where my ideas were synthesized and repeated back to me for clarification. To say the process was intense is an understatement. For a full hour, a colleague asked deep questions about my reflective responses, with the expectation that I would clarify everything I stated. As I reflected, my colleagues actively listened to our conversation as keen observers ready to be the questioner in the future. I believe that being present and mindful of the exchange permitted all of us to grow in another dimension of leadership: the authentic listener.

continued

The impact of my experiences with generative dialogue has been threefold. First, each time I have had the opportunity to share my self-reflections there has always been a commitment, an actionable piece of leadership I need to take back to my school environment. This is both empowering and work-specific, two items I value deeply. Secondly, I am beginning to internalize and utilize the generative dialogue process of asking questions and clarifying the answers of staff members and other colleagues. I believe this to be a profound and explicit way of allowing others to take control of their intentions and build improvement. In response, the feedback from others has been full of gratitude and respect for my role as a leader. Lastly, I am interested in moving to the next level of leadership in the near future. As a future principal, I now feel able to identify and clearly articulate intentional impacts I have had on my school culture. Without the generative dialogue experience, I would not be as focused and visibly actionable in my leadership practice.

Marvin: It's All about *the Self*

My self-esteem took a real hit after I failed to gain a spot in the jurisdictional assistant principal pool. A university professor I had known for many years suggested I consider joining an informal leadership group that she was facilitating called the Leaders of Learning Network. I did not know any of the other people in the group and felt grateful that they welcomed a stranger.

The ongoing and predictable nature of our Leaders of Learning Network gatherings meant there was space and place to reflect. I expected dissonance, pain, a need to do some research and more reflection, and, ultimately, I hoped for a shift or growth in my leadership practice. Throughout all our meetings, we paused to practise being **reflective practitioners**. We learned through observing each other engage in the questioning that guided the generative dialogue. My learning was provoked by questions that elicited deep reflection and action. The space created through this work enabled me to dig into sometimes-painful reflections as I walked alongside others. I was able to connect my own rocky journey to those of my professional colleagues and work through struggles I was having navigating my own identity as a leader.

Throughout our meetings, we practised generative dialogue centred on leadership standards. We were reflective and practised compassionate listening. The tone and environment of our Leaders of Learning Network was characterized by safety and trust, along with an absence of bravado, ego, and competitiveness.

Reflection was a crucial component of our work, as it allowed space and time to think about myself. My journey through leadership was the journey to understand myself. We have all read the research about how we need to reflect in order to know ourselves and understand the decisions we make. However, in our profession, there seems to be a normalization of being "crazy busy," putting students' and teachers' needs and managerial tasks ahead of the space required to know oneself and to grow as a leader.

In my Master of Education program, I became convinced that reflection is essential to leading educational change wisely. The Leaders of Learning Network provided me with the intentional space (no excuses, no putting off), and the reflective work of understanding myself in this work. I find it strange that in such a selfless profession, where I often feel guilty about spending time on my growth, reflection is so often avoided or neglected. I have realized that this might be one factor why progress is so slow and shifts in professional practice often never occur. We—me included—are often afraid of digging into ourselves for fear of what we might see. The overall goal of this work and this journey for me was to envision and realize how to be true to thine own self. It took a collaborative group process to help me grow as an individual.

Case Study Reflections: Considering Professional Reflection

- How and when do you spend time reflecting on your leadership practice? In what ways and to what extent do your professional networks purposely facilitate the reflective process?
- In what ways do you model and facilitate reflective practice with your staff and/or colleagues?
- What are some of the most important themes about reflection that were identified by the Leaders of Learning Network participants?
- Why is reflection often not given its due in the professional development of leaders?

LEADERSHIP *FOR* AND *OF* REFLECTION

To what extent can reflection enhance practice? In what ways can leaders promote reflective practice? For many years, we have relied on the theories of Stephen Brookfield (1984, 1995, 2009, 2017) and Jack Mezirow (1991) to guide our thinking and research around the role of reflection, and to examine ways that nurturing a reflective state of mind can be accomplished by leaders as a primary strategy to enhance organizational learning. Of course, we also acknowledge the seminal work of Donald Schön (1983) in providing a sophisticated conceptual framework of professional reflection.

The previous chapter presented a theoretical framework for these ideas as they pertain to generative dialogue. Mezirow (1991), however, situated reflection in a much more prominent place of importance:

> Much of what we learn involves making new interpretations that enable us to elaborate, further differentiate, and reinforce our long-established frames of reference or to create new meaning schemes. Perhaps even more central to adult learning than elaborating established meaning schemes is the process of reflecting back on prior learning to determine whether what we have learned is justified under present circumstances. (p. 5)

Reflection thus extends meaning by examining presuppositions. Mezirow (1991) continued, "While all reflection implies an element of critique, the term *critical reflection* will here be reserved to refer to challenging the validity of presuppositions in prior learning" (p. 12). At this point, Mezirow posited, transformation has occurred and, if sustained, will result in the habit of mind that Sullivan, Glenn, Roche, and McDonagh (2016) referred to as "the habit of critical reflection for improving practice" (p. 2).

Facilitating this critical reflection (Brookfield, 2017) is more challenging, requiring the following:

- A sustained attempt to keep the focus on uncovering assumptions, particularly those having to do with power and hegemony
- A mindful effort to bring into the discussion as many different perspectives as possible
- An acknowledgment of the importance of each person's contribution, irrespective of seniority, status, or institutional role
- An agreement to try out inclusive conversation protocols that [avoid] one response to a problem (p. 119)

An essential requisite of generative leadership is the ability and willingness of leaders to model reflection in their own practice, as well as to foster a culture of reflection in the organizations they lead. In doing so, we contend, leaders will increasingly adopt and promote many of these aspects of professional learning.

SHIFTING PARADIGMS FROM PROFESSIONAL DEVELOPMENT TO PROFESSIONAL LEARNING: SEMANTICS MATTER FOR REFLECTION

Several years ago, when the vocabulary of professional development was starting to be seen as too limiting or as not attending to research around adult learning and human growth, we registered in an event that was advertised as *The Best in Adult and Professional Learning.* Eureka! We were looking forward to innovative and provocative ways of learning that were a departure from the traditional conventions we were accustomed to. At 8:45 a.m., we and about 500 other participants were herded into a medium size, generically decorated conference room and sat among the 30 rows of chairs. The keynote speaker talked the audience through an array of 37 humorous, motivating slides and, 90 minutes later, we went to break. For the next two days, we attended several very interesting 45-minute sessions on a wide variety of topics, each with handouts, each with the usual Q & A section for the final five minutes of the session. On the car ride home, we debriefed our conference learnings by trying to identify unique structures or processes that distinguished this experience from others that were not advertised as adult learning or professional learning. Other than the promotional title, we were mostly unsuccessful in doing so. The conference didn't implement any noticeable processes in adult learning or in best practices of professional learning. However, the conference did reiterate for us the tendency to adopt phrases, words, and titles that appear to be fresh and trendy, without a full understanding of nuance and accuracy.

> If you were to attend a conference labelled with a similar title, what would you expect? How should it be different than the standard "sit and get" dominant in education?

So, too, with terms such as *reflective practitioner*, *professional development*, and *adult learning*, clarity and consistent understanding of terms matters, lest we fall into a trap of conceptual relativism. We have found that this cavalier attitude can surface when leaders engage in or organize opportunities for the professional learning of staff. Yet, in both substance and practice, there are several key characteristics that differentiate historical practices of professional development (PD) from *professional learning* (PL).

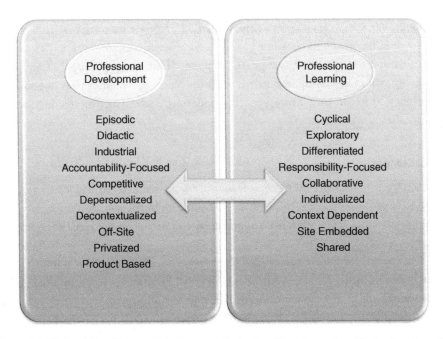

Figure 5.1: Distinguishing Characteristics between Professional Development and Professional Learning

The concept of PD was grounded in a training model made popular all the way back in the Industrial Revolution. Even as the term and many of its activities have evolved from images of incessant repetition and drill, rote memorization, and persistent external evaluation, vestiges of vocational training models of the past remain in practices and structures of present-day PD. Primary among them is a general lack of acknowledgement or value for the idea that reflection is linked with, and possibly at the core of, improved performance.

As figure 5.1 illustrates, there are at least 10 elements that distinguish professional development from professional learning and that contribute to reflective practice. We next will elaborate on each of them.

Cyclical

Recently, a school leader used the term *professional development attention deficit disorder* (PD ADD) to describe the tendency for educators to be enticed by multiple initiatives. He suggested that educators are unable to focus for any sustained period on a deep and coherent understanding and application of strategies that might lead to improved practice. Rather, he observed, they are too easily distracted by the latest book, most recent conference, short-lived trends, and simple fads. We refer to these disparate activities as *being professionally developed*, as opposed to engaging in learning. The process through which learning occurs is not a singular event, although a critical event might provide an impetus for learning. Rather, professional learning is evidenced through multiple iterations (cycles, if you will) of pondering, deconstructing, reconstructing, and actualizing practices in a time frame that varies with each individual. We see cycles of professional learning among educators that last as little as a few months or as long as a few years. In fact, when educators ask us "How long will it take me to learn this?" we gently respond, "How long is a rope?" One phase of learning will take as long as needed, until the learning becomes part of conscious competency, at which time a new cycle of pondering, deconstructing, reconstructing, and actualizing will occur.

Exploratory

We often refer to a didactic form of professional development as "sit and get." In theory, this type of professional development places educators in the role of passive receivers, pedagogically tabula rasa, with little opportunity to internalize the locus of control for content or reflection.

Conversely, exploratory professional learning is based on the early notions of andragogy, as defined by Malcolm Knowles (1984, 2015). Knowles was a seminal author in advocating adult learning experiences that rejected linear, *transmissional*, **rationalist models of professional development**. He presented a portrait of the professional learner in which the following are true:

- Autonomy and the capacity for self-assessment, self-improvement, and professional discovery are acknowledged and supported.
- Prior learning, life experiences, and goals constitute the topics and direction of professional learning.

Reflection is critical to an exploratory element of professional learning and is one reason inquiry-based professional learning is predicated heavily on pursuing an answer to an individual or team question. The extent to which leaders model, share, promote, and celebrate reflection will determine the likelihood that all members of the organization will embark upon exploration of their own learning.

Differentiated

It would be the uncommon school or district that has not at least broached the challenges associated with meeting student learning needs through differentiated instruction, assessment, or programming. It is more likely that strategies of differentiation have been discussed and implemented for several decades now. Yet we rarely see the same considerations given to professional learning. Think back to when you observed a leader anticipating, encouraging, and engaging in the self-identified professional learning needs of a teacher colleague. What would professional learning for a staff look like if the content was individualized, if the process was customized, and if the assessment of learning was unique and personalized? And how might this differentiation strengthen, rather than weaken, the integration of system and school goals?

> Have you ever thought about differentiating learning for your team or your staff? What might that look like? How would that be different from what you do now?

Responsibility-Focused

In our work with school and school district personnel, we come across an inherent cynicism related to the term *PD*. It is a term sometimes associated with lack of responsibility for learning or, in some of the most extreme cases, an example of accountability run amok. We can't count the number of times we have heard reports of workshop binders that never found their way off a dusty shelf, of handouts or PowerPoint summaries that filled recycling bins at the end of sessions, or of educators attending PD events in isolation or without any expectations for sharing; in short, low levels of engagement in learning in favour of being seen at, or "doing" conferences or conventions. In fact, it wasn't so long ago that the three of us received our monthly paycheque handed out by the principal and superintendent at the end of a teachers' convention so that they could ensure we were in attendance right up to the closing keynote session.

We also hear on a regular basis that when school and school district personnel make the leap across the divide separating PD from PL, it is accompanied by a greater assumption of responsibility for learning. Teachers and school leaders who assume direct responsibility for their own learning, often framed in the vernacular of an inquiry question, also put in place measures and evidence that will demonstrate that impact on student learning is occurring. These teachers and school leaders link their own learning with that of the students.

Collaborative

As we will outline in much greater detail in chapter 6, professional learning is greatly enhanced when done collaboratively. Very often, in the traditional mode of teacher and school leader PD, the work of learning is done in isolation; unnervingly, we have even seen solitary PD in a room with dozens of other educators. Traditional PD is frequently viewed as an act of selfish learning: done by self, for self.

This is a difference described by Susan Cain in her book *Quiet*. Cain (2012) presents a strong case that, for some, learning is an independent and analytical process that is dishonoured in "a world that can't stop talking." PL assumes collaboration, but in a way that supports an array of learning preferences. PL is maximized when teachers and school leaders plan to learn after a careful analysis of student learning needs coupled with a thorough review of current knowledge and skill. Collaboration leads to learning being focused on need, and blends intuitively with increased levels of responsibility for the learning of both teacher and student alike.

Individualized

Despite what we just said about collaboration being a hallmark of PL, another hallmark is that it is also individualized. The individualization in this case comes from a recognition that the resulting growth comes from an internal locus, not an external one. PL is maximized when teachers and school leaders take inventory of their own knowledge, skills, and attributes in association with the learning needs of their students. Once these elements are determined, teachers and school leaders plan for and acquire that which is needed to move their learning and, in turn, student learning forward. In this context, the reason for learning is individualized, but the means through which it is best attained and gains maximum impact on students is collaborative.

Context Dependent

Context, then, becomes an important factor when assessing the inherent differences between the impact of traditional PD and the ways in which we have seen PL influence learning. We refer once again to the need for the genesis of PL work to be the students of the class, school, and district. Even though many learners require many similar universal strategies, it is in understanding and attending to the individualized needs of students, teachers, and school leaders that maximum growth will occur. The old adage of *it all depends* does make a difference when student, teacher, and school leader learning are addressed.

Site Embedded

Site embeddedness logically follows the requirement for consideration of context. With a clear focus on in-dividualized needs of students driving the review and analysis of teacher and school leader growth factors, it also should follow that the site of learning be as close to the students and the work as possible. In our work with schools and school districts, we have witnessed multiple ways through which school leaders have en-sured that PL is site embedded and where teachers are freed of teaching responsibilities so that they can at-tend to their own learning done in collaboration with colleagues.

> Take a few minutes to consider the many different ways that professional learning for educators can be more purposeful and appealing when it occurs in the workplace. Have you experienced the benefit of flexible timetabling that allows for weekly team meetings? Observations of colleagues? Time for reflection with district leadership teams? What would it take to increase the level of job-embedded PL in your workplace?

Shared

As we will discuss more thoroughly in the following chapter, **constructivism**, illus-trated through practices of collaboration and sharing, as proposed by Lev Vygotsky (1978) in his theory of social cognition, envelops concepts of shared, collective, and interdependent reflection and learning. Conversely, the term *private* conjures up syn-onyms such as *individual*, *isolated*, *personal*, or *separate*. In practice, professional learning has a core expectation that learning will be disseminated, discussed, and laid bare for examination. This, as identified in figure 5.1, contravenes conventional models of pro-fessional development that rarely place such expectations on the process, the individual, or the teams that participate.

One superintendent referred to this expectation for sharing as "raising the roof" on professional learning as it was implemented in practice. In his mind's eye, he pictured the analogy of classrooms without ceilings, teachers and leaders learning together, peer-ing with well-intentioned curiosity at others' practice as a way to reflect on, examine, and share their own expertise.

WHY REFLECT? CONSIDERING INQUIRY-BASED PROFESSIONAL LEARNING

Townsend and Adams (2009) described inquiry-based professional learning to be the result of a history of practice in three types of professional development (see figure 5.2):

- Rationalism—the sage-on-the-stage model in which teachers and leaders are expected to conform their understanding of best practices to a guru's set of ac-cepted truths about effective practice.

- Behaviourism—steeped in behaviourist practices, this is where most conventional coaching models of professional development reside. The model is also referred to as the "try-retry" model of professional development in which a specific technical skill is outlined and then practised until meeting a standard of acceptable competence determined by an external expert.
- Constructivism—built on principles of sharing, sense-making, and learning with peers, constructivism frees professional development from the persistent external locus of control of rationalism and behaviourism by encouraging self-assessment, social construction of effective practice, and collaboration.

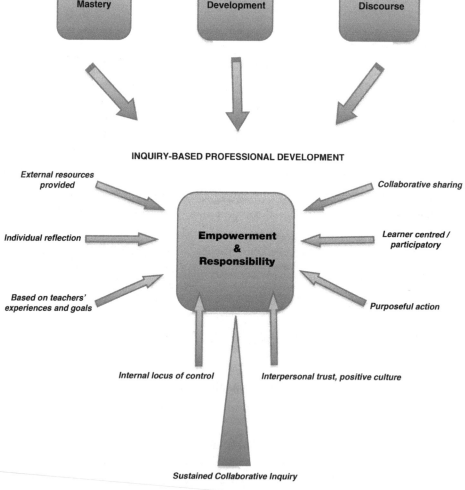

Figure 5.2: Constituent Parts of Inquiry-Based Professional Learning

Educators who we have observed demonstrating some of the most impressive gains in overall growth of practice have used inquiry-based growth plans, such as *The Guide for Teacher Professional Learning*, *The Guide for School Leader Professional Learning* (Adams, 2012), or *The Guide for Superintendent Professional Learning*, depending on their primary role. These documents require teachers, school, and district leaders to begin with a self-assessment of their levels of confidence in meeting the standards of practice based on a four-point scale of efficacy. Figure 5.3 illustrates one possible template that might guide how system leaders reflect on their levels of efficacy and effectiveness.

After reflection, educators synthesize their thinking into two or three key areas to guide their planning for professional learning for the coming year. The next step broadens their reflection to include school goals and school initiatives, and how these external considerations align with their own self-identified areas of growth. Two possible templates that might foster this next step are illustrated in figures 5.4 and 5.5.

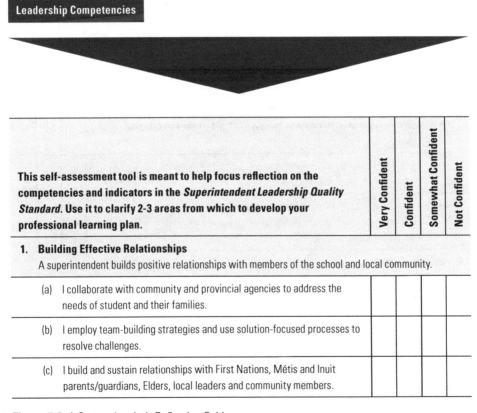

Leadership Competencies				
This self-assessment tool is meant to help focus reflection on the competencies and indicators in the *Superintendent Leadership Quality Standard*. Use it to clarify 2-3 areas from which to develop your professional learning plan.	Very Confident	Confident	Somewhat Confident	Not Confident
1. Building Effective Relationships A superintendent builds positive relationships with members of the school and local community.				
(a) I collaborate with community and provincial agencies to address the needs of student and their families.				
(b) I employ team-building strategies and use solution-focused processes to resolve challenges.				
(c) I build and sustain relationships with First Nations, Métis and Inuit parents/guardians, Elders, local leaders and community members.				

Figure 5.3: A System Leader's Reflection Guide

continued

This self-assessment tool is meant to help focus reflection on the competencies and indicators in the *Superintendent Leadership Quality Standard*. Use it to clarify 2-3 areas from which to develop your professional learning plan.	Very Confident	Confident	Somewhat Confident	Not Confident
2. Modeling Commitment to Professional Learning A superintendent engages in professional learning and critical reflection.				
(a) I communicate a research-informed, student-centred philosophy of education.				
(b) I collaborate with teachers, principals, jurisdiction leaders and other superintendents to build expertise.				
(c) I actively seek feedback to enhance my leadership practice.				
(d) I apply educational research to inform my practice.				
(e) I provide leadership to support school authority research initiatives.				
(f) I engage school and local community members in building shared understandings and priorities.				
3. Embodying Visionary Leadership A superintendent engages the school community to implement a vision for student success.				
(a) I ensure our vision is informed by research on effective learning, teaching and leadership.				
(b) I promote innovation, continuous improvement and support professional collaboration.				
(c) I promote a common understanding of and support for our goals, priorities, and strategic initiatives.				
(d) I ensure our vision is responsive to the ongoing review of our achievements, meets provincial legislation requirements, while incorporating school perspectives.				
4. Leading Learning A superintendent establishes and sustains a culture of learning.				
(a) I foster equality and respect.				
(b) I provide learning opportunities to support the capacity building of all members of the school community.				
(c) I ensure all instruction addresses learning outcomes in programs of study.				
(d) I promote collegial relations, collaboration, critical thinking and innovation.				

This self-assessment tool is meant to help focus reflection on the competencies and indicators in the *Superintendent Leadership Quality Standard*. Use it to clarify 2-3 areas from which to develop your professional learning plan.	Very Confident	Confident	Somewhat Confident	Not Confident
(e) I ensure resources are available for staff to meet the learning needs of all students.				
(f) I build principal and school jurisdiction leader capacity and provide instructional leadership through effective support, supervision and evaluation practices.				
(g) I ensure student assessment practices are evidence-informed and enhance learning, teaching and leadership.				
5. Supporting the Application of Foundational Knowledge about First Nations, Métis and Inuit A superintendent establishes structures and provides resources to support the acquisition and application of foundational First Nations, Métis and Inuit knowledge for the benefit of all students.				
(a) I support staff in acquiring professional learning to meet the learning needs of First Nations, Métis and Inuit and all other students.				
(b) I engage and collaborate with First Nations, Métis and Inuit leaders and organizations to optimize learning success for all students.				
(c) I have foundational knowledge of treaties, agreements and residential school legacies.				
(d) I align resources and build organizational capacity to support First Nations, Métis and Inuit student achievement.				
(e) I facilitate the goals and practices of reconciliation.				
6. Managing School Operations and Resources A superintendent directs operations and manages school authority operations and resources.				
(a) I provide direction in accordance with statutory, regulatory and authority requirements.				
(b) I ensure human resources align with our education plan.				
(c) I delegate responsibility to staff to enhance efficiency and effectiveness.				
(d) I provide for the support, ongoing supervision and evaluation of all staff.				
(e) I establish data-informed planning and decision-making processes.				
(f) I respect cultural diversity and appreciate differing perspectives.				
(g) I recognize student and staff accomplishments.				
(h) I implement mentorship, capacity-building and succession planning programs.				

continued

This self-assessment tool is meant to help focus reflection on the competencies and indicators in the *Superintendent Leadership Quality Standard*. Use it to clarify 2-3 areas from which to develop your professional learning plan.	Very Confident	Confident	Somewhat Confident	Not Confident
7. Supporting Effective Governance A superintendent provides information and support to the board and reports to the Minister of Education.				
(a) I sustain a productive working relationship with the board.				
(b) I ensure a caring, respectful and safe learning environment for all students and staff.				
(c) I ensure all students have the opportunity to meet the standards of education.				
(d) I ensure the board's plans, resource allocations and procedures align with system goals and priorities.				
(e) I ensure the board's fiscal resource management is in accordance with statutory, regulatory and board requirements.				
(f) I support the board in fulfilling its governance function.				
(g) I implement board policies and support regular review of their impact.				
(h) I ensure the support, supervision and evaluation of all staff.				
(i) I facilitate collaboration among the board, staff, and First Nations, Métis and Inuit community members to establish policy directions focused on student achievement.				
(j) I build the capacity of the board and staff to respond to emergent circumstances.				
(k) I support the board as it engages with the school community to develop a vision for student success.				
(l) I facilitate public communication of the board's operations, achievement of goals and priorities.				
(m) I promote constructive relations between the board and all education stakeholders.				

Guide for Teacher Professional Learning

Assessing Professional Needs

Using the self-assessment tool, I recognize the following areas that could guide my planning for professional learning this year:

-
-
-

Planning for Growth

Relevant School Goals:

-
-

Other School Initiatives:

-
-
-
-
-

Planning for Learning

GOAL 1:

Goal:

Related KSA	Strategies	Resource/Support Required	Evidence of Success	Timeline

Inquiry Question:

GOAL 2:

Goal:

Related KSA	Strategies	Resource/Support Required	Evidence of Success	Timeline

Inquiry Question:

Teaching Quality Standard:

Competencies and Indicators to guide professional learning

TEACHERS FOSTER EFFECTIVE RELATIONSHIPS
Teachers build productive relationships with students, parents/guardians, peers 'and others in the school and local community to support student learning.

TEACHERS ENGAGE IN CAREER-LONG LEARNING
Teachers engage in career-long professional learning and ongoing critical 'reflection to improve teaching and learning.

TEACHERS DEMONSTRATE A PROFESSIONAL BODY OF KNOWLEDGE
Teachers apply a current and comprehensive repertoire of effective planning, instruction, and assessment practices to meet the learning needs of every student.

TEACHERS ESTABLISH INCLUSIVE LEARNING ENVIRONMENTS
Teachers establish, promote and sustain inclusive learning environments where diversity is embraced and every student is welcomed, cared for, respected and safe.

TEACHERS APPLY FOUNDATIONAL KNOWLEDGE ABOUT FIRST NATIONS, METIS AND INUIT
Teachers develop and apply foundational knowledge about First Nations, Métis and Inuit for the benefit of all students.

TEACHERS ADHERE TO LEGAL FRAMEWORKS AND POLICIES
Teachers demonstrate an understanding of and adherence to the legal frameworks and policies that provide the foundations for the Alberta education system.

Teachers plan for professional learning ...

- to improve instructional practice and optimize the learning of all students,
- thoughtfully, over time, and in a sustained manner,
- appreciating school and jurisdictional priorities,
- independently and collaboratively within their learning communities,
- by recognizing professional strengths and successful attributes which support the development of enhanced practice.

Effective Teachers...

Quality teaching occurs when the teacher's ongoing analysis of the context, and the teacher's decisions about which pedagogical knowledge and abilities to apply, result in optimum learning for all students.

Teaching Quality Standard (2018)

Figure 5.4: A Teacher's Template for Creating a Professional Learning Action Plan

Planning for Professional Learning as an Educational Leader

Assessing Professional Needs

Using the self-assessment tool, I recognize the following areas that could guide my planning for professional learning this year:

-
-

Connecting My Professional Learning to:

Relevant School Goals:

-
-

Other School Initiatives:

-
-
-
-
-

Learning Goal #1:

Leadership Quality Standard Competency:

Inquiry Question:

Possible Resources:

Strategy	Timeline	Indicators of Success

Formative Reflection:

Summative Reflection:

Learning Goal #2:

Leadership Quality Standard Competency:

Inquiry Question:

Possible Resources:

Strategy	Timeline	Indicators of Success

Formative Reflection:

Summative Reflection:

The purpose of educational leadership is to ensure quality learning experiences: every student, every day, no exceptions.
College of Alberta School Superintendents. *Alberta Leadership Framework*

Figure 5.5: A Leader's Template for Creating a Professional Learning Action Plan

With an understanding of student need and a reflection on their practice, teachers and school leaders enter into what we refer to as "inquiry guided research into their own practice." Similar to models employed by a number of disciplines such as law, medicine, architecture, and accounting (Cacari-Stone, Wallerstein, Garcia, & Minkler, 2014; Decker-Lange, 2018), this is a process in which educators commit to posing and answering essential questions about their professional practice over a sustained period of time. One compelling result of their participation in this process is the praxis generated through iterative cycles of **deconstructing knowledge** and reconstructing professional understanding and instructional leadership practices (DeLuca, Bolden, & Chan, 2017; Emihovich & Battaglia, 2000). That is, inquiry-based goal setting can encourage school leaders to think about and, more often, dialogue about the contentions made by leadership theories, the realities of schools and districts, the gap between the two, and the next-day strategies they might implement within an area of nexus that may include creative action.

Such actions—with their potential to make educators more vulnerable—require an environment of trust in which system leaders must play a vital role. Research shows educators are more motivated to collaborate, invite, and demonstrate a commitment to learning in a collaborative climate of trust (Campbell, Zeichner, Lieberman, & Osmond-Johnson, 2017; DuFour & Marzano, 2011; Leithwood, Harris, & Hopkins, 2008).

In many ways, it is this step that differentiates so much of what we do with teachers and school leaders from what is typically found in schools. The questioning mindset lies at the heart of getting teachers and school leaders to enter into a realm of research. Inquiry leads them to look for evidence of growth in their own practice and, in turn, more effective ways of optimizing learning for all students. In essence, inquiry causes teachers and school leaders to examine their practice by asking and answering a research question; essentially, this looks like a form of rudimentary action research. This practice requires that they gather evidence of meeting their goals, answer their own research question, share the answer, and reflect on the process.

Professional growth plans become living, working documents that take on an importance and life of their own. Traditionally, teachers would provide principals a copy of their growth plans in September and then, at the end of the school year, provide a short and often hastily assembled write-up about what they achieved (Fenwick, 2004). Alternately, learning and practising in an inquiry-based model involves sharing work on a monthly or quarterly basis with a school leader; school leaders share their work on a monthly basis with a school district leader; and, ideally, system leaders share their work with cohorts of colleagues or external trusted advisors. With professional growth plans written (usually in pencil on a large multifold planning document and with many revisions, reflections, and additions), teachers, school leaders, and school district leaders enter into an ongoing and comprehensive process of enacting their inquiry. To enhance reflection using the generative dialogue, generative leaders meet with teachers and colleagues on a frequent (monthly) basis to explore their progress toward answering their differentiated inquiry question by asking four questions:

- What have you done since we last met specific to your professional inquiry question?
- What did you learn as a result of those activities?
- What evidence of your learning would you like to share?
- What will you do in the next 30 days to help yourself answer your guiding question?

INDIVIDUAL AND COLLABORATIVE INQUIRY

Our methodology of choice is collaborative inquiry. Under its authority, we work with schools and districts to answer essential research questions. All participants in our projects—and that has often included all educators in a school, or all those who hold a job in a district—come to participation with a growth plan, some goals identified, and some ideas about strategies they would like to try. Most of them, individually or in a team, quickly come up with a guiding question, the answer to which will provide them with evidence of the extent to which they have been able to achieve their goal or goals.

While not officially credited with authoring the terms *action research* or *collaborative inquiry*, John Dewey (1910) proposed a concise five-step model of inquiry that guides contemporary professional learning, including: (1) identifying curiosities, (2) intellectualizing the context, (3) hypothesizing strategies, (4) reasoning through possible explanations, and (5) testing through action. This recursive process of scientific investigation is essential to most collaborative inquiry processes.

Collaborative inquiry begins when a group of educators commits to asking, exploring, and answering a compelling question about their practice. Common threads such as the value of experience, the importance of relationships and respect, and pragmatic sustainability are woven into collaborative inquiry. All forms of knowledge are valued; all professional experiences are integral to learning. We have participated in collaborative inquiry with many group compositions: parents, students, academics, leaders, and corporate managers. In all cases, we have measured increased levels of confidence and efficacy, empowerment, identity, belonging, and shared responsibility.

The Question Matters

Crafting an inquiry question that is succinct yet inclusive, exploratory yet practical, relevant yet challenging is an important part of collaborative inquiry that requires persistence and patience. The process involves lengthy conversations, often mediated by a skilled facilitator of generative dialogue who asks clarifying questions that may touch on values, beliefs, philosophies, and world views. These discussions are made all the more complex by the history and existing culture of each school or group. Norms and mores of acceptable levels of professional commitment, the understanding of professional learning, the value placed on collegiality versus collaboration, and the position of student learning can also come to bear in these conversations. Furthermore, an expectation that the inquiry question should contribute to or align with school or system goals is omnipresent, and often limits authentic reflection. And yet, a well-articulated inquiry question can capture the heart of the organization's work and can motivate and focus the efforts of learning teams for extended periods of time.

The Anatomy of a Question

While we believe that the inquiry question crafted by individuals and teams must be authentic and unique to their interests, wonderings, and curiosities, we have also facilitated the construction of thousands of questions and contend that there is a general formula for effective questions that can guide reflection and action.

The Opening of the Question

The opening phrase of an effective professional learning question signals information about the type of data that will be gathered to answer the question. We suggest that the prefix "To what extent" is appropriate if evidence will be gathered that is quantitative in nature. For example, if a leader were to seek Likert-scale descriptive statistics of the extent to which students felt the school climate was safe; if a vice-principal hoped to gather data about changes in increased amounts of collaboration time; if a teacher were curious about the impact of new formative assessment instruments on standardized achievement results; if an associate superintendent wondered about the effect of increased levels of literacy professional development for teachers. These might all be instances where quantitative measures might be sought and where an inquiry question might use the "To what extent" prefix. Examples include the following:

- To what extent can differentiated reading instruction …
- To what extent can increased collaborative learning time …
- To what extent can rote drill in math …
- To what extent can the use of video in physical education …

Alternately, "In what ways" is more often used as a prefix to signal that qualitative data will be gathered to answer the inquiry question:

- In what ways can increased feedback in language learning …
- In what ways can journal writing …
- In what ways can reciprocal classroom observations …
- In what ways can increased parent involvement …

Of course, many educators who are adept at creating inquiry-based learning questions seek to gather both quantitative and qualitative data to inform their professional action. They begin their questions with both prefixes:

- In what ways and to what extent might student leadership opportunities ...
- In what ways and to what extent might the use of action research ...
- In what ways and to what extent might various structures of distributed leadership ...

The Interior of the Question: The Who, Why, and How

We construct the interior of the inquiry-based question around three guiding parameters. First, we insist that the pronouns *I* or *my* be an integral part of the question to ensure a higher level of individual professional responsibility for the inquiry. In the case of team inquiries, *we* or *our* must be included in the interior of the question. Second, we ensure that specific strategies are removed from the question; rather, we focus on pedagogies, goals, and themes. We also remove authors or other resources from the question in order to elevate reflection about the larger topic under examination. Third, we promote correlational thinking by linking an action (the verb) with an audience (the noun). By applying these three guidelines, the examples provided previously can be extended.

- In what ways will my differentiated use of literacy resources with second language learners ...
- To what extent will my increased use of professional collaborative time during staff meetings ...
- In what ways can I increase use of reflective journals with high school drama students to ...
- In what ways and to what extent can we increase opportunities for student leadership in middle school ...

The Conclusion of the Question: How Will You Know?

It is at this point that the question loops back and links the goal with measures or evidence. For example, if increased levels of literacy in grade two students will be determined by Fountas and Pinnell measures, this will constitute the suffix of the question. If increased levels of staff collaboration will be determined by numbers of peer classroom observations, these variables will form the conclusion of the question. Perhaps indicators of parent engagement will be determined by attendance at advisory council meetings; if so, this will be reflected in the last part of the question.

An Extended Example

We have found that many teachers and principals are curious about the impact of engagement on student learning. Teachers will often include a student engagement goal in their growth plan, while school leaders will include some type of whole-school initiative connected to engagement in school improvement plans. A teacher goal may very well look like one of the following:

> When we first approach the generative dialogue to craft an inquiry question, we have the following anatomy in mind: In what ways and to what extent can I enhance … in … to … as determined by …?

- My focus for the year is on building engaging activities for my students.
- I intend to increase the levels of student engagement in my class this year.
- Student engagement is a passion of mine and I want to see if I can increase student participation in their own learning.

Unfortunately, when teachers craft these statements, they often get too busy with the act of teaching to go back and see if any of their changes are actually making an impact on student learning. Let us turn these goal statements into collaborative inquiry questions. The questions are predicated on teachers having come together to examine the needs of the students, having done a review of the standards to which they are accountable, and having entered into conversation about committing to a project that they can work on together and in turn answer a question that they now pose.

- In what ways will my implementation of three of Marzano's high-yield instructional strategies impact student engagement with my at-risk students?
- To what extent will my use of mini whiteboards impact class participation in the formative assessment aspect of mathematics learning?
- In what ways and to what extent will my use of structured journal writing impact student reflection on their own learning of science concepts?

Answering the question then becomes the focus when teachers get together. Whether they meet with a school leader or on their own, they will explore their current state of practice. To do so, they will develop tools and instruments, put a process into place, and eventually come to an answer.

In one school that we worked with, a group of grade six teachers gathered to answer this question: In what ways and to what extent will our introduction of high-yield instructional strategies impact student achievement on standardized tests in reading, writing, math, science, and social studies? This group (six teachers and the vice-principal) met every week for 60 minutes. They planned the use of high-yield instructional strategies in their classes on an individual basis and then watched each other put them into practice when they brought all 150 of the grade six students together. When the group came together, one teacher led the learning while the other teachers watched and addressed individual student needs. By the end of the year, the group was able to answer their own question. By the end of three years with the same question, the school had moved from the very bottom of the city rankings to the very top, based on test results: same type of student enrolment, same teachers, very different results.

HELPFUL RESPONSES TO UNHELPFUL ASSUMPTIONS: LEADING REFLECTION

We have encountered educators of all stripes and positions who are skeptical of our efforts to engage them in reflection: the tough 38-year veteran teacher who shed tears when, through our repeated efforts to have him reflect on his long practice, finally confessed, "Why has no one ever asked me these questions before? I would have told them what I *really* wanted to be doing in my professional practice. Now it is probably too late!"; the highly respected and influential educational assistant who commented, after three years of being patiently invited to become involved in the teachers' professional reflection activities, that "I know I told my fellow EAs that these reflective things weren't part of our contract. But now that we do them with the entire staff, they make me feel as though I am included and valued, like I'm part of the professional team rather than just a worker bee dealing with the bad kids"; the principal in our graduate class whose cellphone conveniently rang about 30 seconds into each lesson's free-form write and who approached us at the end of the course to ask "Could you come to my school and to do this 'reflection stuff' with my staff?"; or the deputy superintendent who assured us during central office leadership team meetings that "she had done all of this reflection in her previous positions in a different province, that it had worked great," but that "in this more demanding position that I have now, it is just not as necessary to reflect. I have a pretty clear idea of what needs to be done."

The most frequently heard resistance is, of course, expressed in the guise of "I don't have time for reflection. Let me tell you what my day looks like!" We thought perhaps this *curse of busy* was limited to one group or the other; however, we have observed educators who are, paradoxically, in positions that have mandated responsibility in their role to lead reflection who inform us they are too busy to reflect. Conversely, we have also met superintendents of large systems who could easily claim that their job is "24/7" but who find time to model reflective practice to various groups of employees.

We see the *busy* concern as both a challenge and an invitation. How can we find time within existing structures to enter into reflection with educators and, particularly, leaders? When are conversations being held about growth plans, and are they of the type that can foster reflection? Do educators meet regularly to discuss their responsibilities and achievements with colleagues? Has anyone asked them about their careers, the things that keep them awake at night, what got them into education in the first place? How and when are the people in the highest positions in the organization modelling reflection?

One successful superintendent recently told us that she has had surprising success with seemingly recalcitrant educators in her district by being "extra curious" about the reasons they feel or act the way they do. She spends a great deal of time outside her office visiting them at the school, engaging them in non-judgmental conversations, and building solid, trusting relationships with them. We know that this is not easy for her in any given day but we have observed how well it works.

Some educators who oppose our work with schools that are trying to improve student achievement also resist our efforts to model and engage them in written or verbal reflection. Our research has consistently noted the sense of success that teachers and leaders feel when they work together; the variety of strategies that they use to reflect on and influence student learning; the **differentiation** of learning and growth opportunities that reflection affords students and educators; and the attention that many educators pay to measures of success that go beyond numerical results to include student attitudes, parent satisfaction, staff morale, and wellness. In effect, through disciplined reflection, the impact of educators' efforts can be validated.

KEY CONSIDERATIONS FOR LEADING REFLECTIVE PRACTICE

- Model it
- Model it publicly
- Model it publicly and be prepared to share it frequently
- Model it, share it, and learn from it
- Model it, share it, learn from it, and act on it
- Model it, share it, learn from it, act on it, and talk about it

JOURNAL REFLECTIONS AND WRITING PROVOCATIONS AS YOU REFLECT ON REFLECTION

The writing provocations in this chapter are designed to slowly ease reluctant reflectors into the process of introspection, insight, and problem solving. We have found that a hesitance to engage in deep reflective practice can often be attributed to the following:

- Distrust in the process or in the facilitator. Am I going to be judged if I reveal too much? Too little? Something that is not as "deep" as (read "as good as") others' ideas?
- Lack of awareness of the purpose or results of reflection. Isn't this just like keeping a diary? What if I can't think of anything to write about? Where am I supposed to be going with this?

- Fear of responsibility. Shouldn't someone else really be thinking about these problems? Why am I the only one doing this? How will my reflection matter if "the boss" won't do anything about it?
- Impatience and pessimism. How is this going to immediately help with the problems of practice that I have? Isn't this reflective writing just another fad in education? Couldn't I be doing something more practical with my time?

And yet we have observed the most resistant reflectors engage in free-form writing if, over time, they observe an environment of vulnerability demonstrated by leaders, a suspension of judgment and evaluation by colleagues, and a sense of collaboration and camaraderie in which norms of curiosity are nurtured.

Remember, free-form writing requires leaders to make only two commitments to thinking about their leadership experiences: don't stop writing until an agreed-upon time limit is reached, and don't correct, censor, judge, or otherwise evaluate the thoughts that are being written. If you have been experimenting with the free-form writing we have outlined in the previous chapters, you are probably quite comfortable with extending the time period in which you are reflecting. Are you up to 20 minutes by now?

We have used the following provocation stems to encourage reflection around the concept of reflection:

- I don't usually reflect on my practice because …
- When I think of reflection, it conjures up images of …
- If necessary, I would prefer to reflect …
- Reflecting on my practice is like …

CONCLUSION

We end with the question that we presented as the title of this chapter: "Why do we have to reflect so much?" At the level of philosophy, Plato reminds us of the value of reflection as an epistemological exercise highlighting the power of "possibility" in his metaphor of the cave; Socrates insists that an unexamined life is not worth living; and, at the level of human development, Margaret Wheatley (1992) claimed that without reflection, educators may stumble on their way, creating more unintended consequences and failing to achieve very much.

At the level of practice, we have found that regular dialogue about educators' planned growth is sometimes enough to help them commit to desired change and, over time, become increasingly skillful in identifying and owning evidence, derived through reflection, of their purposeful efforts. For others, the dialogical process is not sufficient. So, since the mid-1980s, we have experimented with the use of video to help educators observe, reflect on, and refine their practice. Still, many remain unconvinced of the potential of video. For us, the *successful* use of video remains an area that deserves a great deal more exploration in fostering reflective practice.

Sometime prior to 1796, Robbie Burns authored his famous quote "O wad some Power the giftie gie us to see ourselves as others see us." Could that gift possibly be the process of reflection?

SUGGESTED READINGS FOR LEADING REFLECTION

Campbell, C., Osmond-Johnson, P., Faubert, B., Zeichner, K., Hobbs-Johnson, A., Brown, S., …
Steffensen, K. (2016). *The state of educators' professional learning in Canada.* Oxford, OH: Learning Forward.

This study is aimed at understanding what educational policies and practices contribute to success and specifically ask "What is the current state of educators' professional learning in Canada?" While Canada has been recognized in international assessments, benchmarks, and research, there is limited pan-Canadian research or data, due to the school education system being the responsibility of ten provinces and three territories. The study's main finding is that there is a mosaic of professional learning experiences, opportunities, promising practices, and challenges within and across Canada. This mosaic speaks to the conclusion drawn by the research that there is no one-size-fits-all approach to professional learning. Commonalities were found across Canada that include the importance of combining evidence, inquiry, and professional judgment to inform professional learning and the need for relevant, practical, and collaborative learning experiences within and beyond school walls. Commonalities also included problems such as finding time for professional learning embedded in the school day, inequities in access to or funding of professional learning, and contentions between system-directed and/or self-selected professional learning.

Dana, N., & Yendol-Hoppey, D. (2014). *The reflective educator's guide to classroom research.* Thousand Oaks, CA: Corwin.

Although this text was written as a guide for teachers and their inquiry into practice, it describes aspects of the reflective process that are also applicable to leaders. Notably, Dana and Yendol-Hoppey explain the importance of "finding a wondering" as a starting point for undertaking authentic professional inquiry. The book's contents are presented in the steps typically found in collaborative action research: developing a plan, considering ethics, analyzing findings, drawing conclusions, and sharing results. Chapter 8, in particular, offers helpful questions to reflect upon and to use to ascertain the extent to which an inquiry-based professional learning cycle has been effective. Such questions include, "Did I connect my wonderings with existing knowledge about this topic related to a literature base?" "Did my inquiry result in action or changes to my practice?" "Do I have a further plan for assessing, reflecting upon, and studying my changes in practice?"

Groen, J., & Kawalilak, C. (2016). *Pathways of adult learning.* Toronto, ON: Canadian Scholars Press.

The authors are two University of Calgary professors whose interest and research in the role of reflection in adult learning goes back over a decade. Although the book has a strong academic foundation, it is also filled with case studies and anecdotes that give voice to those who are and who teach adult learners. In this sense, the book lends an important narrative to the process of adults' reflection; the authors write about "pondering" and "learning from our lives" (p. 5) by asking the question "Out of my entire educational life history, what would I select as important to my learning process? What stories do I tell?" For those leaders who are serious about how their staff members and colleagues come to—and then engage in—learning, this is an important addition to the bookshelf of resources.

Schön, D. (1983). *The reflective practitioner: How professionals think in action.* New York, NY: Basic. In this often-cited and seminal book, Schön uses the profession of architecture to exemplify his contentions about how to bridge the practical craft knowledge required in other professions with the necessary foundational academic knowledge that underlies theoretical aspects of the profession. His invitation in the preface is particularly enticing: "The contributions I have found most helpful ... are those people for whom research functions not as a distraction from practice but as a development of it." Schön's expansive historical exploration of the nature of technical versus professional knowledge leads to his notion of tacit knowledge, an intuitive understanding of skills-during-practice, which he refers to as reflection-in-practice. It is this process, Schön explains, that characterizes "the professions." He presents an interesting conundrum about the influences exerted upon educators by bureaucratic structures. "What happens in an educational bureaucracy when a teacher begins to think and act not as a technical expert but as a reflective practitioner? Her reflection-in-action poses a potential threat to the dynamically conservative system in which she lives" (p. 332). In the end, he submits that reflection is a political—sometimes activist—process that has inherent implications for the role of the professions in a contemporary, consumer-minded society.

York-Barr, J., Sommers, W., Ghere, G., & Montie, J. (2006). *Reflective practice to improve schools.* Thousand Oaks, CA: Corwin.
These authors begin their discussion of reflection with the question "Is reflection new, or even New Age?" Their historical précis include authors such as Buddha, Socrates, Dewey, van Manen, Zeichner, and Schön. Collaborative inquiry, while not explicitly referenced, is a through-line in the book, and in particular in their chapter entitled "Reflective Practice with Partners." In it, they outline structures for reflection such as cognitive coaching, journaling, dyads, and action research.

NOTES

1. As of writing, the 2018 results had not yet been publicized.
2. The Leaders of Learning Network is a small informal group created by one of the authors. It is composed of principals and vice-principals that meet quarterly to discuss and practise the use of generative dialogue and generative leadership skills.

REFERENCES

Adams, P. (2012). *Framework for professional learning: Implementing a collaborative inquiry model to personalize professional learning for educators.* Edmonton, AB: Alberta Education Workforce Planning Branch.

Barth, R. S. (2001). *Learning by heart.* San Francisco, CA: Jossey-Bass.

Brandon, J., Friesen, S., Koh, K., Parsons, D., Adams, P., Mombourquette, C., & Hunter, D. (2018). *Building, supporting, and assuring quality professional practice: A research study of teacher growth, supervision, and evaluation in Alberta.* Edmonton, AB: Alberta Education.

Brookfield, S. (1984). *Adult learners, adult education, and the community.* New York, NY: Teachers College, Columbia University.

Brookfield, S. (1995). *Becoming a critically reflective teacher.* San Francisco, CA: Jossey-Bass.

Brookfield, S. (2009). The concept of critical reflection: Promises and contradictions. *European Journal of Social Work, 12*(3), 293–304. doi:10.1080/13691450902945215

Brookfield, S. (2017). *Becoming a critically reflective teacher* (2nd ed.). San Francisco, CA: Jossey-Bass.

Cacari-Stone, L., Wallerstein, N., Garcia, A. P., & Minkler, M. (2014). The promise of community-based participatory research for health equity: A conceptual model for bridging evidence with policy. *American Journal of Public Health, 104*(9), 1615–1623.

Campbell, C., Zeichner, K. M., Lieberman, A., & Osmond-Johnson, P. (2017). *Empowered educators in Canada: How high-performing systems shape teaching quality.* San Francisco, CA: Jossey-Bass.

Decker-Lange, C. (2018). Problem- and inquiry-based learning in alternative contexts: Using museums in management education. *The International Journal of Management Education, 16,* 446–459. doi:10.1016/j.ijme.2018.08.002

DeLuca, C., Bolden, B., & Chan, J. (2017). Systemic professional learning through collaborative inquiry: Examining teachers' perspectves. *Teaching and Teacher Education, 67,* 67–78. doi:10.1016/j.tate.2017.05.014

Dewey, J. (1910). *How we think.* Boston, MA: DC Heath.

DuFour, R., & Marzano, R. (2011). *Leaders of learning: How district, school, and classroom leaders improve student achievement.* Bloomington, IN: Solution Tree Press.

Emihovich, C., & Battaglia, C. (2000). Creating cultures for collaborative inquiry: New challenges for school leaders. *International Journal of Leadership in Education, 3*(3), 225–238. doi:10.1080/13603120050083918

Fenwick, T. (2004). Teacher learning and professional growth plans: Implementation of a provincial policy. *Journal of Curriculum and Supervision, 19*(3), 259–282.

Jones, C. M., & Thessin, R. A. (2015). A review of the literature related to the change process schools undergo to sustain PLCs. *Planning & Changing, 46*(1/2), 193–211.

Leithwood, K., Harris, A., & Hopkins, D. (2008). Seven strong claims about successful school leadership. *School Leadership and Management, 28*(1), 27–42. doi:10.1080/13632430701800060

Mezirow, J. (1991). *Transformative dimensions of adult learning.* San Francisco, CA: Jossey-Bass.

Organisation for Economic Co-operation and Development. (2014). *TALIS 2013 results: An international perspective on teaching and learning.* Paris, France: OECD.

Schön, D. (1983). *The reflective practitioner.* New York, NY: Basic Books.

Sullivan, B., Glenn, M., Roche, M., & McDonagh, C. (2016). *Introduction to critical reflection and action for teacher researchers.* New York, NY: Routledge.

Townsend, D., & Adams, P. (2009). *The essential equation: A handbook for school improvement.* Calgary, AB: Detselig.

Vygotsky, L. (1978). *Mind in society: The development of higher psychological processes.* Cambridge, MA: Harvard University Press.

Wheatley, M. (1992). *Leadership and the new science.* Oakland, CA: Berrett-Koehler.

CHAPTER SIX

Collaboration and Leadership

How Can Leadership Create Synergy?

Alone, we can do so little; together, we can do so much.
  —*Helen Keller*

"I wonder what Piglet is doing," thought Pooh. "I wish I were there to be doing it, too."
  —*A. A. Milne*

THE POWER OF COLLABORATION

Several years ago, we were presenting findings from a study we had conducted that sought educators' perceptions of the most important conditions for leaders to nurture when initiating and sustaining school improvement projects. One finding was that teachers were firm in their view that opportunities to collaborate were high on their list of priorities. At that time, we recommended several possible ways of reorganizing school and system processes and structures to better accommodate this view. During question period of the presentation, an academic from another university gave us a real grilling on this particular recommendation, suggesting that we were simply championing a neo-socialist ontology that risked causing "groupthink," that "limited creativity," that supported "union mentality," and that disempowered autonomous professional thinking. We couldn't help agreeing with the reasoning of some of his arguments, and we have spent years since then trying to find a balance between the tenets of individualism and communalism as they pertain to education.

Despite what our academic colleague had to say, studies continue to point to the value of collaboration. Recently, Brandon et al. (2018) confirmed that teachers appreciated and wanted more opportunities to engage in collaborative discussions with school leaders and colleagues about professional growth and, more broadly, about aspects of school operations as they might pertain to student learning. Conversations that facilitated reflection on practice were viewed as an integral part of professional learning. However, we acknowledge that individuality exists, even as we continue to observe over and over the necessary condition of human interdependence. Human beings are not born alone, do not nourish and educate themselves, and we can find myriad examples that point to the greatest achievements of humankind being generated through collaborative social action.

Prolific author Peter Senge identified four additional pillars necessary to create learning organizations (Senge, 2006). In the book *The Fifth Discipline: The Art and Practice of the Learning Organization*, Senge presents *shared vision* as a collective driver of effort; he recognizes that reactionary moves in any direction sacrifices the strength that arises from individuality and creative thought. His second pillar recognizes individuality by celebrating the uniqueness of *mental models*. The third pillar involves ongoing learning and development as a lifetime goal. In identifying *personal mastery*, Senge adds that growth, honing skills, and enhancing capacity are important for all individuals in a learning organization. Yet he pairs each of these with his fourth pillar: *team learning*. New discoveries, he contends, are only beneficial to the extent that they are shared and beneficial to the group; he promotes sharing the concept so that new insight and collective capacity are enhanced. While his work was initially developed as a view of organizational life across a wide variety of workplaces, he later collaborated with a team to focus on education systems alone (Senge, Cambron-McCabe, Lucas, Smith, & Dutton, 2012).

Once again, we refer to recent TALIS (OECD, 2014) results to begin our examination of the power of collaboration and its enormous potential to be used by leaders to achieve numerous results in improved culture and climate, professional learning, building community and trust, and accommodating diverse perspectives of purpose and direction. The 2014 results confirm the importance of collaboration and note that teacher collaboration is more common in schools with strong instructional leadership. However, one in three principals does not encourage collaboration among the teaching staff. There is room for improvement, and both policy and practice can help achieve it.

In this chapter we present the case of Pariter Middle School and invite you to think about the ways that a leader may invite, participate in, and cause a school to benefit from collaborative structures and processes. We then offer the thoughts of myriad authors who began exploring the phenomenon of collaboration in education as early as the 1950s. Following a review of the societal trajectories of individualism and collectivism, we discuss what we believe to be some of the essential components of collaboration in schools leading to an understanding of the important conditions for leaders to nurture if they aim to initiate and sustain school improvement. Of course, all theories have their limitations, and we present several of these for your critical consideration. And, as in past chapters, we provide you with some writing provocations that might cause you to explore your assumptions and actions as you lead collaboration.

Pariter Middle School presents an interesting case of collaboration: teacher with teacher, school leaders with teacher, and university professors with teachers and school leaders. The case also highlights the role of individuals placing great value on their own contributions to the group cause, this being increased student learning. However, this case of Pariter is just that, one case. Successful, yes, but not something whole-school reorganization should be predicated on.

Case Study: Better Together at Pariter Middle School

Since the 1980s, all students in grade six at Pariter Middle School have been required to write standardized tests in language arts, math, science, and social studies. The exams are developed and updated annually by the government, then administered near the end of each school year. Results are reported in considerable detail on the ministry website. As well, every district and each school receives an annual copy of results showing, among other information, individual student results, class-by-class results, school and district averages compared to overall provincial averages, participation rates, and five-year trends.

> As we begin the story of Pariter Middle School, think about your own perceptions of the role of standardized examinations of student learning. Are they of hindrance or help in the promotion of student achievement? How about your school community: What would members think?

The value of this testing regimen has been debated constantly, and, at times, heatedly, over the last 35 years but, with few changes, the annual external exams have endured. However, in many schools, animosity toward external testing and, more particularly, frustration at the way results are used to compare schools and districts, remains close to the surface. Pariter Middle School was no exception.

It was a Tuesday morning in September, the day after the standardized test results had been released to the public. Middle school principal Rodney Black put in a call to an old friend at the city's university, a professor in the Faculty of Education. "Have you seen our test results?" he asked with a mixture of dismay and anger. Of course his colleague had seen them. They were headlined on page two of the morning paper, highlighting a comparison between the results of private school students and those of public school students.

"We bombed again," moaned Rodney. "I've just had my annual visit from the superintendent telling me, for the fourth year in a row, that our school's results are not good enough. He says I have to come up with a plan to fix the situation." Rodney's situation evoked empathy. His school was crowded. Designed for 650 students, it was currently serving nearly 750. For years, this area of the city had seen a steady increase in lower socioeconomic demographics and migrant families. In addition, a provincial report had just concluded that this area of the province was experiencing an exceptionally high rate of childhood poverty. In a 10-year span, the school had gone from being a desired destination for teachers to one that many teachers preferred to avoid. Rodney got right to the point: Would any university professors be willing to work with members of Rodney's staff to see if they could come up with an improvement plan?

Two professors agreed to meet with Rodney the next morning to explore possibilities with him and his vice-principal, Sharon. They brainstormed ideas for an

continued

hour (with only a bit of time for lamentation), planning a meeting to be held two weeks hence that would include the seven staff members responsible for teaching all subjects to a pilot group of 150 grade six students. When the appointed day arrived, the meeting with these staff members proved difficult. Several resented giving up any after-school time for such a purpose. Most of them were openly angry that they were being blamed, once again, for results that were clearly beyond their control. In addition, four of the teachers had been students of one or both of the university professors. They were not happy having their old professors telling them, still, how they could teach better.

The teachers needed to vent. They wanted everyone to know just how many of their students required individual education plans, how many could not read, and how many came to school hungry every day. An experienced teacher who had been on this staff for 14 years declared, "These kids can't even read the directions on the exam. Some of them are reading at a grade two level. I'll guarantee more than 40 percent of them will fail the grade six language arts exam next June!" Another teacher chimed in, "Have you seen our student population? More than 30 percent from single-parent families, and so many children from other countries. With no extra resources, how can we be expected to improve student achievement?"

It was obvious that no big agreements were going to come from this first meeting. Even though Rodney was quite specific about additional support they could access, the teachers were reluctant to make any commitments. Sharon then asked if she could summarize some of the outcomes of the meeting. She noted all the concerns that teachers had raised and highlighted two positive points. First, most of the teachers said they wanted to work more closely together and, second, most were willing to talk about teaching strategies they might be able to use to help students do better.

One of the professors put forward the following question: "For five years, you've been identified as the lowest-achieving middle school in the city. You say it hurts. Are you prepared to try something a bit different? If we all work together, I'm sure we can turn these results around."

As the meeting was ending, the principal asked if everyone would be willing to meet again the following Wednesday, from 2:00 to 3:00 p.m. He would arrange coverage of teachers' classes so everyone could attend. The purpose of the next meeting would be to make a binding decision about ways to proceed. Some teachers were more willing than others. Yet, as soon as the next meeting began, it was apparent that the teachers had decided to adopt a more positive approach to this opportunity. Sharon had worked with staff members to produce a simple agenda, and that document guided the conversation. Knowing they would be receiving support from a provincial Department of Education grant, the teachers spent a lot of time trying to figure out how they could create blocks of time during the school week when they could work together without interruption. Guided by their school leadership team and a commitment that the university professors would meet with staff teams every Wednesday morning, the teachers negotiated 75 minutes of collaborative planning time every Thursday afternoon. They then decided to use the first planning session to study the data generated by five years of test results in their school.

As university people do, the two professors encouraged the teachers to think about their work as a form of collaborative inquiry, but it would be many months before any of the teachers showed much interest in the research side of this initiative. They did use their Wednesday meetings with professors to talk about their team goals and the teaching strategies they were using to help students improve. Initially, they were much more likely to give themselves lists of tasks to complete than to identify evidence that their purposeful efforts were having any impact on student learning. Nevertheless, everyone persevered.

The team planning sessions produced one particular strategy that gave teachers greater confidence that they were being appropriately strategic in addressing the learning gaps revealed through their analysis of the achievement exam results data. As a group, the teachers decided to use the last two hours every Friday to team-teach sets of carefully planned lessons. As one teacher confessed, "We may as well use Friday afternoons. Most of us just show videos then." Teachers and education assistants would collaborate to design one math/science lesson and one humanities lesson. On Friday afternoon, students would be divided into two groups of 75. For the first 50 minutes of the afternoon, the teams of five staff members would present their lessons to each group. Then, the groups would switch, and the team would teach the same lesson to the second group of students.

This strategy was successful beyond the expectations of even the most hopeful teachers. The lessons included time for direct teaching, time for students to work in pairs, time for working in groups of four, and time for games. Week after week, staff members reported that there were no instances of student misbehaviour when the large-group team-teaching was happening. One teacher told of students asking constantly about the Friday sessions, and expressing disappointment on those few occasions when the lessons could not be presented.

The teacher team soon came to realize they had found some efficient ways to narrow learning gaps by using innovative high-yield teaching methods. Through collaboration, they were able to prepare and present excellent lessons that promoted student engagement and enjoyment. Each teacher in the team was also aware of their individual responsibility to ensure that the lessons were well planned and delivered. Teachers took increasing responsibility for the work they committed

continued

to doing in the days leading up to team meetings and the Friday afternoon team-teaching sessions. They were more conscious of meeting the needs of all learners, more adventurous in differentiating their practice, and more purposeful in using a variety of teaching and assessment strategies to solidify learning gains.

In March, these teachers were sure enough about their accomplishments that they offered a presentation of their work to approximately 40 other teachers at a district professional learning day. Unfortunately, it did not go well. Even though most of those in attendance showed interest and were respectful, a few participants offered derogatory comments: "This is just teaching to the test." "I think you're working outside the collective agreement." Spirits were dampened for a while. But not for long. The teacher teams studied videos of their teaching. They spent more time in each other's classrooms. They reached out to known experts within their school district and invited them to come and help them grow. They had momentum, and they would not be held back. As one teacher explained, "With team-teaching, I love teaching certain parts of the math curriculum more than others. I can concentrate on my areas of specialization. Other teachers can do the same thing in their subjects. We share the load. We're not all trying to teach everything, so every lesson gets our best shot."

> Why do teachers sometimes make comments that hold each other back? Have you experienced this in your career? If so, what have you internalized as a result of the comments made? If not, what have you done in your career to avoid the situation?

By April, the teacher teams had begun talking openly about their work as a form of collaborative inquiry. As their confidence grew and the impact of their teaching became more obvious, they adopted much more reflective time. Each team had experimented with a guiding question, the answers to which would show how far they had come in achieving their goals. As an example, the math/science team's question became "How has our attention to differentiation through team-teaching impacted grade six student achievement in mathematics?"

> Take time to reflect on the information presented in past chapters. Why did it take the teachers at Pariter until April to really focus on their guiding collaborative inquiry questions? How might the results of this case have changed if teachers had worked from simple goal statements, rather than working through a process of inquiry?

In the weeks leading up to June's standardized tests, these teachers maintained their focus on the needs of every child, and on helping each other. They had formed strong professional partnerships through this initiative and they were certain that student results would improve. Teachers were also taking individual responsibility for student learning by making sure they took care of all items to which they had committed. Of course, it is unwise to compare results only from one year to the next, and many other factors must be considered when educators seek to show reasons for achievement gains but, in this case, it would have been a shocking disappointment for these teachers if student results had not improved.

Improve they did. In mathematics, there was a 9.6 percent increase in the number of students achieving the acceptable standard; in language arts, a 7.2 percent increase; in science, a 6.3 percent increase; and in social studies, a 3.3 percent increase. Also, in social studies, there was an 8.1 percent increase in the number of students achieving the Standard of Excellence. According to the principal, "These results represent five-year highs!"

In summing up her experiences with this initiative, one of the humanities teachers offered the following comment:

> When we started out, I thought we were just trying to teach to the test. As I became more involved in this work, I realized it's hardly about the tests at all. It's really about finding ways to reach every student in collaboration with my colleagues.

Case Study Reflections: Leading, Collaborating, and Leading Collaboration

- What activities or structures do you encourage as a leader to ensure that all teachers have a deep understanding of exemplary teaching? In what ways does collaboration figure into these activities?
- What structures and involvement will you promote as a school leader that will foster collaboration around the analysis of student learning data?
- How will you ensure that the teachers in your school or system are engaged in multiple sustained conversations with their colleagues about their instructional practices?
- As a leader, what impact do you hope to have on student learning? What evidence of practice will you gather to demonstrate this impact? How does collaboration fit into these decisions?

SITUATING COLLABORATION IN LEADERSHIP

Since the turn of the new millennium, the term *collaboration* seems to have achieved the status of master discourse in many segments of social life, including education. Based on its use as a strategy to impact student achievement via pedagogical change, collaboration is widely recognized as a de facto standard for leading schools. Yet, despite its current ubiquitous nature in our collective narrative, the notion of collaboration has not always been associated with daily embedded practices. During the first half of the 20th century, curriculum was heavily influenced by the conservatively framed social

efficiency ideals of American curriculum theorists such
as John Franklin Bobbitt, Ross Finny, Ralph Tyler,
James Popham (Au, 2011; Franklin, 1982), and David
Snedden (Labaree, 2011). At the same time, conceptualizations of school leadership were being increasingly
influenced by Ellwood P. Cubberley's endorsement of
Frederic Winslow Taylor's principles of scientific management (Au, 2011; English, 2006; Shepard, 2000),
Max Weber's characteristics of the ideal bureaucracy,
and Henri Fayol's general principles of management
(Leonard & Leonard, 2001).

> Think back to your days in
> graduate school. Review
> the principles of scientific
> management. Where do you see
> the overlaps between Taylorism
> and the school you went to work
> in every day? What lingering
> effects do we still see in the
> schools of today in the general
> principle of management?

The combination of these and other sociopolitical influences contributed to the professionalization of education, categorization of subject material into courses and modules
(Franklin, 1982), and subsequent formalization of role distinctions between teachers
and principals (Au, 2011). According to Stoller (2015), the ostensible scientific evidence
associated with time and motion studies, standardization, and detailed schemes for organizational planning and control appealed to the technocratic sensibilities of society at
that time. From the turn of the 20th century, educational leadership developed a system
of hierarchical, one-way command structures that exercised top-down decision making
(Leonard & Leonard, 2001). By 1915, administrators throughout several Western countries were adopting the principles of scientific management in an effort to reshape their
schools (Callahan, 1962) and the potential of collaboration was limited to a networking
strategy, rather than a tool to impact teaching and learning.

From these roots, schools became emblematic of knowledge-producing factories
designed to perpetuate a culture of individualism and isolation (Leonard & Leonard,
2001). Lortie (1975) pointed out that social efficiency tenets in schools reinforced an "egg
carton" architecture with a cellular organizational structure that reinforced divisions
between teachers, isolating them within the confines of their classrooms. As another
example, Sarason, Levine, Goldenberg, Cherlin, and Bennett (1966) described teaching
as a lonely profession and drew attention to the scarcity of opportunities for teachers to
discuss their work with colleagues. As yet another example, Goodlad (1984) studied
teacher isolation from a psychological perspective, noting that isolation had become an
infused norm that permeated the physical and social environments of schools. Following that theme, Flinders (1988) posited that teacher isolation could be understood as an
adaptation to characteristics of the school environment that could be observed "by the
manner in which teachers assess instructional priorities and establish day-to-day work
routines" (p. 26). Accordingly, the term *collaboration* became synonymous with *teacher*
collaboration (Goddard, Goddard, & Tschannen-Moran, 2007; Leonard & Leonard,
2001; Vangrieken, Dochy, Raes, & Kyndt, 2015).

Social reform movements during the 1970s and 1980s increased expectations
for educators to close the achievement gap amongst an increasingly diverse student

population in order to promote academic success for all students (Hallinger & Wang, 2015). Reform efforts, such as the effective schools movement and the school improvement movement, sought to identify features, processes, and conditions of those sites that were achieving better than expected levels of performance (Purkey & Smith, 1983). Increased critique of organizational and leadership practices gave impetus to research that focused away from organizational behaviour and toward participative decision making (Follet, 1996).

Uncoupling Leadership from the Leader

A prominent theme in the discourse of school leadership affirms that the performance of schools on any number of metrics is largely dependent on the quality of leadership (Fullan, 2001; Goldring, Huff, Spillane, & Barnes, 2009; Lai, 2015; Leithwood & Azah, 2016; Leithwood, Seashore Louis, Anderson, & Wahlstrom, 2004; Marzano, Waters, & McNulty, 2005; J. Robinson, Sinclair, Tobias, & Choi, 2017; Seashore Louis, Leithwood, Wahlstrom, & Anderson, 2010; Southworth, 2005; Spillane & Seashore Louis, 2002; Thompson, 2017). Evidence suggests that school principals can and do exert significant influence on student achievement (Leithwood, Patten, & Jantzi, 2010). In the pursuit of linkages between leadership and student learning, educational leadership research efforts have pursued various facets of the principalship, including the personality traits of principals (Goldring, Huff, May, & Camburn, 2008; Hallinger, 2011; Leithwood, Harris, & Hopkins, 2008) and the actions and behaviours of principals (Bossert, Dwyer, Rowan, & Lee, 1982; Hallinger & Murphy, 1985; Hallinger, Murphy, Well, Mesa, & Mitman, 1983; J. Robinson, Lloyd, & Rowe, 2008). This concerted focus on the principal-as-individual effectively reinforced romantic notions of the solitary heroic leader capable of saving a failing school (Elmore, 2000; Hallinger, 2005).

During the 1980s and 1990s, a burgeoning volume of literature acknowledged a principal's indirect influence on student achievement, signalling the development of mediated-effects models of school leadership (Blase & Blase, 2000; Hallinger, Bickman, & Davis, 1996; Heck, 1993; Leithwood, 1994; Leithwood, Begley, & Bradley Cousins, 1994). These types of leadership models hypothesized that the principal's leadership is a central determining factor in the instructional organization and culture of the school; thus, they posit that principals affect student achievement through their influence on other people, more so than through honorific power (Hallinger & Wang, 2015; Marks & Printy, 2003). Blase and Blase (2000) recognized indirect leadership as a function of principal behaviours such as making suggestions, providing feedback to teachers, modelling effective instruction, soliciting opinions, supporting collaboration, providing professional development opportunities, and giving praise for effective teaching.

In the latter days of the 20th century, terms such as *distributed leadership* (Gronn, 2000; Harris, 2005; Spillane, 2005), *shared leadership* (Lambert, 2002; Marks & Printy, 2003), and *collaborative leadership* (Hallinger & Heck, 2010) reflected a shift in the ways that leadership influence was described. Each represented a conceptual uncoupling of leadership from positional authority (Bush, 2013), and leadership is now seen to be more of a collective social process, manifested through the interactions of principals and other members of the school community (Bolden, 2011; Lambert, 2002; Spillane, 2005).

Meanwhile, the early 21st century educational landscape has become characterized by trends such as the decentralization of schools, professionalization of education, and development of community-oriented school contexts (Slater, 2004). With these directions, the notion of collaboration has evolved into a common parlance of contemporary schools (Friend & Cook, 2000; Jordan, 1999; Slater, 2004). Decades ago, Schrage (1995) defined collaboration as "the process of shared creation: two or more individuals with complementary skills interacting to create a shared understanding that none had previously possessed or could have come to on their own" (p. 3). Pugach and Johnson (1995) recognized collaboration "when all members of a school's staff are working together and supporting each other to provide the highest quality of curriculum and instruction for the diverse students they serve" (p. 29). In their meta-analysis of literature pertaining to teacher collaboration, Vangrieken et al. (2015) described collaboration as "joint interaction in the group in all activities that are needed to perform a shared task" (p. 23). All three definitions beg the question "What does leading learning through collaboration look like?"

Characteristics of Collaboration

In addition to being voluntary (Leonard & Leonard, 2001), effective collaboration is typically associated with and characterized by mutual/common goals and parity or equality of opportunity to participate/contribute (Cook & Friend, 1991; Welch & Sheridan, 1995); working and reflecting together toward a related focus (Little, 1990; Welch & Sheridan, 1995); and shared responsibility/accountability for outcomes (Friend & Cook, 2000; Tiegerman-Farber & Radziewicz, 1998). However, as we pointed out in chapter 2, one of the most embraced metaphors of collaboration came about with the emergence of the learning community.

Achinstein (2002) described a **professional community** as "a group of people across a school who are engaged in common work; share to a certain degree a set of values, norms, and orientations towards teaching, students, and schooling; and operate collaboratively with structures that foster interdependence" (p. 422). Other authors use terms such as *ongoing, reflective, collaborative, inclusive, learning-oriented, growth-promoting* (Stoll, Bolam, McMahon, Wallace, & Thomas, 2006) and *collective* (King & Newmann, 2001) to outline characteristics of learning communities.

The promotion of these learning communities is based on the assertion that peer conversation and interaction are important in constructing meaning, developing curriculum, and enacting pedagogical reform (Glazier, Boyd, Bell Hughes, Able, & Mallous, 2017; Little, 1990). Sergiovanni (1996) defined these communities as a "collection of individuals who are bonded together by natural will and who are together bound to a set of shared ideas and ideals" (p. 48). Later, Wenger, McDermott, and

Snyder (2002) coined the phrase *communities of practice* as "groups of people who share a concern, a set of problems, or passion about a topic, and who deepen their knowledge and expertise in this area by interacting on an ongoing basis" (p. 4). According to Glazier et al. (2017), this systemic shift from individualism to collectivism is grounded in the assumption that "peer conversation and interaction is important in constructing meaning, developing curriculum, and enacting pedagogical reform" (pp. 4–5), and is thought to promote school cultures in which staff are morally bound to collective goals and ideals. In this way, the concept of teacher collaboration has become widely recognized as a defining quality of schools as morally driven learning communities (Vangrieken et al., 2015).

While this notion of community emphasizes mutually supportive relationships, shared norms and values, and a focus on collective well-being, there remains an undercurrent that values the professional autonomy of teachers (Stoll et al., 2006). Yet healthy autonomy relies on a strong foundation of professional trust.

Trust and Autonomy

According to Tschannen-Moran (2004), trust assumes that teachers and principals will act with the best interests of students. Of the three types of trust conceptualized by Bryk and Schneider (2002), *relational trust* is anchored in the social exchanges associated with key role relationships in schools. Relational trust describes the extent to which there is consonance of expectations and priorities, and the authors identify relational trust as an important organizational characteristic of schools because its "constitutive elements are socially defined in the reciprocal exchanges among participants in a school community, and its presence (or absence) has important consequences for the functioning of a school" (p. 22). According to Kochanek (2005), relational trust is vital in schools because educators need to be able to assume that their colleagues are working to serve the best interests of students behind classroom doors. Further, robust social relationships between and amongst teachers and principals are recognized as critical preconditions for the establishment and maintenance of effective collaboration (Barth, 2006; Bryk & Schneider, 2002; Toole & Louis, 2002).

A study by Havnes (2009) resulted in a hierarchy of levels of educator collaboration: the *preservation of individualism* (focusing on individual teachers' responsibilities and autonomy); *coordination* (coordinating those teacher tasks and responsibilities other than teaching itself); *cooperation* (determining a common ground for collective work by focusing on the substance and process of classroom activities); and *sharing* (mutual sharing and clarification of pedagogical actions and considerations that influence the classroom-based practices of teachers). Different levels of collaboration occurring amongst groups of teachers have also been conceptualized as the evolution from assembled teacher teams to work communities, characterized by deepening levels of reciprocal connectedness, expanding repertoires of interaction, and increasingly shared enterprise (Brouwer, Brekelmans, Nieuwenhuis, & Simons, 2011, 2012).

In some of the most effectively led schools we have witnessed, this balance between the role of the individual and that of the group is struck by addressing issues of norming in which the following questions are discussed:

- Is there a compelling reason for this team's existence? Does the team need a name? Does the team have a clear purpose or clear goals? Does the team need a charter or a covenant?
- Does the team need specific terms of reference?
- Does the team need to meet regularly? How does the meeting agenda get established?
- Who runs each meeting? Does the team have a formal meeting model?
- What are team expectations for starting and finishing meetings on time? Attendance?
- Does the team maintain a record of its meetings? How?
- How does the team ensure that all members' opinions are heard?
- Alternately, how does the team ensure that all members contribute to team decisions?
- How does the team ensure that all members show respect for one another?
- How does the team ensure that all members listen when others are speaking?
- How does the team make decisions? For example, is a consensus model used? If so, what happens in the event of a deadlock?
- If the team arrives at a consensus, how does it deal with any members who may still feel marginalized?
- Similarly, once the team has made a decision that requires action, how does the team ensure that all members do what they have agreed to do?
- How does the team deal with conflict over opinions or values?
- How does the team deal with a chronically disruptive member?
- If the need arises to change one of the team norms, how does that happen?
- How does the team ensure that individual and team successes are celebrated appropriately?

Critique of Collaboration

As mentioned in the case study at the start of this chapter, the notion of collaboration (in process, structure, or both) is not without its critics. The body of literature supporting collaboration is also replete with contrary images of resistance, political infighting, deficient social skills, and over-dependence on formal leaders. Correlating collaboration to improved teaching is tenuous, at best (Havnes, 2009). In addition, scaffolding collaboration with teachers' learning is difficult (Schoenfeld, 2004) while collaborative communities more often focus on practical affairs. These critiques seem to cluster into three larger categories: groupthink, contrived collegiality, and pseudocommunity.

Groupthink

In his book *Victims of Groupthink: A Psychological Study of Foreign Policy Decisions and Fiascos* (1972), author and social psychologist Irving L. Janis offered a compelling critique of socially situated learning as one response to the earlier theory of Lev Vygotsky about social constructivism. Drawing upon Orwell's *1984* use of the expression *doublethink*, Janis authored the term *groupthink* to explain detrimental phenomena occurring within groups. Janis observed group members coming to prioritize their participation in the group above all else, to value the group above anything else, resulting in decision making based on least resistance, simplistic unanimity, false consensus, suppression of personal perspectives, and silencing of dissenting strategies in order to promote the group itself as the ultimate unit of membership. Janis warned that the results of groupthink could be devastating: distorted views of reality, excessive and unwavering optimism, and the neglect of ethical considerations.

Contrived Collegiality

While a collaborative culture may originate from perceptions that professional interactions can be valuable, productive, and pleasant, regulating collaboration can result in artificial or superficial collegiality (Vangrieken et al., 2015). Hargreaves and Dawe (1990) described contrived collegiality as "little more than a quick, slick administrative surrogate for more genuinely collaborative teacher cultures, cultures which take much more time, care, and sensitivity to build than do speedily implemented changes of an administratively superficial nature" (p. 148). Hargreaves (1994) argued that contrived collegiality serves as an insufficient substitute for more spontaneous forms of collaboration and interaction between teachers. Those instances where participation in collaborative opportunities are mandated, prescribed, or otherwise imposed by those other than teachers themselves have also been referred to dismissively as *clobberation* (Slater, 2004).

Pseudocommunity

Grossman, Wineburg, and Woolworth (2001) applied the term *pseudocommunity* to describe situations in which individuals pretend they are already in a community that shares values and common beliefs: the imperative of the pseudocommunity is to "behave as if we all agree" (p. 955). Pseudocommunity refers to those face-to-face relations that appear congenial, mainly because the expression of conflict and dissent has been unresolved. Pseudocommunities distinguish between hidden and revealed, or, using the dramaturgical language of Erving Goffman (1959), a distinction between back stage and front stage. As noted by Grossman et al. (2001), the "key to maintaining a surface esprit de corps is the curtain separating front from back stage and the fact that only some group members are allowed behind it" (p. 956). They contend that the predominant mode of interaction within a pseudocommunity is that of *impression management*, through which individuals adopt roles that often reflect positively on them. Thus, roles within a pseudocommunity are executed smoothly, just as long as everyone gets to play their preferred role without being challenged.

According to Grossman et al. (2001), the most pervasive threat to any pseudocommunity is lingering tension and authenticity. It is of note that educational literature espousing the virtues of relationships, trust, and collegiality seem to be relatively quiet in investigating issues of micro-politics, competition, power imbalance, tension, conflict, and reification of normative ideals associated with the status quo. When it comes to addressing issues and improving student achievement, prevailing wisdom seems to be to put teachers together in a room, close the door, and hope for the best.

The question remains "What can leaders do to avoid groupthink, contrived collegiality, and pseudocommunity?" How can they promote collaboration that leaves room for individual as well as group responsibility for student learning?

Leadership for Collaboration

Our work with schools clearly indicates that a principal who supports collaboration "encourages and nurtures empowerment, risk-taking, and the capacity of other individuals in the school" (Slater, 2004, p. 326). Supportive principal behaviours include *modelling* (setting the tone); *communication skills* (listening and openness in relationships); *valuing people* (applying the input of others to solve problems and make decisions); and *advocacy* (conveying the ongoing visible endorsement of and participation in collaborative activities). These principals display healthy emotional competencies associated with leading a collaborative community: understanding others, self-awareness, and managing emotions and relationships. Principals who lead through solid and supportive collaborative structures have a knowledge base and a set of skills that include highly effective communication, emotional competencies, decision-making and problem-solving skills, conflict management, and team-building. Collaborative principals build capacity in others to assume leadership roles by letting go of their power and control and by calling upon and accessing the expertise of others required for school improvement (Slater, 2004).

We have come to realize that principals need to understand that supportive conditions alone, such as time and spaces to meet, do not ensure the changes required in teachers' collective practices for schools to become professional learning communities. Principals' professional knowledge, expertise, and determination to nurture their teaching staffs as professional learning communities will fall flat if relational trust among the faculty is absent. Importantly, in this sense, trust requires increased focus on and visibility of the adult social relationships in schools. Relational trust has to be built and sustained, and it has to be active. Principals need to work continually in the social network of the school to nurture trust, and this takes time, commitment, and effective communication.

According to Glazier et al. (2017), "Simply putting teachers together will not necessarily lead to positive change. However, that is a critical beginning step" (p. 5). Through mutual engagement, joint enterprise, and shared repertoire, participants in a community of practice can experience meaning and transformative learning. The development of a community of practice often requires substantial nurturing to enable productive collaboration.

CONSIDERATIONS FOR LEADERSHIP

The following key elements characterize leaders who lead learning through collaboration (Bryk and Schneider, 2002; Cranston, 2011):

- Vision and direction for participants to know where the initiative is headed
- Design and structure for the process to get underway
- Flexibility and creativity to encourage ongoing adjustments that further support implementation
- Support and encouragement for all participants to promote a sense of safety and belonging
- Care of self and others
- Acknowledgement of uncertainty, ambiguity, and value of diverse perspectives
- Focus on individual learning and growth needs, as well as attention to the learning and growth needs of the organization
- Trust and communication

As you write the following provocations, think about these key elements and note the ways they weave in and through your leadership and your collaboration with teachers. Reflect upon the Pariter Middle School experience and assess the ways and the degree to which each element was present (or not) in what Rodney and Sharon undertook to lead learning.

JOURNAL REFLECTIONS AND WRITING PROVOCATIONS FOR LEADING COLLABORATION

The writing provocations in this chapter are meant to have you think critically about collaboration, not as a panacea, but as one of many important strategies to support efforts that will positively impact student learning.

- I consider the biggest barriers to collaboration in schools to be …
- One of the most successful collaborative efforts I have been included in has been …
- When I imagine myself working elbow-to-elbow with colleagues or teachers, I …
- The cultural foundations necessary for successful collaboration seem …
- When I think about leading collaborative efforts, I feel that …

CONCLUSION

The literature of collaboration in the leadership of schools is fraught with tension, conflict, and contradiction. Modern conceptualizations of collaboration in the leadership of schools embed assumptions associated with more democratized schools, the empowerment of the marginalized, and the promotion of positive and supportive relationships throughout the extended school community, all while asserting lifelong commitments to the goals of the organization and the promotion of academic success for all students.

SUGGESTED READINGS FOR LEADING COLLABORATION

Brookfield, S., & Preskill, S. (2016). *The discussion book*. San Francisco, CA: Jossey-Bass.

In a departure from his previous works, Brookfield collaborates with Stephen Preskill to offer a manual of strategies for how leaders and teachers of adults can enhance collaborative learning. The book offers 50 such strategies under categories such as promoting good questioning, democratizing participation, getting discussions going, getting learners out of their comfort zones, and building cohesion. Each of the 50 chapters offers the strategy's purpose, how it works, when it works, and what to watch for. Brookfield and Preskill end many of the 50 chapters with questions that provoke use of the strategy and that can be asked of learners to prompt critical reflection.

Glaude, C. (2005). *Protocols for professional learning conversations*. Courtenay, BC: connect2learning.

Glaude offers this handbook to propose a series of guiding structures to promote greater effectiveness of collaborative learning. These ideas originated in her work with teachers who were involved with sharing artifacts of student work to norm assessment standards. She defines *learning conversations* as structured, ongoing dialogues between professionals for the purpose of sharing expertise. Glaude uses the term *provocative question* as one type of protocol to engage teams in conversations about research. Her practical text offers templates and case studies to help educators embark upon professional collaboration by considering some of the preliminary processes necessary for effective decision making in groups.

Isaac, W. (2014). *Dialogue: The art of thinking together*. New York, NY: Double Day. (Original work published 1999)

William Isaac examined organizational challenges in companies such as Shell, Motorola, and Hewlett Packard to conclude that one of the primary contributors to organizational dis-ease is the inability to communicate and, more specifically, to engage in successful dialogue. He defines *dialogue* as "a living experience of inquiry within and between people" and contends that the skills of effective dialogue exist untapped or undeveloped in most leaders, as evidenced by a developmental history of oral communication. He suggests that one important skill in effective dialogue is the ability to overcome internal assumptions about thinking together that have resulted in stagnation and inaction.

Young, S. (2007). *Micromessaging*. New York, NY: McGraw-Hill.

Healthy relationships and solid communication are of utmost importance when people work and learn together and, importantly, when leaders participate in or promote the process of learning. Young contends that doing so is highly dependent upon non-verbal messaging that leaders consciously or unconsciously use as part of effective communication; he refers to this aspect of communication as *micromessaging*. He suggests that this message must be applied in a differentiated and personalized way with each interaction in balance with an approach of equity. Although an expert in corporate contexts, Young attempts to extend the skills of micromessaging to educational leaders and states that "how well educators micromessage shapes how students open up to learning, their accomplishments and self-esteem, and directions of careers" (p. 179).

REFERENCES

Achinstein, B. (2002). Conflict amid community: The micropolitics of teacher collaboration. *Teachers College Record, 104*(3), 421–455.

Au, W. (2011). Teaching under the new Taylorism: High-stakes testing and the standardization of the 21st century curriculum. *Journal of Curriculum Studies, 43*(1), 25–45. doi:https://doi.org/10.1080/00220272.2010.521261

Barth, R. S. (2006). Relationships within the schoolhouse. *Educational Leadership, 63*(6), 9–13.

Blase, J., & Blase, J. (2000). Effective instructional leadership: Teachers' perspectives on how principals promote teaching and learning in schools. *Journal of Educational Administration, 38*(2), 130–141.

Bolden, R. (2011). Distributed leadership in organizations: A review of theory and research. *International Journal of Management Review, 13*, 251–269.

Bossert, S., Dwyer, D., Rowan, B., & Lee, G. (1982). The instructional management role of the principal. *Educational Administration Quarterly, 18*(3), 34–64. doi:10.1177/0013161X82018003004

Brandon, J., Friesen, S., Koh, K., Parsons, D., Adams, P., Mombourquette, C., … Hunter, D. (2018). *Building, supporting, and assuring quality professional practice: A research study of teacher growth, supervision, and evaluation in Alberta*. Edmonton, AB: Alberta Education.

Brouwer, P., Brekelmans, M., Nieuwenhuis, L., & Simons, R. J. (2011). Community development in the school workplace. *International Journal of Educational Management, 26*(4), 403–418. doi:http://dx.doi.org/10.1108/09513541211227809

Brouwer, P., Brekelmans, M., Nieuwenhuis, L., & Simons, R. J. (2012). Fostering teacher community development: A review of design principles and a case study of an innovative disciplinary team. *Learning Environments Research, 15*, 319–344. doi:https://doi.org/10.1007/s10984-012-9119-1

Bryk, A. S., & Schneider, B. (2002). *Trust in schools: A core resource for improvement*. New York, NY: Russell Sage Foundation.

Bush, T. (2013). Distributed leadership: The model of choice in the 21st century. *Educational Management Administration & Leadership, 41*(5), 543–544. doi:https://doi.org/10.1177/1741143213489497

Callahan, R. E. (1962). *Education and the cult of efficiency*. Chicago, IL: University of Chicago Press.

Cook, L., & Friend, M. (1991). Principles for the practice of collaboration in schools. *Preventing school failure: Alternative education for children and youth, 35*(4), 6–9. doi:https://doi.org/10.1080/1045988X.1991.9944251

Cranston, J. (2011). Relational trust: The glue that binds a professional learning community. *Alberta Journal of Educational Research, 57*(1), 59–72.

Elmore, R. (2000). *Building a new structure for school leadership*. Washington, DC: Albert Shanker Institute.

English, F. W. (2006). *Encyclopedia of educational leadership and administration* (Vol. 1). Thousand Oaks, CA: Sage.

Flinders, D. J. (1988). Teacher isolation and the new reform. *Journal of Curriculum and Supervision, 4*, 17–29.

Follet, M. P. (1996). The giving of orders. In J. M. Shafritz & J. S. Ott (Eds.), *Classics of organization theory* (4th ed., pp. 156–162). Albany, NY: Wadsworth.

Franklin, B. M. (1982). The social efficiency movement reconsidered: Curriculum change in Minneapolis, 1917–1950. *Curiculum Inquiry, 12*, 9–33.

Friend, M., & Cook, L. (2000). *Interactions: Collaboration skills for school professionals* (3rd ed.). New York: NY: Longman.

Fullan, M. (2001). *Leading in a culture of change*. San Francisco, CA: Jossey-Bass.

Glazier, J. A., Boyd, A., Bell Hughes, K., Able, H., & Mallous, R. (2017). The elusive search for teacher collaboration. *The New Educator, 13*(3), 3–21. doi:http://dx.doi.org/10.1080/1547688X.2016.1144841

Goddard, Y. L., Goddard, R. D., & Tschannen-Moran, M. (2007). A theoretical and empirical investigation of teacher collaboration for school improvement and student achievement in public elementary schools. *Teachers College Record, 109*(4), 877–896.

Goffman, E. (1959). *The presentation of self in everyday life*. Garden City, NY: Doubleday.

Goldring, E., Huff, J., May, H., & Camburn, E. (2008). School context and individual characteristics: What influences principal practice? *Journal of Educational Administration, 46*(3), 332–352. doi:https://doi.org/10.1108/09578230810869275

Goldring, E., Huff, J., Spillane, J. P., & Barnes, C. (2009). Measuring the learning-centered leadership expertise of school principals. *Leadership and Policy in Schools, 8*(2), 197–228. doi:https://doi.org/10.1080/15700760902737170

Goodlad, J. I. (1984). *A place called school: Prospects for the future*. New York, NY: McGraw-Hill.

Gronn, P. (2000). Distributed Properties: A new architecture for leadership. *Educational Management & Administration, 28*(3), 317–338. doi:https://doi.org/10.1177/0263211X000283006

Grossman, P., Wineburg, S., & Woolworth, S. (2001). Toward a theory of teacher community. *Teachers College Record, 103*(6), 942–1012.

Hallinger, P. (2005). Instructional leadership and the school principal: A passing fancy that refuses to fade away. *Leadership and Policy in Schools, 4*(3), 221–239. doi:10.1080/15700760500244793

Hallinger, P. (2011). A review of three decades of doctoral studies using the Principal Instructional Management Rating Scale: A lens of methodological progress in educational leadership. *Educational Administration Quarterly, 47*(2), 271–306. doi:https://doi.org/10.1177/0013161X10383412

Hallinger, P., Bickman, L., & Davis, K. (1996). School context, principal leadership and student achievement. *Elementary School Journal, 96*(5), 498–518.

Hallinger, P., & Heck, R. H. (2010). Leadership for learning: Does collaborative leadership make a difference in school improvement? *Educational Management Administration & Leadership, 38*(6), 654–678. doi:https://doi.org/10.1177/1741143210379060

Hallinger, P., & Murphy, J. (1985). Assessing the instructional management behavior of principals. *The Elementary School Journal, 86*(2), 217–247.

Hallinger, P., Murphy, J., Well, M., Mesa, R. P., & Mitman, A. (1983). School effectiveness: Identifying the specific practices, behaviors of the principal. *NASSP Bulletin, 67*(463), 83–91. doi:https://doi.org/10.1177/019263658306746314

Hallinger, P., & Wang, W. C. (2015). *Assessing instructional leadership with the Principal Instructional Management Rating Scale.* Switzerland: Springer.

Hargreaves, A. (1994). *Changing teachers, changing times: Teachers' work and culture in the postmodern age.* New York, NY: Teachers' College Press.

Hargreaves, A., & Dawe, R. (1990). Paths of professional development: Contrived collegiality, collaborative culture, and the case of peer coaching. *Teaching & Teacher Education, 6*, 227–241. doi:https://doi.org/10.1016/0742-051X(90)90015-W

Harris, A. (2005). Distributed leadership. In B. Davies (Ed.), *The essentials of school leadership* (pp. 160–172). Thousand Oaks, CA: Sage.

Havnes, A. (2009). Talk, planning and decision-making in interdisciplinary teacher teams: A case study. *Teachers and Teaching: Theory and Practice, 15*, 155–176. doi:https://doi.org/10.1080/13540600802661360

Heck, R. (1993). School context, principal leadership, and achievement: The case of secondary schools in Singapore. *The Urban Review, 25*(3), 151–166.

Janis, I. L. (1972). *Victims of groupthink: A psychological study of foreign-policy decisions and fiascoes.* Boston, MA: Houghton Mifflin.

Jordan, C. F. (1999). Using collaborative action teams to create community schools. *National Association of Secondary School Principals Bulletin* (December), 48–56.

King, M. B., & Newmann, F. M. (2001). Building school capacity through professional development: Conceptual and emperical considerations. *International Journal of Educational Management, 15*(2), 86–93.

Kochanek, J. R. (2005). *Building trust for better schools: Research-based practices.* Thousand Oaks, CA: Corwin Press.

Labaree, D. F. (2011). How Dewey lost: The victory of David Snedden and social efficiency in the reform of American education. In D. Tröhler, T. Schlag, & F. Ostervalder (Eds.), *Pragmatism and modernities.* Rotterdam, Netherlands: Sense.

Lai, E. (2015). Enacting principal leadership: Exploiting situated possibilities to build school capacity for change. *Research Papers in Education, 30,* 70–94. doi:https://doi.org/10.1080/0 2671522.2014.880939

Lambert, L. (2002). A framework for shared leadership. *Educational Leadership, 59*(8), 37–40.

Leithwood, K. (1994). Leadership for school restructuring. *Educational Administration Quarterly, 30*(4), 498–518. doi:10.1177/0013161x94030004006

Leithwood, K., & Azah, V. N. (2016). Characteristics of effective leadership networks. *Journal of Educational Administration, 54*(4), 409–433.

Leithwood, K., Begley, P. T., & Bradley Cousins, J. (1994). *Developing expert leadership for future schools.* Bristol, PA: Falmer Press.

Leithwood, K., Harris, A., & Hopkins, D. (2008). Seven strong claims about successful school leadership. *School Leadership & Management, 28*(1), 27–42. doi:https://doi. org/10.1080/13632430701800060

Leithwood, K., Patten, S., & Jantzi, D. (2010). Testing a conception of how school leadership influences student learning. *Education Administration Quarterly, 46*(5), 671–706. doi:https://doi.org/10.1177/0013161X10377347

Leithwood, K., Seashore Louis, K., Anderson, S., & Wahlstrom, K. (2004). How leadership influences student learning. *Learning from Leadership Project.* Minneapolis, MN: Wallace Foundation.

Leonard, P. E., & Leonard, L. J. (2001). The collaborative prescription: Remedy or reverie? *International Journal of Leadership in Education, 4*(4), 383–399.

Little, J. W. (1990). The persistence of privacy: Autonomy and initiative in teachers' professional relations. *Teachers College Record, 91*(4), 509–531.

Lortie, D. C. (1975). *Schoolteacher: A sociological study.* Chicago, IL: University of Chicago Press.

Marks, H. M., & Printy, S. M. (2003). Principal leadership and school performance: An integration of transformational and instructional leadership. *Educational Administration Quarterly, 39*(3), 370–397. doi:https://doi.org/10.1177/0013161X03253412

Marzano, R. J., Waters, T., & McNulty, B. A. (2005). *School leadership that works: From research to results.* Alexandria, VA: Association for Supervision and Curriculum Development.

Organisation for Economic Co-operation and Development. (2014). TALIS 2013 results: An international perspective on teaching and learning. Paris, France: OECD.

Pugach, M. C., & Johnson, L. J. (1995). *Collaborative practitioners: Collaborative schools.* Denver, CO: Love.

Purkey, S., & Smith, M. (1983). Effective schools: A review. *The Elementary School Journal, 83*(4), 426–452. doi:https://doi.org/10.1080/01619568409538458

Robinson, J., Sinclair, M., Tobias, J., & Choi, E. (2017). More dynamic that you think: Hidden aspects of decision-making. *Administrative Sciences, 7*(23), 1–29.

Robinson, V., Lloyd, C., & Rowe, K. (2008). The impact of leadership on student outcomes: An analysis of the differential effects of leadership types. *Educational Administration Quarterly, 44*(5), 635–674.

Sarason, S. B., Levine, M., Goldenberg, I. I., Cherlin, D., & Bennett, E. (1966). *Psychology in community settings: Clinical, educational, vocational, social aspects.* New York, NY: Wiley.

Schoenfeld, A. H. (2004). Multiple learning communities: Students, teachers, instructional designers, and researchers. *Journal of Curriculum Studies, 36*(2), 237–255. doi:https://doi.org/10.1080/0022027032000145561

Schrage, M. (1995). *No more teams! Mastering the dynamics of creative collaboration.* New York, NY: Doubleday.

Seashore Louis, K., Leithwood, K., Wahlstrom, K. L., & Anderson, S. E. (2010). Investigating the links to improved student learning: Final report of research findings. *Learning from Leadership Project.* Minneapolis, MN: Wallace Foundation.

Senge, P. (2006). *The fifth discipline: The art and practice of the learning organization* (Rev. ed.). New York, NY: Currency Doubleday.

Senge, P., Cambron-McCabe, N., Lucas, T., Smith, B., & Dutton, J. (2012). *Schools that learn.* New York, NY: Penguin Random House.

Sergiovanni, T. J. (1996). *Leadership for the school house.* San Francisco, CA: Jossey-Bass.

Shepard, L. A. (2000). The role of assessment in a learning culture. *Journal of Education, 189*(1/2), 95–106.

Slater, L. (2004). Collaboration: A framework for school improvement. *International Electronic Journal for Leadership in Learning, 8*(5).

Southworth, G. (2005). Learning-centered leadership. In B. Davies (Ed.), *The essentials of school leadership* (pp. 75–92). Thousand Oaks, CA: Sage.

Spillane, J. P. (2005). Distributed leadership. *The Educational Forum, 69*(2), 143–150. doi:https://doi.org/10.1080/00131720508984678

Spillane, J. P., & Seashore Louis, K. (2002). School improvement processes and practices: Professional learning for building instructional capacity. *Yearbook for the National Society for the Study of Education, 101*(1), 83–104.

Stoll, L., Bolam, R., McMahon, A., Wallace, M., & Thomas, S. (2006). Professional learning communities: A review of the literature. *Journal of Educational Change, 7,* 221–258. doi:https://doi.org/10.1007/s10833-006-0001-8

Stoller, A. (2015). Taylorism and the logic of learning outcomes. *Journal of Curriculum Studies, 47*(3), 317–333. doi:https://doi.org/10.1080/00220272.2015.1018328

Thompson, C. S. (2017). Teachers' expectations of educational leaders' leadership approach and perspectives on the principalship: Identifying critical leadership paradigms for the 21st century. *Journal of Organizational and Educational Leadership, 2*(2) 1–29.

Tiegerman-Farber, E., & Radziewicz, C. (1998). *Collaborative decision-making: The pathway to inclusion.* Upper Saddle River, NJ: Merrill.

Toole, J., & Louis, K. S. (2002). Professional learning communities in international education. In K. Leithwood & P. Hallinger (Eds.), *The second international handbook of educational leadership* (pp. 245–279). Dordrecht, Netherlands: Kluwer Academic.

Tschannen-Moran, M. (2004). *Trust matters: Leadership of successful schools*. San Francisco, CA: Jossey-Bass.

Vangrieken, K., Dochy, F., Raes, E., & Kyndt, E. (2015). Teacher collaboration: A systematic review. *Educational Research Review, 15*, 17–40. doi:http://dx.doi.org/10.1016/j.edurev.2015.04.002

Welch, M., & Sheridan, S. (1995). *Educational partnership: Serving students at risk*. Fort Worth, TX: Harcourt Brace.

Wenger, E., McDermott, R. A., & Snyder, W. M. (2002). *Cultivating communities of practice: A guide to managing knowledge*. Boston, MA: Harvard Business School Press.

CHAPTER SEVEN

Instructional Leadership to Instructional Practice

How Can I Be a Leader of Learners?

> To lead people, walk beside them. As for the best leaders, the people do not notice their existence ... When the best leader's work is done, the people say, "We did it ourselves!"
>   —*Lao Tsu*

> There seems to be a lot of hype about focusing on instructional leadership. I'm not really even sure what it is and my fellow principals can't seem to define it either. In fact, my teachers just think that it means that I have been told by central office to supervise them more! But, this just doesn't feel like it is at the heart of what I am supposed to be doing as an instructional leader.
>   —*Jason, first-year elementary school principal*

THE LEADERSHIP OF LEARNING

As Jason expressed to us, there does indeed seem to be a renewed interest in what constitutes instructional leadership, a term that has made appearances in the literature for decades but that seems to be emerging again with new and unique definitions. The term's reconstitution has resulted in questions posed to us over more recent years around the importance of being a *lead learner* and a *leader of learners*. Often, we find that these ideas are understood to only loosely intersect with—and sometimes collide with—instructional leadership.

> As you begin to read this chapter, reflect on the terms *lead learner* and *leader of learners*. Is there a noticeable difference in the way in which the mandate of instructional leadership is actualized?

This chapter begins with the question "How can I be a **leader of learners**?" This question presumes that a primary responsibility of leaders includes supporting in various ways the continued growth and learning of all those within one's sphere of influence, small or large, children or adults; we write this chapter with this presumption in the fore. Yet, there continues to be a great deal written about two larger themes that thread their way through generative leadership and generative dialogue that we have not yet addressed; these two themes present a conundrum that seems to contravene our understandings of leadership using powerful questions. The first is the topic of leading growth and facilitating the learning of competent professionals, employee supervision, and attending to the needs of evaluation of professionals when competence may be called into question. How are these activities written into policy and how are they enacted in various parts of the world? The extent to which the generative dialogue may be a foundational skill set that guides aspects of ascertaining competence and effectiveness is considered in this chapter.

A second area of discussion that we have only briefly presented up to this point is an examination of instructional leadership: its historical underpinnings and definitions, and how it is situated broadly in educational leadership and specifically in teacher evaluation. Germane to this book, is it possible to locate generative leadership in a larger framework of instructional leadership? Are generative leadership and instructional leadership mutually exclusive? Or is there room for both in a toolbox for effective leaders?

Our opening case study from Australia presents ideas about how some educators from New South Wales answered these types of questions.

> In this chapter we will present a thorough review of the literature dealing with teacher growth, supervision, and evaluation. We will then connect this literature to that of instructional leadership. We do so to help you situate generative leadership and the skills of generative dialogue within the broader realm of educational leadership. What do you believe the differences between each to be?

Case Study: An International Experiment with Generative Leadership

A chance meeting led to the creation of the North Coast Initiative for School Improvement in New South Wales, Australia. Since its inception in 2015, this movement has grown to influence professional staff in nearly 100 schools. Dozens of school leaders have sustained their commitment to the North Coast Initiative through exemplary collaboration with colleagues, and with academics from the School of Education at Southern Cross University. In fact, two of the most distinguishing characteristics of the North Coast Initiative are the school-to-school networks that have continued to expand and the active participation of a cadre of 10 academics who have voluntarily maintained a schedule of site visits, documentation, and support that has earned the respect of many educational leaders. Among its successes are the more than 70 school educators who have earned Master of Education degrees in the last three years, and two who have begun doctoral studies that include some aspect of generative leadership.

> Generative dialogue within a model of generative leadership has truly become an inter-jurisdictional, inter-provincial, and international way of leading. As you read the case about the North Coast Initiative for School Improvement, imagine the conversations among these educators as they came to more fully understand their roles associated with teacher growth, supervision, and evaluation.

The original partnership between North Coast schools and the university began with an invitation to 24 school leaders and three school directors to attend a two-day workshop at the university. There, participants were offered an overview of two successful international leadership growth projects, a review of current literature on instructional leadership, and demonstrations of skills, structures, and processes associated with collaborative inquiry and generative dialogue. One of those leaders who attended the first session was Glen, who was serving a large area of the North Coast in the role of principal of school leadership, an experimental designation introduced by the New South Wales Department of Education. Buoyed by his relentless focus and looking to explore new possibilities in their own leadership of learning, a strong core of experienced school leaders made a serious commitment to the initiative's structure of regular site visits, professional learning, partnerships, networking, and evidence-based practice. Glen established and maintained a website that became a repository of videos, artifacts, documents, and records of growth and impact.

Prior to the start of this initiative, many schools on the North Coast had an established record of inter-school collaboration in matters of curriculum, assessment, and innovation. They were not easily persuaded that any new forms of professional engagement would add significantly to what they were already doing. It is to their credit that they did not reject the new ideas about generative leadership out of hand but, rather, took their time to learn how key conceptual shifts could be mapped onto their existing methods. Some were skeptical; a few were resistant. Still, they attended workshops and symposia; they invited external teams into their schools; they shared ideas and opportunities with their executive teams; and they changed their leadership practices.

The North Coast Initiative was given a boost in late 2015 when a team of educators from the North Coast region organized an international study tour, visiting sites across Western Canada where schools, and whole districts, had been using collaborative inquiry/generative dialogue methods and processes, some for over five years. That tour triggered a reciprocal response from 15 leaders who visited selected North Coast schools and participated in several workshops in July of the following year, and who have continued to do so as annual events.

Participation in the North Coast Initiative was further encouraged when the NSW Department of Education introduced a professional development plan (PDP) that resembled many of the conceptual and practical strategies that are at the heart of generative leadership and generative dialogue. At approximately the same time, the North Coast Initiative was given additional status and recognition when it was awarded two NSW Department of Education grants—first, a grant of $15,000, followed by another grant of $100,000 for innovation in education. And, by 2017,

continued

workshops and seminars sponsored by the North Coast Initiative and Southern Cross University had exceeded 5,000 attendees. University professors had been the recipients of a university community service award for their work in the initiative and, in addition, they published several journal articles related to this work.

The period June 2017 to June 2018 saw a consolidation of North Coast Initiative activities centred on approximately 50 schools in which leadership growth, and the growth of teacher teams, contributed greatly to goal achievement and higher levels of staff commitment. In many schools, measures of student achievement demonstrated steady increases and, in some of the early-adopting schools, student achievement exceeded by significant margins the previous five-year averages. There has been growth, too, in the number of schools that have formed various partnerships of a kind not seen before. In one example, four high schools came together to share monthly visits of their executive team members. Their collective goal was to ensure that all schools progressed and all students were successful. In another instance, a small elementary school and a large elementary school partnered with a director and a university researcher to make sure their monthly meetings provided opportunities to discuss their progress toward achieving their goals. Another small school maintained a vibrant relationship with two academics, one of whom had recently retired but continued to show up every month. Still another elementary school enjoyed a partnership with the principal of the largest high school in the region.

In 2018, another policy shift by the NSW Department of Education brought renewed attention to the North Coast Initiative. In conjunction with a substantial increase in the number of directors (similar in some ways to North American superintendents), their roles were targeted to include a major emphasis on instructional leadership. Several directors in areas impacted by the initiative already had a focus on instructional leadership as part of their portfolio. Most were very strong supporters of the initiative. Yet this policy change seemed to have broadened the appeal of the North Coast Initiative, resulting in an expansion of schools and directors wanting to participate in a new way of thinking about and doing educational leadership.

Case Study Reflections: Instructional Leadership

- In what ways can partnerships such as the North Coast Initiative contribute to enhanced leadership practices? In what ways might it hinder?
- How are the instructional leadership practices identified in the case study similar to those you have experienced? How are they different from those you have experienced?
- What are some practical lessons about instructional leadership that emerge from the case study?

BUILDING, SUPPORTING, AND ASSURING QUALITY PROFESSIONAL PRACTICE[1]

Much has been written about leadership of professional growth over the past decade that highlights several broad themes: teacher professional growth is an essential condition for student learning and achievement; collaborative and inquiry-based approaches are most effective for supporting teacher growth; and, when professional learning is embedded in practice, reflected in professional standards, and articulated through rubrics and exemplars, educators feel supported and guided.

Untangling Professional Growth, Supervision, and Evaluation

Wei, Darling-Hammond, Andree, Richardson, and Orphanos (2009) noted that "efforts to improve student achievement can succeed only by building the capacity of teachers to improve their instructional practice and the capacity of school systems to advance teacher learning" (p. 1). Thus, professional learning has become a "vitally important dimension of the educational improvement process" (Guskey & Yoon, 2009, p. 495), and education reform in general is assumed to be a function of enhancing the quality of teacher learning (Desimone, 2011). Bakkenes, Vermunt, and Webbels (2010) contend that teachers are "the most important agents in shaping education for students and in bringing about change and innovation in educational practices" (p. 533). This statement has stood as uncontested. The key message is that impact on student learning is the *raison d'être* of leading professional growth planning; growth planning that is divorced from the specific impacts on students is both incongruent and ineffective.

> Throughout this book we have argued that for the growth planning cycle to make an impact on student learning, it is best done when guided by an inquiry question that is written after a thorough review of the applicable teaching standard and in conjunction with an assessment of student need. How does this relate to your understanding of the cycle?

The link between teacher learning and student achievement bears out internationally as well. Burns and Darling-Hammond (2014) linked collaborative and relevant professional learning to effective teaching practices. Based on 2013 TALIS results, which represent views of teachers and principals in lower secondary schools from 34 jurisdictions around the world, they posit that leaders who support professional learning will strengthen teaching and contribute to high-quality learning for students. As a result of comprehensive data analyses focused on a range of practices related to the way teachers are trained, supported, and prepared for the classroom; the working environments they face when they get there; the level of interaction they have with colleagues; the way they are formally appraised; their professional growth; their levels of confidence in their abilities; and their satisfaction with their work, Burns and Darling-Hammond (2014) concluded the following:

> Teachers are the most valuable resource available to schools. They are the most influential in-school factor upon student learning, and also the greatest financial

investment in terms of their training and ongoing compensation. Thus, attracting high-quality individuals into the profession, providing them with the supports they need to make the transition from teacher candidate to experienced teacher, and retaining them in the profession are of critical importance to educational systems. Doing so requires policies that support teachers' continual professional growth, including working with and learning from colleagues, to ensure that teaching practice develops to meet the continually changing demands on the profession. (p. 46)

This essential link between teacher growth and student learning has necessitated a paradigm shift in the way that teachers' professional development happens. In their report on the status of teacher development, Wei et al. (2009) called for "much more intensive and effective professional learning than has traditionally been available in the past" (p. 1). Hirsh and Killion (2009) described this paradigmatic shift to a focus on teacher growth in four ways: (1) from in-service education and professional development to professional learning; (2) from individual learning to team-based, school-wide learning; (3) from separate individual teacher, school, or district professional development plans to effective professional learning embedded into team-, school-, and district-improvement efforts; and (4) from improving teaching practices to improving teacher quality and student learning.

> Butler and Schnellert, and Darling-Hammond and Richardson provide the foundational statements for the necessity of moving toward inquiry-guided professional growth and the impacts provided by generative dialogue. Which aspects of their list do you incorporate into your leadership practice?

Fundamentally, "change must be meaningfully situated and sustained at the classroom level" (Butler & Schnellert, 2012, p. 1206), meaning that teachers learn when they have opportunities to reflect upon and critique their practice vis-à-vis student learning over extended periods of time (Darling-Hammond & Richardson, 2009).

Teacher Professional Growth: Embedded in Context, Reflected in Standards of Practice, and Articulated through Rubrics and Exemplars

What is the nature of teacher growth? Literature suggests that teacher professional learning and growth happens best when it is embedded in context, reflects standards of practice, and is articulated through rubrics and exemplars. These three components are described next.

Professional Growth as Situated and Contextualized

Literature of the past decade supports the notion of teachers learning during and through teaching. Bruce, Esmonde, Ross, Dookie, and Beatty (2010) described authentic teacher growth to be "embedded in the

> Consider your current school context. How do these four key considerations for the nature of teacher growth play out? If they do not, are items such as teacher growth plans compliance documents or do they act as agents of change?

classroom context and constructed through experience and practice in sustained iterative cycles of goal setting/planning, practicing, and reflecting" (p. 2). Similarly, Brady (2009) suggested that while teacher learning is a broad and complex process that can occur in many ways and in various contexts, "it is always embedded in the daily lives of teachers in the classroom, in the school community, in the corridors, in courses and workshops" (p. 337).

While suggesting a reflective model for teacher learning initiated and controlled by educational authorities, Kiss (2016) acknowledged the centrality of the teacher in professional growth: "The teacher learner should be in the centre of learning. [This] should be built into the everyday work of the school. It must offer a chance to collect evidence of and opportunities for examining student learning with the aim of improving the syllabus and fine-tuning its execution in the school context" (p. 55). Clearly, teacher professional growth considerations must first and foremost emerge from the context of the classroom and the pedagogical needs of the teacher. This will require a renewed understanding of what constitutes effective teacher professional growth and, as Darling-Hammond and McLaughlin (2011) argued, will be incumbent upon educational organizations to provide opportunities for reflection and discussion related to standards of practice.

> We often mention the connection between teacher growth and standards of practice. The following paragraphs highlight why we pay particular attention to standards of practice when addressing issues of teacher growth, supervision, and in some cases, when necessary, evaluation.

Professional Growth Reflected in Standards of Practice

Standards of practice "provide a vision for the profession. They define what teachers should know and do [and] they establish a foundation upon which all aspects of teacher development from teacher education to induction and ongoing professional development can be aligned" (Virginia Department of Education, 2012, p. 1). Moreover, by providing a common language within an articulated set of professional expectations, these standards "support teachers as they establish professional goals and engage in continuous and purposeful professional growth and development" (California Commission on Teacher Credentialing, 2009, p. 16). Asserting that improving teaching must be focused on improving student outcomes, the Australian Professional Standards for Teaching (Australian Institute for Teaching and School Leadership, 2014) are outlined as follows:

> To improve teaching, it is necessary to have a clear vision of what effective teaching looks like. [The Standards] outline what teachers should know and be able to do at four career stages. These Standards present a comprehensive picture of the elements of effective teaching organized around the domains of professional knowledge, professional practice and professional engagement. (p. 3)

High-quality professional growth experiences, described as relevant, collaborative, and future-focused, are the means of improving teacher practice (Australian Institute for Teaching and School Leadership, 2012). Variously stated, Canadian provincial policies emphasize that professional learning is integral to effective teaching practices and student learning (Ontario College of Teachers, 2016), the hallmark of professionalism (British Columbia Ministry of Education Governance and Legislation Branch, 2016), and a necessary reflective process associated with high-quality teaching (Province of Nova Scotia, 2016). Australia, Texas, California, Virginia, and Hong Kong, among many others, base teacher growth on standards of practice, as do British Columbia, Ontario, and Nova Scotia. In short, teacher learning and growth is an essential criterion of a standard of professional practice and engagement. Standards of practice articulate agreed-upon professional expectations for teaching excellence and ensure that teachers' growth planning and learning are purposeful, and that teachers understand in what areas they are expected to grow.

Professional Growth Articulated through Rubrics and Exemplars

If standards point to a territory of teacher excellence, rubrics and exemplars are the road map for potential pathways toward enhanced practice and professional growth. In Canadian jurisdictions, exemplars are often viewed as representative of broad conceptual frameworks. Conversely, jurisdictions such as Australia, California, Texas, and Hong Kong have created rubrics and exemplars to guide teacher learning. Australia's is worth noting for its specificity and use of increments. In addition to the *Australian Charter for the Professional Learning of Teachers and School Leaders* (Australian Institute for Teaching and School Leadership, 2012), which details the characteristics of high-quality professional learning, the *Australian Professional Standards for Teachers* (Australian Institute for Teaching and School Leadership, 2014) describes practice across four career stages of teacher development. These resources recognize that professional knowledge and skills develop throughout a teacher's career in response to changing contexts; thus, articulated standards, accompanied by rubrics and illustrations of practice at four stages of development differentiate for teachers' professional learning needs, goal setting, collaboration, and growth over time.

LEADING GROWTH AND SUPERVISION

The term *supervision* has been variously defined over the past several decades. Glanz (2000) listed no fewer than 36 modern definitions of the term before concluding that "supervision is of vital importance to promote instructional improvement, promote teacher growth, foster curriculum development, and support instruction" (p. 77). The consensus that emerges from most literature is that supervision's primary purpose is to foster teacher growth (Blase & Blase, 1998, 2000; Glanz, 2000; Glickman, Gordon, & Ross-Gordon, 2017; Pajak,

2003; Zepeda, 2017; Zepeda & Lanoue, 2017). Sergiovanni (1992) explained that "We supervise for good reasons. We want schools to be better, teachers to grow, and students to have academically and developmentally sound learning experiences; and we believe that supervision serves these and other worthy ends" (p. 204). Included in Glickman's orientation to teacher supervision are a variety of strategies and tasks: curriculum development, staff development, action research, and mentoring (Glickman, Gordon, and Ross-Gordon, 2017).

Glanz (2000) called for supervision that "utilizes a wide array of strategies, methodologies, and approaches aimed at improving instruction and promoting educational leadership as well as change" (p. 85). Pajak (2003) described four options: collegial supervision (peer coaching and cognitive coaching), self-directed supervision, informal supervision, and inquiry-based supervision (action research).

We have categorized the approaches to supervision into the following clusters: developmental supervision, differentiated supervision, clinical supervision, constructivist supervision, and informal supervision.

> Often, the word *supervision* conjures up images of a principal sitting in the back of the room with a clipboard (or, more recently, a tablet) taking notes on the activities of the students and teacher. This "visit" is followed by some sort of telling activity during which the principal informs the teacher of what went well and what needs more attention. We contend that this type of supervision produces reams of notes, but very little change in teacher practice. The connection between growth and supervision is often lost. What is your response to our contention?

Developmental Supervision

Developmental supervision is an integrated supervisory model first presented by Carl Glickman in 1985. In its most recent iteration, developmental supervision is described as a "match of initial supervisory approach[es] with the teacher's or group's developmental levels, expertise and commitment" (Glickman, Gordon, & Ross-Gordon, 2017, p. 197). Glickman et al. call for analyzing teachers' developmental levels by doing the following:

- Choosing the best entry-level supervisory approach
- Applying the chosen approach
- Fostering teacher development while gradually increasing teacher choice and decision-making responsibility (p. 204)

The Glickman, Gordon, and Ross-Gordon (2017) model is designed to respond to principles of adult learning and teachers' stages of development through clinical supervision and peer coaching, group development, professional development, curriculum development, action research, and school improvement.

> Within Glickman et al.'s description lies what we consider to be an important characteristic of traditional understandings of supervision: *giving, telling,* and *offering* are all verbs that imply one-way conversations. Generative dialogue differs: don't tell, ask questions!

Differentiated Supervision

Glatthorn (1997) described the term *supervision* as "a process of facilitating the professional growth of a teacher, primarily by giving the teacher feedback about classroom interactions and helping the teacher make use of that feedback in order to make teaching more effective" (p. 2). In this approach, supervision can take a variety of forms:

- Trained supervisors provide clinical supervision for novices and experienced teachers encountering difficulty.
- Cooperative professional development provides a range of group and paired growth activities—peer observation and reading groups, for instance.
- Self-directed development involves the fashioning of an individualized plan for professional growth, where the administrator serves as a resource.
- Administrative monitoring consists of brief and unannounced classroom visits "to ensure that the staff are carrying out assignments and responsibilities in a professional manner." (Glatthorn, 1997, p. 5)

Clinical Supervision

Pajak (2003) presented a "style-guided" approach to clinical supervision, based on an understanding of teacher development as "a recurring cycle of growth that begins with (1) concrete experience, followed by (2) empathic reflection, (3) construction of meaning, and (4) active experimentation" (p. 88). The responsibility of the supervisor is to make a "deliberate effort to honor and legitim[ize] perspectives and practices that differ from their own preferred styles of perceiving, judging, and communicating about reality" (p. 4). Pajak offered strategies commensurate with five stages of clinical supervision. These five stages include (1) pre-observation conference, (2) classroom observation, (3) data analysis and strategy, (4) conference, and (5) post-conference analysis.

Our experiences with collaboration, inquiry, and generative dialogue lead us to endorse what Pajak presents. We also note that, like so much of the literature, Pajak's findings are connected to the "what" of instructional leadership. Throughout this book we have presented a way of working alongside teachers to do the work. We continue to offer suggestions on the "how." In what ways do you see Pajak's five stages linked to generative leadership processes?

To accommodate various teachers' styles, Pajak (2003) posited four families of clinical supervision:

- *Original clinical* models (developed by Goldhammer and Cogan) "emphasize the importance of collegial relationships with teachers, cooperative discovery of meaning, and development of unique teaching styles" and are based on "empirical, behavioral, phenomenological, and developmental perspectives."

- *Artistic/humanistic* models (developed by Eisner and Blumberg) "forsake step by step procedures and emphasize open interpersonal relations and personal intuition, artistry, and idiosyncrasy" and are based upon "aesthetic and existential principles."
- *Technical/didactic* clinical supervision models (developed by Gall and Acheson; and Hunter) comprise "techniques of observation and feedback that reinforce certain 'effective' behaviors or predetermined models of teaching to which teachers attempt to conform."
- *Developmental/reflective* models (Glickman; Costa and Garmstrom; and others) comprise the final family. These models are "sensitive to individual differences and the social, organizational, political, and cultural contexts of teaching" and "encourage reflection among teachers, foster growth, and promote justice and equity." (p. 8)

Glanz (2000) similarly offered three approaches to supervision: (1) *applied science*, (2) *interpretive-practical*, and (3) *critical emancipatory*. The *applied science* model is a directive, behaviouristic, and positivist approach within the modernist paradigm that involves supervisors observing teaching, diagnosing classroom problems, and prescribing or suggesting research-based ideas for improvement. The other two approaches fall within the postmodern paradigm. The *interpretive-practical* approach focuses on person-centred communication and collegial relationships to facilitate a shared understanding of pedagogic problems and to generate context-specific responses. The *critical-emancipatory* approach to supervision goes "beyond mere collaboration in the development of instructional goals" by challenging teachers to "examine the moral, ethical, and political dimensions embedded in everyday thinking and practice" and to "take risks and construct knowledge for themselves" (Glanz, 2000, p. 79).

Constructivist Supervision

Zepeda (2017) developed a constructivist supervisory model that provides teachers with "multiple opportunities to transfer information and to construct deeper understanding of their own practices and those of others" within a capacity-building learning community (p. 96). Such supervision involves reciprocal processes that respect the differing developmental learning needs of novices and veterans. Like other forms of professional development, constructivist supervision is embedded into the fabric of the school to provide a "tailor-made approach for assisting teachers with their growth" (p. 100). Embedding supervision means "new skills are implemented *during* the supervisory process, not *after*. Moreover, new skills can become part of the teacher's *practice as they are learned*" (p. 102). Five features characterize this model:

- Differentiated forms of supervision (e.g., peer coaching, mentoring, and portfolio development)
- An environment rich with dialogue

- Autonomous relationships so teachers can negotiate their own learning based upon what makes sense to them
- Activities extending reflection
- Self-analysis of practice (Zepeda, 2017, p. 96)

Informal Supervision

Informal supervision is an element of several supervisory models (e.g., Ginsberg & Murphy, 2002; Glatthorn, 1997; B. Marshall, 2013; Pajak, 2003). Glatthorn (1997) referred to these *drop-ins* as *administrative monitoring* and advocated short, regularly scheduled classroom visits by administrators for openly communicated and mutually understood purposes as one part of a more comprehensive supervision program. Similarly, K. Marshall (2005) monitored classrooms to get a sense of the big picture and to find answers to five key questions:

- Are teachers on track with the curriculum?
- Are students learning?
- Are teachers "happy campers" in terms of their jobs and their lives?
- Do some teachers deserve special praise?
- Do some teachers need redirection, emergency support, or a negative evaluation? (p. 703)

Even though we include Marshall's key questions in our book, we have reservations about them. Think about what you have read and ask yourself "How do you think teachers would respond to being called 'happy campers'? Is praise another form of judgment? What about 'negative' evaluation?"

Ginsberg and Murphy (2002) also saw value in *walkthroughs* as one component of a more comprehensive supportive program of learning and teaching. Their five-minute visits are framed by supervisory questions about the existence of a clear academic focus, level of student engagement, and demonstrations of critical-thinking skills. Walkthroughs "can foster focused, reflective, and collaborative adult learning: generally, teachers welcome the opportunity for discussion that walkthroughs provide" (p. 34). The manner of supervisors as they participate in this program is a crucial aspect of its success. As Sergiovanni and Starratt (2007) pointed out, informal supervision can be viewed negatively as "informal surveillance" (p. 258) if the practice is not embedded within an overall program that fosters reflection, trust, and professional growth.

Instructional rounds (City, Elmore, Fiarman, & Teitel, 2009) are a similar form of informal supervision. The idea is to help school leaders and teachers develop a shared understanding of what high-quality instruction looks like and what is needed to support it. Inspired by the medical-rounds model used by physicians, the premise is to help educators develop a shared practice of observing, discussing, and analyzing learning and teaching.

SITUATING EVALUATION

For the most part, evaluation procedures across the provinces and territories in Canada are similar. All teachers are evaluated against a set of provincial/territorial standards or competencies, and teachers new to the profession must go through an evaluation process in order to receive permanent teacher certification and ongoing contracts. For veteran teachers, though, there is some variance in how and when evaluation takes place. In British Columbia, teachers are required to participate in the evaluation process, but these processes vary for each school district. Evaluation methods are outlined in a school district's collective agreement and are slightly different from one district to another in terms of process and procedure commensurate with the British Columbia School Act (British Columbia Ministry of Education Governance and Legislation Branch, 2016). One example is from the Vancouver Board of Education (2013), where teacher evaluation occurs through a teacher request or a principal's decision and is based on criteria outlined in the School Act and school regulations. The basis of this criteria includes standards for planning, context of teaching, instructional techniques, classroom management, and inclusion of parents and community.

Now we come to the one item that, all by itself, can distort the wonderful work achieved through growth-focused supervision. When evaluation is deemed to apply to all aspects of supervision, the language of supervision begins to sound like judgment. Evaluation must remain in its own neat little box—one that is used for accountability purposes when there is evidence indicating that the teaching standard is no longer being met or when evidence is to know if it is being met.

Other provinces that follow a similar model of tasking school boards with responsibility for evaluation procedures include Manitoba (Manitoba Teachers' Society, 2017), New Brunswick (Bouchamma, 2005), and Nova Scotia (Halifax School Board, 2007). Some processes may vary from the Vancouver School Board, where they use more frequent cycles of formal evaluation; however, most are similar in nature and intent.

In other provinces and territories, such as Saskatchewan, Ontario, and the Northwest Territories, ministries of education establish provincial and territorial teacher supervision and evaluation policies that all school boards follow. In Saskatchewan, policies and procedures for the evaluation of teachers must comply with the Education Act (Goverment of Saskatchewan, 2015). Professional associations, such as the Saskatchewan Teachers' Federation (STF), also have guideline policies for school officials to follow (Saskatchewan Teachers' Federation, 2016). These policies and positions do not specify detailed procedures for principals to follow, such as a four-year cycle, and there is no set timeline for evaluations to occur.

Saskatchewan's policy differs from Ontario's Education Act (Government of Ontario, 1996/2007) that stipulates experienced teachers are to be evaluated or appraised at least once every five years. A set of guidelines and procedures for principals to follow are outlined in the *Teacher Performance Appraisal: Technical Requirements Manual.* The Northwest Territories operates similarly, where teachers are evaluated at least once every five years and where principals adhere to set procedures and policies (Northwest Territories Ministry of Education, 2004).

Internationally, other countries present other options. For example, in Australia, teacher evaluation or appraisal is required to gain and maintain professional registration/accreditation, with teachers being evaluated against specific national standards (Australian Institute for Teaching and School Leadership, 2017). Implemented in 2012, the Australian *Teacher Performance and Development Framework* focuses on improving student outcomes, improving teaching, and the role of principals in improving school performance and creating a culture of performance and development (Education Services Australia, 2012). This framework is a cycle with five components (focus on student outcomes, clear understanding of effective teaching, leadership, flexibility, and coherence) with no associated timelines outlined in policy. Schools in Australia implement independent procedures for evaluation. The foundational premise for this practice rests on performance management processes, which are linked to educational goals set at the national, state, or school levels; school improvement initiatives; and the annual improvement plan. Evaluation is also requested by teachers as a way to measure the quality of their teaching performance for probation, promotion, or pay increments.

In the Netherlands, individual school boards are required to create human resource policies for their schools, keep competency files on teachers, and ensure sustained achievement of certain competencies. Regular performance interviews with teachers are stipulated in policy, but there are no articulated guidelines on how to evaluate teachers. School leaders assume this responsibility and procedures vary from school to school. The Education Professions Act describes 56 competencies for teachers and the Inspectorate of Education provides indicators for lesson observations. A supplementary peer assessment program allows teachers from one school to visit and assess teachers from another school.

Teacher evaluation in Chile is compulsory for all teachers who work in public schools. There are four possible results for teachers upon evaluation: *outstanding, competent, basic,* and *unsatisfactory.* Evaluators are external to the school and, as a result, school leaders usually remain distant in their support for teachers' professional growth. The National Teacher Evaluation has four main parts: (1) self-evaluation, (2) third-party reference report, (3) peer evaluation, and (4) teacher performance portfolio. Teachers evaluated as *competent* or *outstanding* may receive monetary remuneration, as long as they have high results in another voluntary content test called the Variable Individual Performance Allowance program (AVDI). The AVDI assesses teachers' knowledge of each subject/content area. If teachers do not take the AVDI, their results from the national Chilean teacher evaluation are nullified. Teachers who are evaluated as *basic* or *unsatisfactory* are expected to receive further training from the local education department. Overall, Chilean teachers tend to have a negative perception of the national teacher evaluation program (Taut, Santelices, Araya, & Manzi, 2011) because (1) it is time-consuming and stressful, (2) there is little support provided at the school level, (3) teachers fear being labelled, (4) the evaluation tends to add more work for teachers, which increases an already heavy workload, and (5) overall, the evaluation provides few opportunities to improve teachers' professional practice.

After a comprehensive review of literature, Brandon et al. (2018) found the following to be key connections between the requirement for teacher evaluation and instructional leadership leading to enhanced teaching practice and student learning:

- Effective evaluation emphasizes teacher growth and improvement in relation to student learning outcomes.
- Effective evaluation models reference clearly articulated standards to ensure teaching excellence.
- A culture of continuous learning and improvement is nurtured when evaluation is part of a broader sustained process of growth for teachers at all career stages. The sole use of summative evaluations for high-stakes purposes such as job security or reward incentives demotivates and de-professionalizes teachers. These high-stakes summative evaluations jeopardize teacher learning as an integral aspect of evaluation processes.
- To address contextual variances in the teaching environment (e.g., teaching experience, subject, grade level, class composition) and make performance feedback meaningful for teachers, strategies include (1) using multiple artifacts of evidence for teaching performance, (2) differentiating evaluation based on career stage, and (3) incorporating collegial processes.

It certainly is evident that many school systems require some type of judgment to be made about the quality of teaching, yet Brandon et al. (2018) found that leaving evaluation solely in a paradigm of judgment is not sufficient to improve teaching practice. The answer, then, to our query about utility of generative dialogue within a generative leadership model lies in the power of using teacher growth conversations as the focal point for ongoing and purposeful teacher supervision and using this information as a starting point for the evaluation of teachers, should the need arise. The need for tenured teacher evaluation considerably decreases through (1) purposeful, intentional, ongoing conversations with teachers about areas in which they would like to explore and grow, (2) following these conversations with classroom observations, (3) incorporating cycles of generative dialogue over a sustained period of time.

When we work with school leaders, we emphasize the need for adherence to the requirements of the jurisdiction's teacher evaluation policy. However, we also stress the need to focus conversations with teachers on growth and improvement, and for the teachers to embrace the process as an opportunity to reflect on their own practice. Even those who are undergoing a formal process of evaluation can benefit immensely from this shift in perspective. By so doing, teachers continue to grow in professional ability and still maintain a healthy respect for their own ability to identify areas for growth and plan for it to occur.

SCAFFOLDING THE INSTRUCTIONAL LEADERSHIP LITERATURE

Throughout this chapter we have presented the research-based literature supporting the concepts of teacher growth, teacher supervision, and teacher evaluation. We have also made direct links to the role of the school leader in using teacher growth, supervision, and evaluation processes to work alongside teachers with the aim of improving instruction and, in turn, student learning. What we have not addressed is the link between growth, supervision, and evaluation and the school leader's role to the larger idea of *instructional leadership*. Where are the connections? Do the connections even matter? Is it desirable, or even possible, for a "leading without answers approach" to be an appropriate one in linking growth, supervision, and evaluation?

The term *instructional leadership* is as diverse as it is popular, and includes a variety of interpretations and conceptualizations that simultaneously offer incongruence and overlap. The concepts of influence and change are central to instructional leadership, reflected through three central themes: personality traits of leaders; leadership actions and behaviours; and levels of leadership influence within organizational contexts.

> As you read this section of the chapter, begin to reflect on the "what" of instructional leadership and the "how" of generative dialogue within generative leadership.

The term *instructional leadership* surfaced in the United States during the 1950s as a practice-based prescription rather than a theory-driven construct (Bridges, 1967) and gained further prominence in the 1970s and 1980s during the effective schools movement. At that time, researchers were interested in examining the reasons contributing to differences in student achievement between schools (Hallinger, Murphy, Well, Mesa, & Mitman, 1983; Purkey & Smith, 1983). A particular thrust within this research was the pursuit of potential relationships between leadership and student achievement (Heck, 1993; Leithwood, Seashore Louis, Anderson, & Wahlstrom, 2004; Spillane, Halverson, & Diamond, 2001).

Early instructional leadership research prioritized the personal characteristics of principals as a primary mechanism for determining student achievement. In 1979, a seminal article by Ronald Edmonds posited that schools that demonstrating increases in student achievement were led by strong principals who were "more likely to be an instructional leader, more assertive in [their] institutional leadership role, more of a disciplinarian, and perhaps most of all, [assume] responsibility for the evaluation of the achievement of basic objectives" (p. 18). Principals who demonstrated the ability to establish high professional expectations for teachers and learning goals for students were considered to be effective instructional leaders (Bossert, Dwyer, Rowan, & Lee,

1982; Elmore, 2000; Hallinger, Bickman, & Davis, 1996; Purkey & Smith, 1983). Instructional leaders were also characterized as goal-oriented (Bossert et al., 1982), able to define a clear vision and mission for the organization (Murphy, Elliot, Goldring, & Porter, 2006) and to generate a collective focus on teaching and learning (Edmonds, 1979; Hallinger et al., 1996).

In their extensive review of the literature, Bossert et al. (1982) developed an *instructional management* framework representing actions and strategies employed by principals to impact the instructional practices of teachers, with the intention of increasing student achievement. The term *instructional management* referred to those aspects of the principal's roles and responsibilities associated with the coordination of curriculum and instruction. The scope of influence of the framework posited by Bossert et al. (1982) is seen in subsequent research in the areas of *activities of principals* (Robinson, Lloyd, & Rowe, 2008); *personal characteristics of principals* (Goldring, Huff, May, & Camburn, 2008; Hallinger, 2011; Leithwood, Harris, & Hopkins, 2008); and *organizational context* (Goldring et al., 2008; Hallinger, 2011; Leithwood et al., 2008).

Another example of early models of instructional leadership focused on the actions and behaviours of principals developed by Hallinger et al. (1983). These researchers represented the term *instructional management* through three general dimensions: defining the school's mission, managing curriculum and instruction, and promoting a positive school learning climate. This research contributed to the development of associated research instruments such as the Principal Instructional Management Rating Scale (Hallinger & Murphy, 1985), designed for empirical investigations to elucidate the antecedents, practices, and effects of the principal's instructional leadership practices. The dimensions of this instructional leadership model were interpreted as being solely situated with the principal as the formal leader of the school. Thus, research into the concept of instructional leadership in this era subsequently reinforced notions of the solitary, heroic leader capable of saving the failing school (Elmore, 2000; Hallinger, 2005).

The frameworks posited by Bossert et al. (1982) and Hallinger and Murphy (1985) signalled the emergence of instructional management as a research-based construct for understanding how principals affect student learning (Bush, 2011; Hallinger & Murphy, 1985; Hallinger & Wang, 2015). As noted by Hallinger and Wang (2015), the term *instructional management* gradually became more commonly referred to by American scholars and practitioners as *instructional leadership*, the distinction being based on a growing awareness that principals who operate from this frame of reference rely more on expertise than on formal authoritative positions of power to influence others (Blase & Blase, 1999).

The literature builds upon the three aforementioned dimensions of instructional leadership initially offered by Hallinger et al. (1983), associating instructional leadership with an increasing multiplicity of actions and behaviours such as developing a vision and giving direction, understanding people and developing people, redesigning the organization, and managing the teaching and learning program. As noted by Neumerski

(2012), the actions and behaviours of principals most commonly recognized as being conducive to increasing student achievement included the systematic monitoring of student progress, classroom visits, teacher observations, and generating a common vision amongst staff.

Conceptualizations and definitions of instructional leadership have continued to develop over time. Much of the research toward instructional leadership conducted in North America over the past 30 years reflects a *direct-effects* model, with the assumption that leadership has a direct effect on student achievement. Motivated to increase student achievement on normative-referenced government exams, these models often focus explicitly on the manner in which principals influence changes to the pedagogical practices of teachers (Hallinger et al., 1996; Heck, 1993; Heck, Larson, & Marcoulides, 1990). The direct-effects orientation assumed that these effects can be measured reliably, and separately from other related variables such as organizational climate, teacher commitment, socioeconomic status, and instructional organization (Hallinger & Heck, 1998).

A burgeoning volume of *mediated-effects* models of instructional leadership emerged in the 1980s and 1990s (Hallinger et al., 1996; Heck, 1993; Leithwood, 1994), hypothesizing that principals achieve their effect on school outcomes along indirect paths. In the mediated-effects model, instructional leadership was seen as having an indirect influence through which principals changed instructional organization and culture within the school. Mediated-effects models of instructional leadership recognized that principals effect school outcomes primarily through their influence on other people in the school community, using influence more than positional power to motivate staff toward collective goals (Hallinger & Wang, 2015; Marks & Printy, 2003). Blase and Blase (2000) defined a *mediated version of instructional leadership* as a series of seven principal behaviours: making suggestions, providing feedback to teachers, modelling effective instruction, soliciting opinions, supporting collaboration, providing professional development opportunities, and giving praise for effective teaching.

Contemporary instructional leadership research takes a more inclusive approach, adopting notions of shared, distributed, collective, or reciprocal instructional leadership. For example, Spillane et al. (2001) examined the actions and behaviours of formal leaders, such as principals, and informal leaders, such as teachers, as central elements of instructional leadership practice. They described how principals and teachers co-performed instructional leadership functions and shared instructional leadership roles and responsibilities. As another example, the shared instructional leadership model posited by Robinson et al. (2008) viewed the principal as seeking out the ideas, insights, and expertise of teachers in the areas of curriculum and instruction and working with teachers for school improvement, while the responsibility for staff development, curricular development, and supervision of instructional tasks is shared between teachers and principals.

This expanded view of instructional leadership is shifting from a principal-centred practice to a shared or collective practice, encouraging the authority and empowerment of teachers to influence decisions related to instructional programming, organizational structure, and other activities associated with formal and informal leadership roles (Leithwood & Jantzi, 2006; Seashore Louis, Dretzke, & Wahlstrom, 2010). Contemporary conceptions recognize that instructional leadership affects conditions that promote positive learning environments for students (Hallinger & Heck, 2010; Leithwood et al., 2008; Robinson et al., 2008); establishes high expectations embedded in curriculum standards, structures, and processes (Seashore Louis, Dretzke, et al., 2010); and supports the ongoing professional learning of teachers and promotion of sustainable change (Robinson et al., 2008; Seashore Louis, Leithwood, Wahlstrom, & Anderson, 2010).

The literature also highlights several important limitations associated with the instructional leadership model. For example, the complex demands and structural and contextual conditions of daily life in schools are known to limit the ability of individual principals to enact the management of instructional programs and coordination of the curriculum (Hallinger & Murphy, 2012). The classroom has traditionally represented the exclusive domain of the teacher, in which principals may, or may not, be welcome (Hallinger & Wang, 2015). Moreover, the literature recognizes instances in which principals possess less subject-specific expertise than the teachers whom they supervise (Bossert et al., 1982; Hallinger, 2003).

Despite these limitations, the instructional leadership model offers considerable research opportunity in the contemporary context of public education. Throughout much of the English-speaking world, principals are formally expected to demonstrate a list of descriptor statements that reflect government's and society's conceptualization of instructional leadership, such as the following:

- Building the capacity of teachers to respond to the learning needs of students
- Implementing professional growth, supervision, and evaluation processes to ensure that all teachers meet an accepted standard
- Ensuring that student instruction addresses learning outcomes outlined in a program of study
- Facilitating mentorship and induction supports
- Demonstrating a strong understanding of effective pedagogy and curriculum
- Facilitating the use of a variety of technologies to support learning for all students
- Ensuring that assessment and evaluation practices are fair, appropriate, and evidence-informed for all students
- Interpreting a wide range of data to inform school practice and enable success for all students
- Facilitating access to resources, agencies, and experts within and outside the school community to enhance student learning and development

We contend that the definition and frameworks of instructional leadership presented in this chapter outline the "what" of school leadership that produces teacher instructional growth, leading to improved student learning. In other words, we lay out the foundation of necessary conditions for instructional leadership. Threaded throughout these conditions, generative dialogue is the means through which school leaders can actualize their instructional leadership mandate in a manner that supports their work with teachers to promote growth, participate in ongoing supervision that focuses on growth, and move to summative evaluation if teachers are demonstrating that they are not meeting the applicable standard of practice.

JOURNAL REFLECTIONS AND WRITING PROVOCATIONS AS YOU LEAD LEARNING

- I imagine the process of instructional leadership to look like ...
- In my mind, the difference between leading learning and being the lead learner is ...
- Growth, supervision, and evaluation differ by ...
- Growth, supervision, and evaluation are related by ...

SUGGESTED READINGS FOR INSTRUCTIONAL LEADERSHIP AND LEADING LEARNERS

Aguilar, E. (2013). *The art of coaching: Effective strategies for school transformation*. San Fransisco, CA: Jossey-Bass.

In this book, Elena Aguilar presents three types of coaching that, she argues, serve a wide variety of purposes in education: directive, facilitative, and transformative. Perhaps more than any other single source that we have encountered over the past five years, *The Art of Coaching* most closely aligns with the skills, practices, assertions, and content of the book you are presently reading. Much of the material contained here about the generative leadership model can be crossed referenced to Aguilar: building relationship and trust; checking unmonitored beliefs; effective listening, questioning, and conversing; positive habits of mind; reflective practice; and collaboration.

Brown, B. (2018). *Dare to lead: Brave work, tough conversations*. New York, NY: Random House.

Brown contends that "leadership is not about titles, status and wielding power." Her book incorporates many terms and phrases that are central to our notion of generative leadership: *vulnerability, curiosity, asking the right questions, trust*. She outlines the heart of daring leadership as threefold: (1) coming to terms with vulnerability, (2) identity and leadership (who we are is how we lead), and (3) empowering others by demonstrating ethical courage. Section 5, in particular, describes what Brown refers to as "grounded confidence," or a form of efficacy that is the result of "learning and unlearning, practicing and failing, and surviving a few misses." Her ideas are grounded in her experiences and observations in corporate leadership, but have a direct link and applicability to educational leadership.

Petta, K., Smith, R., & Chasling, M. (2018). Generative dialogue: A concept analysis. *Management in Education, 33*(2), 53–61. https://doi.org/10.1177/0892020618780978
This analysis offers an exploration of the concept of generative dialogue, written about as an emerging model in educational leadership and, additionally, in the areas of counselling education and psychology, business studies, and vocational education. The authors conclude that the primary common thread of generative dialogue's underpinnings and strategies is the engagement, shared trust, and mutual respect that results from "meaningful collegiate interactions." Petta et al. conclude that a generative dialogue is of value when leaders must straddle the dual roles of manager and practitioner. Furthermore, the authors contend that generative dialogue is a particularly useful set of skills that can contribute to Spillane's notion of distributed leadership.

Zepeda, S. J., Parylo, O., & Klar, H. W. (2017). Educational leadership for teaching and learning. In D. Waite & I. Bogotch (Eds.), *The Wiley international handbook of educational leadership* (pp. 227–252). Hoboken, NJ: John Wiley & Sons.
This chapter by Zepeda, Parylo, and Klar examines the state of educational leadership in relation to teaching and learning in the context of the fluid educational milieu that has developed since the 1980s. They touch on the trends in learning-centred leadership, instructional leadership, and distributed leadership. Additionally, Zepeda et al. consider the shifting role of the principal, the effect that central office inaction has on sustainable learning, and the possible future direction of leadership for teaching and learning.

NOTE

1. This section is adapted from Brandon, J., Friesen, S., Koh, K., Parsons, D., Adams, P., Mombourquette, C., & Hunter, D. (2018). *Building, supporting, and assuring quality professional practice: A research study of teacher growth, supervision, and evaluation in Alberta.* Edmonton, AB: Alberta Education.

REFERENCES

Alberta Education. (2018). *Leadership quality standard.* Edmonton, AB: Alberta Education. Retrieved from https://education.alberta.ca/media/3739621/standardsdoc-lqs-_fa-web-2018-01-17.pdf

Australian Institute for Teaching and School Leadership. (2012). *Australian charter for the professional learning of teachers and school leaders: A shared responsibility and commitment.* Melbourne, Australia: ATSCL.

Australian Institute for Teaching and School Leadership. (2014). *Australian professional standards for teachers.* Retrieved from http://www.aitsl.edu.au/ australian-professional-standards-for-teachers/standards/list

Australian Institute for Teaching and School Leadership. (2017). *Australian professional standards for teachers.* Retrieved from https://www.aitsl.edu.au/teach/standards

Bakkenes, I., Vermunt, J. D., & Webbels, T. (2010). Teacher learning in the context of educational innovation: Learning activities and learning outcomes of experienced teachers. *Learning and Instruction, 20*(6), 533–548.

Blase, J., & Blase, J. (1998). *Handbook of instructional leadership: How really good principals promote teaching and learning.* Thousand Oaks, CA: Corwin Press.

Blase, J., & Blase, J. (1999). Principals' instructional leadership and teacher development: Teachers' perspectives. *Educational Administration Quarterly, 35*(3), 349–378. doi:https:// doi.org/10.1177/0013161X99353003

Blase, J., & Blase, J. (2000). Effective instructional leadership: Teachers' perspectives on how principals promote teaching and learning in schools. *Journal of Educational Administration, 38*(2), 130–141.

Bossert, S., Dwyer, D., Rowan, B., & Lee, G. (1982). The instructional management role of the principal. *Educational Administration Quarterly, 18*(3), 34–64. doi:10.1177/00131 61X82018003004

Bouchamma, Y. (2005). Evaluating teaching personnel. Which model of supervision do Canadian teachers prefer? *Journal of Personnel Evaluation in Education, 18*(4), 289–308. doi:10.1007/s11092-007-9025-8

Brady, L. (2009). Shakespeare reloaded: Teacher professional development within a collaborative learning community. *Teacher Development, 13*(4), 335–348.

Brandon, J., Friesen, S., Koh, K., Parsons, D., Adams, P., Mombourquette, C., … Hunter, D. (2018). *Building, supporting, and assuring quality professional practice: A research study of teacher growth, supervision, and evaluation in Alberta.* Edmonton, AB: Alberta Education.

Bridges, E. (1967). Instructional leadership: A concept re-examined. *Journal of Educational Administration, 5*(2), 136–147. doi:https://doi.org/10.1108/eb009614

British Columbia Ministry of Education Governance and Legislation Branch. (2016). School Act. Victoria, BC: Queen's Publisher. Retrieved from http://www2.gov.bc.ca/assets/gov/ education/administration/legislation- policy/legislation/schoollaw/d/bcreg_26589.pdf

Bruce, C. D., Esmonde, I., Ross, J., Dookie, L., & Beatty, R. (2010). The effects of sustained classroom-embedded teacher professional learning on teacher efficacy and related student achievement. *Teaching and Teacher Education, 26*(8), 1598–1608. doi:https://doi. org/10.1016/j.tate.2010.06.011

Burns, D., & Darling-Hammond, L. (2014). *Teaching around the world: What can TALIS tell us.* Stanford, CA: Stanford Center for Opportunity Policy in Education.

Bush, T. (2011). *The importance of leadership and management for education* (4th ed.). Thousand Oaks, CA: Sage.

Butler, C., & Schnellert, L. (2012). Collaborative inquiry in teacher professional development. *Teaching and Teacher Education, 28*(2), 1206–1220.

California Commission on Teacher Credentialing. (2009). *California standards for the teaching profession.* Retrieved from https://www.ctc.ca.gov/docs/default-source/educator-prep/standards/cstp-2009.pdf

City, E., Elmore, R., Fiarman, S., & Teitel, L. (2009). *Instructional rounds in education: A network approach to improving teaching and learning.* Cambridge, MA: Harvard Education Press.

Darling-Hammond, L., & McLaughlin, M. W. (2011). Policies that support professional development in an era of reform. *Phi Delta Kappan, 92*(6), 81–92. doi:10.1177/003172171109200622

Darling-Hammond, L., & Richardson, N. (2009). Teacher learning: What matters? *Educational Leadership, 66*(5), 46–53.

Desimone, L. M. (2011). A primer on effective professional development. *Phi Delta Kappan, 92*(6), 68–71.

Edmonds, R. (1979). Effective schools for the urban poor. *Educational Leadership, 37,* 15–24.

Education Services Australia. (2012). *Teacher performance and development framework.* Retrieved from http://www.aitsl.edu.au/docs/default-source/professional-growth-resources/performance-and developmentresources/australian_teacher_performance_and_development_framework_august_2012.pdf

Elmore, R. (2000). *Building a new structure for school leadership.* Washington, DC: Albert Shanker Institute.

Ginsberg, M. B., & Murphy, D. (2002). How walkthroughs open doors. *Educational Leadership, 59*(8), 34–36.

Glanz, J. (2000). Supervision: Don't discount the value of the modern. In J. Glanz & L. Behar-Horenstein (Eds.), *Paradigm debates in curriculum and supervision: Modern and postmodern perspectives* (pp. 71–92). Westport, CT: Bergin and Garvey.

Glatthorn, A. A. (1997). *Differentiated supervision.* Alexandra, VA: Association for Supervision and Curriculum Development.

Glickman, C., Gordon, S., & Ross-Gordon, J. (2017). *Supervision and instructional leadership* (10th ed.). New York, NY: Pearson.

Goldring, E., Huff, H., May, H., & Camburn, E. (2008). School context and individual characteristics: What influences principal practice? *Journal of Educational Administration, 46*(3), 332–352. doi:https://doi.org/10.1108/09578230810869275

Government of Ontario. (2007). Education Act. Toronto, ON: Queen's Printer. (Original work published 1996). Retrieved from https://www.ontario.ca/laws/regulation/020099#BK4

Goverment of Saskatchewan. (2015). The Education Act. Regina, SK: Queen's Printer. Retrieved from http://www.publications.gov.sk.ca/freelaw/documents/English/Statutes/Statutes/E0-2.pdf

Guskey, T., & Yoon, K. (2009). What works in professional development? *Phi Delta Kappan, 90*(7), 495–500. doi:10.1177/003172170909000709

Halifax School Board. (2007). *Supervision and appraisal for school-based teaching and staff policy.* Retrieved from http://www.hrsb.ca/sites/default/files/hrsb/Downloads/pdf/board/policy/sectionD/D.008-appraisal-school-based-teaching-staff.pdf

Hallinger, P. (2003). Leading educational change: Reflections on the practice of instructional and transformational leadership. *Cambridge Journal of Education, 33*(3), 329–352.

Hallinger, P. (2005). Instructional leadership and the school principal: A passing fancy that refuses to fade away. *Leadership and Policy in Schools, 4*(3), 221–239. doi:10.1080/15700760500244793

Hallinger, P. (2011). A review of three decades of doctoral studies using the Principal Instructional Management Rating Scale: A lens of methodological progress in educational leadership. *Educational Administration Quarterly, 47*(2), 271–306. doi:https://doi.org/10.1177/0013161X10383412

Hallinger, P., Bickman, L., & Davis, K. (1996). School context, principal leadership and student achievement. *Elementary School Journal, 96*(5), 498–518.

Hallinger, P., & Heck, R. H. (1998). Exploring the principal's contribution to school effectiveness: 1980–1995. *School Effectiveness and School Improvement, 9*(2), 157–191.

Hallinger, P., & Heck, R. H. (2010). Leadership for learning: Does collaborative leadership make a difference in school improvement? *Educational Management Administration & Leadership, 38*(6), 654–678. doi:https://doi.org/10.1177/1741143210379060

Hallinger, P., & Murphy, J. (1985). Assessing the instructional management behaviour of principals. *The Elementary School Journal, 86*(2), 217–247.

Hallinger, P., & Murphy, J. F. (2012). Running on empty? Finding the time and capacity to lead learning. *NASSP Bulletin, 97*, 5–21. doi:https://doi.org/10.1177/0192636512469288

Hallinger, P., Murphy, J., Well, M., Mesa, R. P., & Mitman, A. (1983). School effectiveness: Identifying the specific practices, behaviors of the principal. *NASSP Bulletin, 67*(463), 83–91. doi:https://doi.org/10.1177/019263658306746314

Hallinger, P., & Wang, W. C. (2015). Assessing instructional leadership with the Principal Instructional Management Rating Scale. Switzerland: Springer.

Heck, R. (1993). School context, principal leadership, and achievement: The case of secondary schools in Singapore. *The Urban Review, 25*(3), 151–166.

Heck, R., Larson, T., & Marcoulides, G. (1990). Principal instructional leadership and school achievement: Validation of a causal model. *Educational Administration Quarterly, 26*, 94–125.

Hirsh, S., & Killion, J. (2009). When educators learn, students learn. *Phi Delta Kappan, 90*(7), 464–469.

Kiss, T. (2016). School-based teacher learning: A reflective approach. *Journal of Nusantara Studies (JONUS), 1*(2), 50–62.

Leithwood, K. (1994). Leadership for school restructuring. *Educational Administration Quarterly, 30*(4), 498–518. doi:10.1177/0013161x94030004006

Leithwood, K., Harris, A., & Hopkins, D. (2008). Seven strong claims about successful school leadership. *School Leadership & Management, 28*(1), 27–42. doi:https://doi.org/10.1080/13632430701800060

Leithwood, K., & Jantzi, D. (2006). Transformational school leadership for large-scale reform: Effects on students, teachers, and their classroom practices. *School Effectiveness & School Improvement, 17*(2), 201–227. doi:10.1080/09243450600565829

Leithwood, K., Seashore Louis, K., Anderson, S., & Wahlstrom, K. (2004). How leadership influences student learning. *Learning from Leadership Project.* Minneapolis, MN: Wallace Foundation.

Manitoba Teachers' Society. (2017). *Teacher evaluation.* Retrieved from http://www.mbteach.org/mtscms/2017/01/02/teacher-evaluation/.

Marks, H. M., & Printy, S. M. (2003). Principal leadership and school performance: An integration of transformational and instructional leadership. *Educational Administration Quarterly, 39*(3), 370–397. doi:https://doi.org/10.1177/0013161X03253412

Marshall, B. (2013). *Rethinking teacher supervision and evaluation: How to work smart, build collaboration, and close the achievement gap.* San Francisco, CA: Jossey-Bass.

Marshall, K. (2005). It's time to rethink teacher supervision and evaluation. *Phi Delta Kappan, 86*(10), 727–735.

Murphy, J., Elliot, S. N., Goldring, E., & Porter, A. C. (2006). *Learning-centered leadership: A conceptual framework.* Minneapolis, MN: Wallace Foundation.

Neumerski, C. M. (2012). Rethinking instructional leadership, a review: What do we know about principal, teacher, and coach instructional leadership, and where should we go from here? *Educational Administration Quarterly, 49*(2), 310–347.

Northwest Territories Ministry of Education, Culture and Employment. (2004). *Evaluation and promotion of professional growth for teachers in Northwest Territories schools.* Retrieved from https://www.ece.gov.nt.ca/sites/www.ece.gov.nt.ca/files/resources/ministerial_directive__evaluation_and_promotion_of_professional_growthfor_teachers_in_nwt_schools_2004.pdf.

Ontario College of Teachers. (2016). *Standards of practice.* Retrieved from https://www.oct.ca/public/professional-standards/standards-of-practice

Pajak, E. (2003). *Honoring diverse teaching styles: A guide for supervisors.* Alexandria, VA: Association for Supervision and Curriculum Development.

Province of Nova Scotia. (2016). *From school to success: Clearing the path: Report of the Transition Task Force.* Halifax, NS: Province of Nova Scotia. Retrieved from https://www.ednet.ns.ca/docs/fromschooltosuccess-clearingthepath.pdf

Purkey, S., & Smith, M. (1983). Effective schools: A review. *The Elementary School Journal, 83*(4), 426–452. doi:https://doi.org/10.1080/01619568409538458

Robinson, V. M. J., Lloyd, C. A., & Rowe, K. J. (2008). The impact of leadership on student outcomes: An analysis of the differential effects of leadership types. *Educational Administration Quarterly, 44*(5), 635–674.

Saskatchewan Teachers' Federation. (2016). *Teacher supervision and evaluatoin policy.* Retrieved from https://www.stf.sk.ca/sites/default/files/governance_handbook_policy_2_4.pdf

Seashore Louis, K., Dretzke, B., & Wahlstrom, K. (2010). How does leadership affect student achievement? Results from a national US survey. *School Effectiveness & School Improvement, 21*(3), 315–336. doi:10.1080/09243453.2010.486586

Seashore Louis, K., Leithwood, K., Wahlstrom, K. L., & Anderson, S. E. (2010). *Investigating the links to improved student learning: Final report of research findings Learning from Leadership Project.* Minneapolis, MN: Wallace Foundation.

Sergiovanni, T. J. (1992). Why we should seek substitutes for leadership. *Educational Leadership, 49*(5), 41–44.

Sergiovanni, T. J., & Starratt, R. J. (2007). *Supervision: A redefinition* (8th ed.). Boston, MA and Toronto, ON: McGraw-Hill.

Spillane, J. P., Halverson, R., & Diamond, J. B. (2001). Investigating school leadership practice: A distributed perspective. *American Educational Research Association, 30*(3), 23–28.

Taut, S., Santelices, M. V., Araya, C., & Manzi, J. (2011). Perceived effects and uses of the national teacher evaluation system in Chilean elementary schools. *Studies in Educational Evaluation, 37*(4), 218–229.

Vancouver Board of Education. (2013). *Provincial and local matters collective agreement.* Vancouver, BC. Retrieved from https://www.vsb.bc.ca/_layouts/vsbwww/arch/default/files/school-files/Employment/39-LK-2013-2019%20Final%20for%20signature%20Jan%2022%202016.pdf

Virginia Department of Education. (2012). *Virginia standards for the professional practice of teachers.* Retrieved from http://www.doe.virginia.gov/teaching/regulations/uniform_performance_stds_2011.pdf

Wei, R. C., Darling-Hammond, L., Andree, A., Richardson, N., & Orphanos, S. (2009). Professional learning in the learning profession: A status report on teacher development in the U.S. and abroad. Dallas, TX: National Staff Development Council.

Zepeda, S. J. (2000). *Instructional supervision: Applying tools and concepts.* New York, NY: Routledge.

Zepeda, S. J. (2017). *Instructional supervision: Applying tools and concepts* (4th ed.). New York, NY: Routledge.

Zepeda, S. J., & Lanoue, P. D. (2017). Conversation walks: Improving instructional leadership. *Educational Leadership, 74*(8), 58–61.

Zepeda, S. J., Parylo, O., & Klar, H. W. (2017). Educational leadership for teaching and learning. In D. Waite & I. Bogotch (Eds.), *The Wiley international handbook of educational leadership* (pp. 227–252). Hoboken, NJ: John Wiley & Sons.

CHAPTER EIGHT

Measuring Success

What Impacts Can Be Generated by Leading without Answers?

You have planted them, and they have taken root; they grow and bear fruit.
    —Jeremiah 12:2

In the midst of very busy jobs, where it is easy to get caught up in the day-to-day chaos, generative dialogue helps maintain clarity, making goals more attainable through specific actions. The process helps me recognize all the things we do and achieve together.
    —Retired superintendent

MEASURING SUCCESS

Over the last 15 years, nearly 1,000 schools that we are aware of have engaged with key principles, practices, and processes of the collaborative inquiry/generative dialogue model of leadership growth that is described in detail in this text. They range in size from large high schools with 1,500-plus students on the West Coast of Canada to a cohort of seven one-teacher schools in a remote district of New South Wales. They cover climatic zones from frigid to sub-tropical, and socioeconomic strata and diversity across the spectrum. What their leaders have in common is a willingness to explore new ways of thinking about the leadership of learning, a commitment to continuous growth, and a belief that schools—wherever they are—have a responsibility to provide the best possible quality of education to every student who comes into their care. We have been privileged to work with these educators, to learn and grow with them; it has been our good fortune to have observed their challenges and witness their successes and celebrations.

Fittingly, we have saved the final words for several of these powerful leaders who embrace the title of our book: who effectively inspire purpose and direction; who motivate, guide, and provoke collaboration and reflection; and who are tenacious in their commitment to growth, theirs and others'. And throughout the vicissitudes of leadership, they do it all with the tenet that doing so is more effective by simply asking powerful questions, rather than by preaching, telling, or judging.

Now, in this final chapter, we have invited superintendents, school leaders, and teachers to share their experiences, wisdom, and perspectives regarding the impact of generative leadership on professional practice. We begin with the case study of a most dramatic turnaround in school improvement using generative leadership. Next, three superintendents offer a systems perspective on the impact of generative leadership. This is followed by the views of four principals and two classroom teachers. We then present reflections from one international scholar who has been involved with generative leadership for seven years and conclude with final thoughts on our journey through generative leadership.

Case Study: Buffalo Berry High School Leaders Maximize Impact

We came from a very dark place. When we go back to the beginning and talk about the reputation of the school, reputation of the community, headlines in regional papers about us, it was bad. The large, big-city newspaper nearest to us printed an article titled "Violence Stalks the Halls of Buffalo Berry." That is what we were up against. So, we began this leadership work on the heels of what we considered to be a really negative school review and a professional and geographic community that had taken a lot of hard hits over the past four or five years. Although, at home, my partner reminded me that it could be worse: in the neighbouring community, the elementary school kids hadn't been able to use the playground for almost 18 months because raw sewage was settling into the land around the school and the facilities director wasn't able to find a company to drive the 90 minutes to the school to fix it.

To begin, our leadership team had to remove themselves emotionally from the public battering we were taking. I was in my office in July, staring at my bookshelf, and recalled reading a book called *The Wounded Leader* in a course taken as part of a professional development summer series. I had to admit, I hadn't given the book another thought since then; as with so many valuable resources on my desk, I just couldn't find the time to read anything other than report cards, budgets, annual plans, new system policies, and the occasional teacher growth plan. After taking a few days of purposefully setting some things aside to begin my reading (and allowing myself a short pity party!), I decided that I was going to choose to continue leading the school. On the advice of one of my young, new vice-principals, I reached out to an old mentor from my undergraduate days to see if she could offer us a new perspective on the situation. Maybe it wasn't as bad as I was imagining? Maybe there was an easy fix that someone from the outside could share?

Of course, it wasn't going to be as simple as that! After the first visit from my mentor, during which she visited all classrooms, she asked the leadership team some tough questions about the school culture, our vision for student success, our leadership styles, and the competence of our teachers. She then introduced us to the idea of generative leadership and asked us to consider if we were willing to commit to a three-year process to engage in a comprehensive and coordinated plan to improve the school. My athletic director, also a member of the leadership team, responded, "Of course! How much worse can it be than what we are doing now?"

Unfortunately, it had the potential to get even worse because we first had to tear down some walls of resistance that staff had built up. To do that, we were going to have to address a challenge that many high schools face—rethinking and reconstructing the time-honoured towers of subject-area isolation. Our team arranged to use our professional development money to attend a leadership conference and, on the last day of the conference, we had a one-on-one session with a researcher who spoke to our need to get into classrooms, have teachers focus on learning pedagogy in balance with content curriculum, and have teachers observe and learn from one another.

Our first success came when, in consultation with my mentor, I organized the October professional development day as one where all members of the school— including the caretakers— took a look at academic data, what parents were saying, what grades we were reporting, what teachers were saying about us, and, generally, whether we considered the school's path to be positive and conducive to student learning. After analyzing the school review data, we had the central office team and some other school principals come in for discussion. We identified areas within the school where we were doing okay, as well as areas that we believed needed some change. That seemed to provoke staff into wanting to act, so we immediately adjusted our work as leaders of learning to include four new components:

- We needed a triad of people involved in professional learning. We moved away from the idea that an administrator needed to be one of those people. We had a script for participants around their goals and had them construct an inquiry question. In short, we provided a fairly structured system for collaboration and modelled our leadership goals to staff in the form of inquiry-based professional learning.
- We scheduled classroom visitations for no less than once each month, meaning that every teacher was observed once a month by another teacher from another content area. Prior to this, every teacher was observed once a month by a member of the leadership team, as well as once a month by the assessment specialist and another teacher. We built on this system of supports by linking the observations to areas that teachers identified in their growth plans.
- We originally started the generative leadership project with math teachers sitting in math classes or English teachers sitting in English classes, but then we began removing these limits. We revised the timetable to allow the chemistry teacher to sit in an art class and look at the art teacher teaching. This allowed for some interesting questions that began to remove the isolation and divide among teachers.

continued

- Everything was driven by the generative dialogue questions—all of our strategies. When we talked about outcomes, assessments, or an attendance strategy, everything was driven by "in what ways" and "to what extent." We have this built into a professional goals plan, but we also threaded this format through everything in terms of strategy. If we wanted to give a detention to a student, we had to think about in what ways and to what extent we would improve the outcome for the student through the detention.

I think we have had a lot of successes over the past three years, but for the most part I think the biggest one is most shown through the huge buy-in from all staff. They are now willing to own responsibility for being the largest impact on student achievement and engagement. The school bus driver and the principal and the secretary are also part of the support, but it's the classroom teachers who have the largest interaction with the students and have the largest stake in this. From our perspective, there were three big areas of impact on our school that made the biggest difference in our school as we travelled down the generative leadership road:

- Leadership groups—I knew we had teachers in every bubble. Whether they were hostile to change or deeply committed to change, we had to move everyone along the continuum of growth. At different stages we were able to do that.
- Shared decision making—When we talked with the teachers, they often felt all these new things were coming from the principal. We needed to be sure that teachers felt they had input and this wasn't all top-driven.
- Changing classrooms—From places of teaching to places of learning. We had teachers who had planned their classes for the year and nothing was going to deter them. But it wasn't about their teaching breakdown; it was whether or not the children understood it.

Case Study Reflections: Leading for Impact

- What areas of impact are identified in this case? Which resonate most with you?
- Compare the advantages and disadvantages of traditional high school models that minimize interdisciplinary collaboration and inquiry-based professional learning.
- How can leaders effectively present student learning or other data to staff in ways that avoid defensiveness, disengagement, or hostility?
- What is the biggest assumption about high schools that prevents paradigmatic shifts in teaching and learning?
- What do you accept as measures of impact of your leadership?

SUPERINTENDENTS' PERSPECTIVES

The following three Canadian superintendents—Piet Langstraat, Cheryl Gilmore, and Kurt Sacher—illustrate how their commitment to generative leadership has impacted various aspects of their organization.

Superintendent Piet Langstraat

One of the things I found over my time as a school and system leader is that sitting in my office coming up with wonderful plans for the improvement of my school district got us nowhere. What I really needed to do was tap into the passions of the individuals within my school district—all of them, including students. After multiple years of trying the top-down approach, I came to the realization that this is not what it is all about.

In my view, 70 percent of all change initiatives fail. Why is that? I would argue the reason is that there is a very top-down approach, with hierarchical reporting lines, and with expectations that those being directed would enthusiastically join in simply because they were told to do something. But that's not how it works. Learning and leadership are very personalized and internalized. I would stand up and flap my arms, carry on and say "This is the direction we all need to go." What I got in return was people charging off in all directions, but what I really wanted was people to reflect and think about how my ideas connected with theirs. I now think of planning in terms of generative dialogue, but also in terms of generative planning. I start by asking people "What keeps you up at night?" and "What is the one thing that you are passionate about changing within your school?"

In Canada, each school district is expected to have a district education plan, and each individual school is expected to have a school plan. When going through the process of building an education plan, I start by getting input through face-to-face meetings and online sources. I also implement supports unique to our version of generative planning that go beyond the 30-day generative dialogue conversations I have with my school leaders. During this stage, I start by asking:

1. What's important around here?
2. What troubles you about the education system?
3. What hopes, aspirations, and needs are not being met?

The answers to these fundamental questions allow our leadership team to then build our school district education plan, reflecting the goals of our school district. Now, when I go out and talk to school principals and ask how they see themselves reflected in the plan, they can answer, because they were involved in collectively building it. I firmly believe that being able to see oneself within the plan leads to real commitment, and evidence from our practice of generative planning clearly supports that conclusion.

Once every month, I schedule time for generative dialogue with all my school leaders. This consists of two interconnected elements that I call intentional inquiry and deliberate dialogue.

Intentional Inquiry

It's not about setting a goal; it's about asking a question. It is interesting to set a goal such as "I want to improve the graduation rates of Indigenous students by 5 percent." However, I would argue that it is more impactful for me to ask a question such as "If I combine culture, language, and pedagogy for Indigenous students, can I improve their academic outcomes?" That promotes a very different kind of process and, if I think about myself as an adult learner, it very much connects for me. Once I started asking deeper and richer questions, my work was transformed.

Deliberate Dialogue

As I learned more about the generative dialogue process, I just kept showing up and questioning school leaders about what they really needed and what they were really curious about. In the beginning it took about six months to get them to identify the real question they were passionate about. At first, busy principals saw it as just another box to check. It took them a little while to realize that I was authentically curious about that which they were most curious about in their own practice. Once people understood that I actually wanted to know, they began to fully engage.

What I found to be so fascinating about the whole generative dialogue process was that I never once had to say to anyone "Our goal is to increase literacy or increase high school completion rates." I simply had to ask "What do you want to work on; what are you passionate about; what are you worried about; how can I support you?" They took ownership of the process and truly ran with the ball that was given to them.

Yet my experience tempers my naïveté. I have had some very resistant principals. While it may sound simplistic, I just kept showing up even with the most resistant ones. I remained a genuinely curious person and, in the end, I even developed a curiosity about the nature of the resistance I encountered. When I ran into someone who was resistant, I just kept asking them questions. I didn't return to a telling mode. I reminded myself that everybody is competent. At the same time, I recognized that this didn't necessarily mean they were functioning at all times at a level that would truly promote student learning. I would say to myself, "A leader can be competent but also low functioning." When I would say that to my school leaders, they didn't really believe me at first. But when they realized that I had a five-year contract and was going to keep coming back, most engaged in the process. This meant they took increasing levels of responsibility for their own learning and professional growth.

One of the neat extensions that I embedded into our practice of generative dialogue was focus on collective inquiry. We would ask our school-based leadership teams questions, such as "What's your team inquiry?" or "What are you curious about as an individual and what are you curious about as a team?" The practice of asking for a collective inquiry question was something that had a great impact on those who were resistant. For example, if I was working with a grumpy old principal who was not really engaged but who had two really engaged deputy principals, the process naturally encouraged the principal toward greater participation. I really worked hard at doing both: individual inquiry and collective inquiry. The collective inquiry wasn't meant to be a pressure technique, but it did tend to light some fires that led to increased participation.

Somewhere along the way, I realized that typical leadership development programs simply do not work. When I think about leadership development programs that I have been involved in as a participant or that I have subjected others to over the years, there is a strange dynamic at play. Typically, a one-size-fits-all approach is delivered managerially, where someone is positioned as having this incredible wisdom to share, and participants will be awed and amazed as they somehow learn. Another problem is that these events are not rooted in the day-to-day challenges faced by leaders. Speakers show up, present ideas, and, come hell or high water, expect to impress the gathered throng with their message. Most of these programs focus on techniques rather than individual needs of participants. Importantly, there is no accountability after these events. People leave these events without the knowledge and skills necessary to implement what they have learned. Consequently, they quickly revert to previous ways of thinking or working.

An important discovery that I made about growth is that learning to lead is developed *in* the work, not in isolation *from* the work. That's a really key principle. When I didn't immerse my learning in my work, it became misguided. Leadership growth has to be embedded in day-to-day work. It needs to be personal, contextual, regular, and collaborative. Most of all, it needs to lead to concrete action and personal accountability. It is this power of personal accountability that makes a huge difference. Muddling through and making mistakes were the things I learned from and remember.

Generative dialogue is not only about causing people to *think* differently, it motivates them to *act* differently. Generative dialogue highlights the unique skills, talents, and needs that we have as individuals. It breaks down hierarchy and reporting lines, and expands influence. Generative dialogue enriches culture. I believe it is not my job as a leader to create a whole bunch of people who think the way I do. The most diverse eco systems are the strongest.

SUPERINTENDENT DR. CHERYL GILMORE

Over the past three years, our school district has supported the development of generative leadership and has infused an inquiry model of professional learning. As an educational leader, I have always believed strongly in the power of coherence across a system. The underlying premise that guided my work was that purposeful and sustained change requires the kind of systems thinking that Peter Senge wrote about in the early 1990s. In my experience, our efforts to implement these strategies met with varying levels of success. While the strategies were successful in moving our system forward in a variety of ways, there was not a strong sense of coherence or evidence that how we *think* about purposeful growth and change was embedded and sustainable.

When our district embarked on the generative leadership project in partnership with the university, I anticipated that there would be particular outcomes based on the researchers' work with other districts within and outside the province of Alberta. These outcomes are coming to fruition. The first part of the project, supported in part through the Alberta Research Network,[1] was implementation of a collaborative inquiry model to examine the readiness and awareness of school leaders preparing to enact the Alberta *Leadership Quality Standard* (Alberta Education, 2018). I anticipated that the process would build knowledge and efficacy among district and school leaders. This proved to be true. I also anticipated that leaders across the district would come to recognize the benefit of an inquiry-based model of professional learning. This proved to be true in a way that far exceeded my expectations. Leaders across the district not only recognize the benefit, they are excited about it and repeatedly express how using generative dialogue has compelled them to become reflective in their leadership practice and grow as leaders.

School and district leaders used an inquiry question as the foundation for their professional growth plans. Their questions were generated through their deep thinking about what made them curious and kept them awake at night in concert with their reflection on the competencies delineated in the *Leadership Quality Standard*. All schools were required to have a school leadership team question and could also choose to have an individual question.

District-level leaders started by visiting schools in pairs to engage all school leadership teams in generative dialogue. University experts modelled the process and provided support and advice. While I expected that the process would compel deeper reflection on leaders' practice and growth, I did not anticipate the level to which they developed commitment to the process of generative dialogue. This was aided by the steadfastness of district leader pairs to keep to their scheduled visitations and adhere to the underlying assumptions of generative dialogue. As district leaders, we learned that generative dialogue is a skill that takes time and practice to develop. Being true to the underlying assumptions, what Dr. Adams and Dr. Mombourquette refer to as "requisite habits of mind," takes more of a conscious effort and planning ahead than one might think. Generative dialogue facilitators cannot have preconceived notions about what they believe the school leadership team needs to work on. This is a shift in mindset. It is not about reviewing school improvement plans, compelling the administrative team to develop strategies to address gaps identified by system leaders, or developing a question or strategies that fit nicely with district priorities. It is about suspending judgment and believing that all leaders are competent and capable of creating a question that will contribute to their growth as leaders. It is about what *they* are passionate about and committed to exploring. It was somewhat surprising to me how much conscious effort it takes to be 100 percent genuine in listening in a manner that helps frame questions to compel deeper thinking about another's inquiry, learning, and strategies, not my own.

To say that the excitement and commitment of school leaders to an inquiry model using generative dialogue was immediate and without some barriers would not be true. While some leaders were early adopters, other school leaders began the process with the conviction that "this too shall pass." Some perceived this work to be an added burden requiring time, effort, and additional commitment that would go away. I believe that three important factors changed this belief. First, as already mentioned, it was imperative that the district leaders did not cancel or postpone meetings. The modelling of absolute commitment to the school teams fostered trust and a belief that they were valued. Second, working hard to adhere to the "habits of mind" resulted in greater trust, with school leaders feeling more supported in their growth. They came to understand that the meetings were not about judgment or hidden agendas. Third, having the university experts work with the entire district leadership team on an ongoing basis gave the process a research-based credibility that was direct and effective. Sessions were scheduled throughout the year for all leaders, which deepened their understanding of an inquiry model and generative dialogue.

Our next phase, that of implementing the inquiry model using generative dialogue with all teachers in the district, is a challenge that I believe our leaders are up to. What I did not anticipate at the beginning of this initiative is the degree to which school leaders have assumed ownership over the process of implementing the model with their staff. I was somewhat surprised when administrators collaboratively developed implementation structures and worked diligently to develop a roll-out that would be common across schools. Our work with university colleagues provides guidance and time for reflection on how the process is going. School leaders recognize the barrier of time but are being creative in finding time to engage their staff. This commitment can be attributed to their strong belief in the difference reflective inquiry can have on instructional practice. There is variance across the school teams with respect to their perceived level of expertise in engaging staff in generative dialogue, but there is no shortage of commitment to a process they believe in. This commitment is an outcome of their own successful journey in self-reflection and their development of a growth mindset.

After three years of collaboration with our university partners, maintaining a strong commitment to a process that began with foundational knowledge and progressed to the development of skills through practice, I feel that generative leadership is changing how we think about learning as leaders, professionals, and staff across a district. This way of thinking can be described as a culture becoming imbued with a growth mindset and greater coherence. There is a common belief in the power of reflective practice and a growing understanding of how generative leadership practices impact instruction and student learning. School leaders are becoming more skilled in selecting evidence that will answer their inquiry and better able to imagine what the final step will look like. What is the final step?

The final step is when the inquiry model using generative dialogue becomes seamless with instructional supervision. It will be the staff members' inquiry that focuses supervisory attention and support. As staff develop skills and move forward with reflective practice in structures that provide for both collaboration and autonomy, and leaders support this practice as skilled facilitators, we will move closer to being a learning system that is coherent. I believe that with continued work we will, indeed, not only have common understandings about purposeful growth and change, we will have capacity at all levels for it to be embedded and sustained.

Superintendent Kurt Sacher

My involvement in collaborative inquiry and generative dialogue has solidified my commitment to staff development that is organic, authentic, learner driven, and supported over time. I am convinced that all meaningful educational change comes from within, where the learner is both challenged and supported by thoughtful questions and an ongoing openness to the latest educational research.

From a skill perspective, I have become better at asking thought-provoking questions, providing quality support, being more in touch with the current reality my colleagues face, and being more aware that people need to be supported to solve their own problems rather than have them solved for them. I have also become more skilled at preparing school board members for the importance of not only having a plan but having one that we stick to for years. This sustained focus of the plan helps school leaders do their best work because they know when we do something that it is not going to disappear in exchange for a different flavour of the month.

I have learned to show my own vulnerability as a learning leader and to model for school leaders how they can do the same at their sites. As I have become better at blending a balance of challenge and support over time with our school leaders, I have learned that I need to be directly involved to demonstrate the importance of our work. I need to promote the notion of standing *beside* rather than *above* my colleagues. When the system aligns in that way, it is powerful, from the classroom to the boardroom. When we engage people from within, in a model that challenges and supports, we get high levels of ownership and learning from everyone.

I have seen our leaders get better at supporting their staff, asking more thought-provoking questions, and listening more than they talk. I have seen leadership confidence grow as they learn the power a question has to promote thought and action, even in areas where they have little or no subject area expertise. I have seen them model higher levels of collaboration to other leaders as a result of our work with the university researchers.

I see our teachers more comfortable with school leaders in their classrooms and working alongside them to grow their professional practice. I see them obtaining increased student achievement results on standardized tests and in key literacy assessments. I see them continuing to be better at effective collaboration with their peers, and I see them bringing our quality learning environments (QLE) to life in every one of our classrooms.

JOURNAL REFLECTIONS AND WRITING PROVOCATIONS ON SUPERINTENDENTS GENERATING IMPACT

- The idea of system leaders asking questions rather than giving answers seems …
- The views of these superintendents are different from or similar to …
- The impact of a superintendent asking questions would cause me to …

CENTRAL OFFICE LEADERS' PERSPECTIVES

Next, we present reflections from three former school leaders who now hold central office positions. Terry Moghrabi, Rob Moltzahn, and James Hansen offer their perspectives on how their involvement in generative leadership has impacted their professional learning.

Associate Superintendent Terry Moghrabi

As I reflect on what practices and research I employed to improve my own leadership skills, I can say with certainty that my time working on generative dialogue has had the greatest impact on my career. It helped me become an effective instructional leader, knowing what to do to influence teacher efficacy and lead learning as the principal of a rural high school. The countless generative dialogue conversations I had with colleagues and university researchers provoked and challenged me to move away from problems and excuses toward practices and solutions that could foster learning for staff and students. I felt it was imperative to shift our classrooms away from places of teaching to places of learning. We did this by focusing on engaged teaching and authentic assessment. It was not easy; it took several years as we learned to work together, reflecting not only on what needed to be taught, but how to engage all learners.

Some of the most powerful inquiry that we undertook ignited thoughtful reflection on questions such as "How will we know that the students have learned the outcomes?" and "What will we do to ensure that those who didn't yet learn will still get the chance to learn the outcomes?" We framed our goal in a guiding question, constantly asking "In what ways and to what extent do our strategies impact student achievement?"

As a leadership team, we were committed to purposeful conversations with teachers and students, always trying to foster growth and learning. As we honed our knowledge and skills, we built greater trust with our teachers. Many became role models for each other by participating in a strategic peer-coaching model. They contributed to a major change in our high school as they led the way with classroom visits and rich conversations about learning. We could see the typical isolation of a department-style school shift to a more collaborative culture. The more teachers took control over their own learning, and classroom leadership, the more confident and competent I felt as a school leader.

In turn, we saw the changes in our students. They felt valued and cared for by all the adults in the building. They tried harder. Their results continued to improve, year after year. The power of collaborative inquiry and generative dialogue came into my learning journey at a most fortunate time, as it did for many of my colleagues. I believe the ripples of the influence of this work will be felt for decades in my school and throughout our district.

Associate Superintendent Rob Moltzahn

Several years ago, my superintendent invited me to participate in a district-wide project that promised to support leadership growth and teacher efficacy. Not only have I been genuinely interested in these two themes over the course of my career, but I have consistently sought out professional learning opportunities that would improve my leadership capacity, especially as it relates to helping teachers.

During the project, we were introduced to processes of instructional leadership focusing on collaborative inquiry and generative dialogue. Almost immediately, I began to work differently with staff and saw success. In the second and third year, I was more convinced that this was valuable work, and I became increasingly invested. I concentrated on helping teachers become more reflective on their own teaching practices and, critically, the impact of their teaching on student achievement. I met with teachers frequently and, using the skills of generative dialogue, I was able to help them experience greater confidence in their teaching practice.

In my opinion, this model of generative leadership transformed my work as a school leader. I learned how to ask questions, but also when to be silent and listen. I was able to hear things I had not heard in the past, which helped me ask better, more pertinent questions. I believe that this process helped me become more useful to teachers in their professional growth and self-reflection, which related directly to the student-centred decisions they were making in the classroom. The process has been effective in changing the way that I think, listen, and speak in both my professional and personal life.

District Principal James Hansen

I began my involvement with the collaborative inquiry, generative dialogue, and generative leadership model over two years ago by spending several days visiting other school jurisdictions that were using them. Then, under the direction of the superintendent, I helped lead the implementation of a leadership growth initiative in our district.

I believe my growth has been particularly profound in learning to work with colleagues using generative dialogue. I learned to make sure to begin with genuine curiosity. I learned to listen more carefully to what people were saying and to concentrate on their ideas rather than trying to direct their thinking. I learned to help people focus on what was particularly important to *them*, to look carefully at their own assumptions, and to help them reflect on strategies and practices they might want to use. I became more skillful in helping colleagues connect their daily work to the big ideas that motivate them. Interestingly, listening better and being more curious about colleagues soon spread to all areas of my practice.

In addition, having someone else *lead me* in the generative dialogue process has been a very effective way of helping me clarify critical aspects of my professional practice, causing me to think more deeply about what I am using as evidence, and bringing passion and enthusiasm more often into my practice. Moreover, when things seem to be getting difficult, I look to meeting with my generative dialogue partner to help me figure out better ways to move forward.

JOURNAL REFLECTIONS AND WRITING PROVOCATIONS ON CENTRAL OFFICE LEADERS GENERATING IMPACT

- School and central office leadership both require ...
- The value of experiencing the generative dialogue as a leader is ...
- I could use generative dialogue in my personal life when ...

PRINCIPALS' PERSPECTIVES

As with so many other aspects of educational transformation, the school principal is at the nexus. We now present the views of four current principals. Janeen Silcock, Greg Armstrong, Topher Macintosh, and David Silcock describe how their participation in generative leadership has impacted nearly every aspect of their professional lives.

Principal Janeen Silcock

As a principal I saw myself as articulate, supportive, and compassionate. In 2015, I began a generative dialogue journey that created an opportunity to take the best parts of my leadership and make them even better.

As educators, we choose to be in a relationship with young people. They come with warts, delights, and much more. These young people have brains that are in a stage of exuberance: challenging, creating, fighting, or taking flight. They are unpredictable, influenced by peers, and trying to find where they fit, who they are, and who they want to be. Some staff are still in these throes as well! Every day, individuals come to school trying to be the best version of themselves at that point in time. Some have a warm bed and a person who cares about them, someone to pack their lunch, someone to come home to at the end of the day. Some are not so lucky and school becomes as important to their well-being as their learning. The social nature of schools and the quality of relationships developed there are central to growth. All of us in schools want to love and be loved, and to be valued for who we are and what we do.

In my leadership journey, I realized that I had been having many conversations in my daily life but was surprised to acknowledge that I had been having the most frequent conversation with one person: me. According to Dene Rossouw (2012), generative dialogue creates something new by generating hope through the flow of meaning.

For me, engaging in generative dialogue gives me permission to be the best kind of teacher by being both a learner and a student. It gives me permission to not know. It allows me to be curious, with no time constraints. Generative dialogue allows me to sit on the edge of being brave and frightened. Generosity of spirit, time, and knowledge is key. I can revel in the suspension of judgment and delight in having the opportunity to chat.

Generative dialogue is a means through which I experience celebratory, considered, and quality conversations. It can also lead to courageous discussions that sometimes need to happen in order to keep students at the centre.

So what has changed, if anything? Everything has changed except the nature of our students and staff: they still want to be loved and respected, they still want to belong, and they still want to learn. We found time to have quality conversations during which we listened, learned, collaborated, and celebrated learning for staff and students. That time was regularized and protect. As well, our participation was evidence based. We had to be brave and accept that being brave meant being a little bit afraid. As a leader, I had to learn to listen with my mouth shut and I had to stop rescuing. Regular participation in generative dialogue has given me a way to be brave, deliberate, and valued. In the words of Dr. Seuss, it celebrates "youness."

In 2015, I started my own exploration of generative dialogue, and eight members of my school executive joined me. In 2016, 42 executives were on board. In 2017, we had 90 staff involved in 30-day conversations. In 2018, it became "just the way we do things." In 2019, we are rolling the process out to our students.

I believe my commitment to the collaborative inquiry/generative dialogue process is the best investment I could have made for myself, for every staff member, and for every student. It has been the best thing I could do for my heart, my head, and my school.

Principal Greg Armstrong

When I became the acting principal of a very large school, I quickly became aware that we did not put students first. The members of our executive were not united and were often argumentative. Our decision-making processes were inadequate at a time of great flux in our organization. I knew we really had to find better ways to focus on students and their needs, but I wasn't sure I knew how to make that happen. I challenged all 23 members of the school executive to help me build the structures and develop the processes that would contribute most to our professional growth and our success with students.

As part of my own learning, I got involved in generative dialogue with a university colleague, a fellow principal, my director, and two researchers. They all helped me formulate my own professional development plan goals. As part of that plan, I set out to develop a more functional and cohesive core executive at my school. In a move that helped us become more trusting of each other, we committed to a once-weekly meeting; a *safe* round table at which we could openly discuss issues and options in a way that promoted collaboration, without prejudice or reprisal. Sometimes we met more often. One of our earliest actions was to create detailed roles and responsibilities for all executive members. A second was the introduction of monthly *conversations for growth* using a generative dialogue approach.

Within a year, we were able to involve all staff in a professional learning day at which everyone contributed to an exploration of the question "What is most important to us?" The results were encouraging. In particular, a large majority of teachers identified impact on students, inspiration of students, and quality of student work as three of the most important answers.

When I moved into a new principal position, I continued to make collaborative inquiry and generative dialogue central to my own growth and leadership. I have maintained an ongoing professional partnership with several members of the university team, meeting with them three times a year for the last four years. Through this collaborative work, I believe I have demonstrated the capacity to build a cohesive leadership team capable of creating and sustaining strategic directions that are focused on improving student performance. My involvement in this work has had a profound impact on my leadership growth more than any other experience in my career.

Principal Topher Macintosh

My experience in learning about and practising generative dialogue stands as a highlight in my career. It has involved some of my most interesting and practical professional learning. The conversational nature of the work has enabled me to bring it directly into my building, where I am now sharing it with my vice-principal and teachers. Beyond the clear benefit of collegial conversations, the generative dialogue process provides genuine growth and leadership opportunities, as colleagues share their ideas, goals, and strategies in order to improve their practice. There is nothing top-down about it.

When I am the focus of a generative dialogue, I find I am able to organize and clarify my thoughts around those aspects of my own practice I am hoping to refine. I respond very positively to the trust and respect modelled by the facilitator.

When I first assumed the questioning role, I was bent on providing advice. Since then, I have learned to start with a genuinely curious approach. This has been a most valuable element of generative dialogue for me. I can now let the questions lead the learning and not try to provide solutions for every problem. It is much more effective when my colleagues, through reflection, are able to make their own decisions about their professional practice.

Principal David Silcock

In 2012, I had been an educator for over 30 years and felt very lucky to have been a part of a profession that had been both rewarding and enjoyable. As a school principal, I had built my leadership practices around a passionate belief in the importance of cooperative practice, quality professional learning, and a commitment to continuous improvement. Yet for a number of years I had experienced a mild, underlying feeling of professional isolation. This puzzled me because I worked regularly and productively with other principals, my school director, and other educational leaders. I came to realize this was because the interactions were primarily task or system orientated; regrettably, meaningful personalized professional interactions seemed to occur only when we were supporting colleagues during critical incidents.

During a chance meeting and conversation with David Townsend in 2012, I was introduced to some of the leadership work that was occurring in parts of Canada. I was introduced to the concepts of collaborative inquiry and generative dialogue, and the differences between cooperation, collegiality, and collaboration. It was at this point that I identified what was contributing to my underlying feeling of professional isolation: I believed that school leaders with whom I associated had high levels of collegiality and cooperation but needed to improve in substantive collaborative practice. I became convinced that the collaborative inquiry/generative dialogue process, with its emphasis on 30-day conversations, provided a sustainable framework for a more authentic form of collaboration for school leaders and school communities.

This is what we have sought to do in northern New South Wales since 2012. A growing number of educational leaders from schools, network offices, and Southern Cross University have supported school leaders, through regular 30-day visits, to reflect on evidence of impact derived from guiding questions linked to professional growth.

In my school we send two members of our leadership team to visit Byron Bay High School every 30 days (twice per school term). Over the course of the school day, we meet with members of their school leadership team (two or three at a time) to talk about the guiding questions that frame their performance and development plan. They describe what they have done over the last 30 days, what they have learned, what their evidence is (often showing us examples), and what they intend to do for the next 30 days. Our role is to be genuinely curious (something that is easy to do), to suspend judgment, and to ask questions that aid the flow of the conversation. We never miss these meetings, and that, in itself, is a powerfully affirming activity. Twice a term, Byron Bay High School sends two school leaders to Alstonville High to replicate the process. We are in our third year of this collaborative inquiry partnership, and commitment to the process continues to grow. Each of our head teachers and deputy principals also holds 30-day conversations with teachers, and I schedule quality conversations with all head teachers each term. In 2019, we are introducing to our students the concept of regular peer-led collaborative inquiry around learning goals. We have built in weekly time slots for all students to meet in small groups with a learning coach so they can develop learning plans and reflect on how these are aiding their progress.

Whilst we still have a way to go in our journey toward building consistent practice across the whole school community, for the first time since I have been a school leader I believe we have a framework and philosophy that offers a way of building healthy and functional teams. We have moved beyond cooperative and collegial practice toward genuinely authentic collaboration. We have learned the lesson that achieving growth occurs one small step at a time.

Personally, in those periods of professional life when things get crazy busy, I now find more success in managing the stress associated with competing demands on my time and energy by coming back to my guiding questions, reflecting on my core priorities, and ensuring that I continue to direct my staff's professional efforts toward inquiry that we consider essential to our growth as a learning community.

JOURNAL REFLECTIONS AND WRITING PROVOCATIONS ON PRINCIPALS GENERATING IMPACT

- When a principal lets go of the need to provide answers …
- The dangers of a principal continually asking questions might be …
- I see the links between the role of a principal and student learning to be …

TEACHER PERSPECTIVES

We turn now to the perspective of a teacher who implemented generative dialogue with two of her colleagues as they collaborated around their professional practice.

Teacher Michelle McNulty

Yesterday, I met with two of my colleagues for our first check-in since we created our initial inquiry question. Both colleagues were eager to start, and both agreed that "they had never been so prepared for a meeting in their entire career" because they had followed through with their commitments and were eager to go.

As I went through the generative dialogue process with one of them, I realized the importance of asking the right question at the right time. At one point, I knew I needed to go deeper so I asked a question (I don't even remember what it was), and my colleague made a face and said, "Oh man, this turned from easy to hard!" I knew I had stumbled onto an area of need, and what was so important was that she knew it too. Interestingly, something similar happened through my questioning of the third member of our team.

It was then that I knew that generative dialogue was working. I was learning a lot, and they were both ready to further challenge themselves. I initially thought that I had taken the easy way out by choosing to work with two colleagues with whom I am very close. However, the process helped us get deeper really fast. They were not afraid to answer deep questions and, together, we were able to explore assumptions that were created from past experiences. We now have a solid foundation of trust, and it is clear that anything can be said during our collaborative time without fear of judgment.

At the end of these sessions, we are drained because we know that we have discovered additional areas of professional growth that we are ready to reflect on and tackle as a team. My colleagues indicated that they may not be so open to doing this with a school leader, but they felt that perhaps they could work with a teacher mentor, especially during their first year. They believe the process is meaningful and are eager to continue to answer their inquiry question.

JOURNAL REFLECTIONS AND WRITING PROVOCATIONS ON TEACHERS GENERATING IMPACT

- When colleagues engage in professional conversations with each other, there is potential for …
- In some schools, the generative dialogue could not occur among teachers because …
- The power of teachers engaging in generative dialogue is …

UNIVERSITY PARTNERS' PERSPECTIVES

We maintain that one of the advantages of the generative dialogue is its applicability to a variety of contexts. We have also observed that the skills of generative dialogue can be used by those in a variety of formal and informal leadership roles: teachers, lead teachers, department heads, learning coaches, school leaders, consultants, directors, district leaders, and superintendents. To this list we add university partners, who can play an important role in igniting, activating, and inspiring commitment to the collaborative inquiry/generative dialogue process as it is embedded in our model of generative leadership. Dr. Chaseling provides such an example.

Professor Marilyn Chaseling

I was an established academic when I first observed the collaborative inquiry approach in Canadian schools nearly 10 years ago. At that time, some schools were being funded through a ministry initiative that infused extra per student dollars into this work. Over time, as I stayed in contact with a respected Albertan academic, I began to imagine the great potential that this could have for my colleagues and me with school leaders in Australia. We took the leap into collaborative inquiry and generative dialogue as a way to support schools' focus on improving teacher effectiveness and student outcomes.

Since 2014, a voluntary alliance has been forged between eight university academics, six ministry senior educators, and approximately 80 principals and assistant principals, aimed at the leadership growth of school leaders. Over this time, most school leader participants have developed skills of conflict management and dialogue beyond what might have reasonably been expected had they not been part of this initiative. As well, most are more confident that, in their professional work, they are better able to demonstrate that they are meeting or exceeding the national standards of practice for school leaders.

Furthermore, in increasing numbers of schools, the formation and growth of teams of educators committed to collaboration around the achievement of agreed-upon goals marks an identifiable shift in the culture of these schools. Similarly, participating schools are better able to use evidence to show areas of improvement, changes in practice, and gaps in development. As research partners, we have identified a critical mass of early-adopting schools in which student achievement outcomes have improved in concert with the schools' participation in this work.

The continuing expansion of networks of schools, all helping each other grow and succeed, has been more evident through this initiative than in any other in which I have engaged. In growing numbers, educators have transformed their professional learning experiences from a series of unrelated events to ongoing inquiries into the many ways in which their growth in practice can impact the most important measures of school success. Importantly, quality relationships between schools and the university have become a signature part of our partnership.

And yet challenges remain. As more schools signal their hope to be included in the initiative, we need more educators ready and willing to serve as leaders of learning. At present, skillful leaders are being asked to give more time and energy than they can reasonably be expected. In addition, in a massive public school system known for its dual elements of centralized and local control, an initiative as organic as this one—in which success depends as much on shared responsibility as on directive leadership—is not easily grafted onto existing cultural values, traditional structures, and taken-for-granted beliefs about what can and should be attempted in the name of public education. Innovative practices take time.

Much of the actual impact of this initiative still needs to be assessed, documented, and reported upon through rigorous research. The process has begun, but the dissemination of verifiable research findings lags behind the lived experiences of a great majority of educators whose commitment to the initiative has been career-altering. Accordingly, in the near future, researchers will produce a thorough documentation of impact on educators, schools, and students. Further efforts will be made to involve more Department of Education directors in leadership of the implementation of processes and practices across a broader range of schools.

Early signs are positive that participation in collaborative inquiry and generative dialogue has strengthened school leaders' capacity to engage all staff in school improvement processes with high levels of initiative-taking, productivity, enthusiasm, and mutual respect, and a focus on learning.

FINAL REFLECTIONS AND WRITING PROVOCATIONS: LEADING FOR IMPACT

Now that you have had at least six opportunities to engage in free-form writing to foster insight reflection, we offer you some final provocations for your 30-minute reflective writing:

- Questions that I would like to ask all of these leaders are ...
- The impact that I hope to have as a result of my generative leadership is ...
- My most enduring conclusions about generative leadership are that ...

OUR FINAL WORDS

Among us, we have a combined 120 years of educational experience as classroom teachers, school and district leaders, university researchers, and university leaders. That fact alone probably makes it more difficult for us to identify with real certainty those aspects of professional practice, culture, and educational leadership that contribute most to student success in public schools. Nevertheless, over the last two decades we have increasingly championed the value of collaboration, curiosity, partnerships, professional discipline, and evidence in helping schools provide an enhanced quality of learning experiences for the students they serve.

We see successful schools as those in which most of the adults are collectively committed to the needs of every student, where every student receives some quality teacher-time every day, where teams of educators work purposefully toward the achievement of agreed-upon goals, and in which the leadership of learning is enacted as a shared responsibility. We don't think many would argue against this proposition. However, in practice, there are times when the day-to-day realities of schools can threaten to overwhelm the best intentions of even the most dedicated educators.

Accordingly, we have not written this text to honour just a small number of teachers and formal leaders who have risen to a lofty pinnacle in some mythical educational pantheon. We are convinced by our lived experiences that the ideas, skills, processes, practices, and methods described throughout this text have direct applicability to any school or district in which educators are prepared to take up the challenge of continuous improvement over the span of their careers. We would argue that includes most of them.

We have seen that a central office staff alone cannot make schools better, nor can school leaders, acting alone. The evidence of our work with more than 450 schools shows that without the energy, enthusiasm, commitment, and ability of both groups, school improvement is less likely to happen. We have abundant documentation of school and system leaders who, through will and skill, have been able to influence the improvement process in districts, individual schools, and single classrooms. Those outcomes notwithstanding, long-term improvement in schools is most likely to happen as a result of effective leadership that is capable of fostering the kind of cultural change that promotes and is supported by changes in educator practice. Such a cultural shift communicates the message to increasing numbers of students that they are valued, respected, useful, and important to their school's community, and that the school is there to help them succeed.

The approach is neither top-down nor bottom-up. Improvement occurs one student at a time, one teacher at a time, one classroom at a time, one school at a time, and one district at a time. It moves from the centre of an organization outward, from the edges of an organization inward, and from anywhere within an organization forward. The impetus for improvement may often appear to be external, but the commitment to improvement must come from within: within the organization itself and within each member of that organization. So many educators engaged in this type of work have shared this common insight with us: "Oh, I get it. It starts with *me!*"

However, a willingness and readiness to start has to be met with the resources, structures, processes, and practices that can help turn commitment into purposeful action. In all our work, we have tried to ensure that educators in any form of leadership are ready and able to lead their school improvement initiatives, provide the recognition and support that nurtures growth, and contribute effectively to the ethos of shared responsibility that characterizes successful schools.

We emphasize the importance of goals to the extent that they can enhance conversations about strategies, which in turn can help build more robust collaborative structures. In collaboration lies the potential for teams of educators to take charge of their work, explore the possibilities inherent in different forms of professional inquiry, and use the evidence of their own effectiveness to inform their ongoing practice. In short, clearer goals can lead to more powerful strategies, more focused guiding questions, more useful evidence, and more effective practice.

Perhaps the structure that lends greatest support to collaboration is regularized meetings, at which participants can show and tell what they have accomplished, what they have learned, what they are accepting as evidence of their progress, and what they will do next. To maximize their success, teams need to meet, but the meetings must have purpose. They must be viewed as increasing the likelihood of continuing success. Obviously, too many meetings, offering too little real value to participants, can have a deleterious impact on any initiative. In reality, the regular meetings should provide a forum for generative dialogue. Generative dialogue is the process that allows for continuing exploration of the impact of refined practice on student learning and achievement.

Through dialogue, teams of educators are able to determine how well they are meeting their goals. The *continuing exploration* is collaborative inquiry.

Another enabling process that affects school improvement relates directly to the actual schedule of activities that guide and support any initiative. For example, we have found that in schools where discussions about next year's goals take place before the end of the current year, and where the pursuit of agreed-upon goals begins as soon as possible, there is a much greater likelihood that those schools will progress. Alternately, school staffs that wait until the new year has started before they begin their conversations about goals for the year face more serious challenges to their possible success.

In improving schools, as in improving districts, the positive outcomes of collaboration depend on and contribute to the growth of trust and mutual respect among the educators involved. We have seen how an increase in trust results from people doing what they have committed to do, making sure they "have each other's back," being slow to judge or criticize others, and, above all, being fair. As well, we have seen that improvements in levels of respect among colleagues can be mirrored in the perceptions of students and parents when they respond to surveys and interviews.

In these final few paragraphs, we'd like to reconfirm, honour, and pay respect to the contributions made to school improvement by superintendents, directors, school leaders, and classroom teachers. The need for their expertise, wisdom, courage, and caring never seems to diminish. At their best, they inspirit our profession with images of hope and humour, love and labour, helpfulness and perseverance.

And they do it for the benefit of *all* the students they serve:

"It's about every kid," said superintendent Kurt Sacher.

"Nothing really happens in public education until it happens for a student in a classroom," according to superintendent Piet Langstraat.

"I didn't know just how much I could care about the welfare of one child until I had to drive a 12-year-old boy home to a trailer park in our so-called wealthy town. When I saw the way he and his mother were suffering, my whole career focus changed. From then on, I knew I had to be more helpful!" This came from a 20-year classroom veteran teacher.

And one more. In an Alberta town, a kindergarten student fell asleep on the school bus. When the driver woke him and asked him what school he attended, the boy cried, "I don't know, but I know my principal loves me!" Straight away the bus driver said, "I know which school *you* go to."

The kind of leadership we champion is more pragmatic than theoretic, emphasizing skills and attitudes more than it focuses on style or traits. It is of the heart *and* the head, a leadership *of* and *for* learning, first and foremost for self, then other educators, then students, then communities. The model of professional growth we have promoted in this text embraces learning by doing, an on-the-job way of committing to continuous growth.

We hope you, the reader, found something of value in every chapter. We hope you saw something of yourself in the anecdotes, case studies, and other examples we have shared. It has been a pleasure for us to be involved in the work, our reflections upon it, the preparation of this text, and the ongoing dissemination of the results of our efforts to contribute something meaningful to the field of educational leadership.

NOTE

1. The Alberta Research Network (ARN) was created as a way for the ministry to support the research needs of Alberta's education system in a collaborative manner. It is a coalition of educators, researchers, and policy-makers who work to improve the way research evidence is collected, accessed, and used across the K–12 education system. The network provides opportunity and support for education partners to collaborate on research relevant to Alberta's education system. Cooperation helps educators identify research trends and gaps, collaborative opportunities, and solutions to address complex education issues.

REFERENCES

Alberta Education. (2018). *Leadership quality standard*. Edmonton, AB: Alberta Education. Retrieved from https://education.alberta.ca/media/3739621/standardsdoc-lqs-_fa-web-2018-01-17.pdf

Rossouw, D. (2012). *Generative leadership*. Retrieved from https://www.possibil.com/generative-dialogue/

Glossary

adaptive communities – *See* **communities: adaptive**

adult learning – First considered by Malcolm Knowles, the model proposes a set of guidelines that outline the characteristics, motives, and environments in which adults most effectively learn. The model was originally meant to supplement theories of pedagogy (children's learning); some literature points to more areas of overlap than distinction.

assumed competence – An approach of positive intentions in which educators presume that their colleagues possess a level of professional skill that meets or exceeds an acceptable standard of practice.

authentic curiosity – A deep and sincere desire to know the thoughts, ideas, insights, and conundrums of teachers and colleagues that provide an environment of acceptance and trust.

benign communities – *See* **communities: benign**

collaborative inquiry – A process of professional learning undertaken by teams of educators who are asking and answering a shared professional inquiry question.

collaborative *learning* time – Based on an intersection point of the concepts professional learning, constructivism, and adult learning.

collaborative *social* time – Also referred to as collegiality, it is more commonly understood to be informal interactions between educators that build goodwill, positive relationships, and preliminary levels of trust.

collaborative *work* time – Based on the premise that the primary purpose for collaborating with colleagues is task completion, the creation of products, of demonstrable artifacts of productivity.

communities: adaptive – Communities that are infused with a sense of initiative taking, productivity, and optimism.

communities: benign – Communities that are most often compliant and content with the status quo.

communities: generative – Communities that consistently undertake actions that demonstrate enthusiastic commitment, mutual respect, and appreciation of inquiry leading to growth.

communities: reactionary – Communities that most often exhibit unresolved conflict, frustrated idealism, and a confrontational stance toward improvement initiatives.

communities: withdrawn – Communities that are least likely to consistently demonstrate the characteristics of effective organizations.

communities of practice – Groups of people who share a concern, a set of problems, or a passion about a topic, and who deepen their knowledge and expertise in this area by interacting on an ongoing basis.

competence: conscious competence – When an educator has had so much practice with a skill that it has become "second nature" and can be performed easily. Decisions about the skill are made purposefully, with a full understanding of the rationale and impact of the skill. The individual may be able to teach it to others, depending upon how and when it was learned.

competence: conscious incompetence – When an educator may not understand or know how to do something, although they recognize the deficit, as well as the value of a new skill in addressing the deficit.

competence: unconscious competence – When an educator performs a skill well, although it may be difficult to articulate what the skill or competency actually is or why choices were made about the use of the skill. When identified, there is heavy conscious involvement in executing the new skill.

competence: unconscious incompetence – When educators may not understand or know how to do something and may not necessarily recognize the deficit; in fact, they may deny the usefulness of the skill or the extent to which learning the skill will positively impact practice.

constructivism – Also referred to as social cognitive theory, first proposed by Russian psychologist Lev Vygotsky and based on Piaget's notion of environment adaptation. This is a model of learning that contends that the process and context of learning is heavily influenced by the social environment.

critical reflection – A form of reflection reserved to refer to challenging the validity of presuppositions in prior learning. Traced to John Dewey and Paulo Freire, who argued the process of reflective thinking can cause educators to teach more deliberately, especially in recognizing the politics of pedagogy.

deconstructing knowledge – Through reflection, re-examining understandings and assumptions about taken-for-granted aspects of professional practice.

differentiation – In the context of professional learning, the term refers to a process through which individual professional strengths are self-assessed, challenges are converted into learning, and forward movement is achieved.

director of education – An educational leadership position, in Australia and other countries, responsible for endorsing the published school plan; monitoring school plan implementation for compliance with legislative and policy requirements including equity or other targeted funding, and for compliance with state and department priorities, such as the literacy and numeracy strategy; and supporting principals to engage in all aspects of the school excellence policy and engaging in regular professional conversations regarding the school's plan, self-assessment, and annual report. *See also* **executive director of education**

ssonant leaders – Dissonant leaders operate more on the authoritative side of the leadership continuum. They maintain a social and emotional distance from others.

They can cause emotional frustration, stress, burnout, and disengagement in others. While a dissonant leader often intends to remain objective and logical in decision making, the approach is commonly viewed by others as cold and distant.

educational mission – A mission statement, along with core beliefs and core values, provides the boundaries in which staff and other stakeholders have agreed to work to achieve a shared vision.

educational vision – A vision statement, or simply a vision, is a public declaration that schools or other educational organizations use to describe their high-level goals for the future—what they hope to achieve if they successfully fulfill their organizational purpose or mission.

effective teams – People of goodwill who are able to work together toward the achievement of agreed-upon goals.

evidence-based practice – Educators working together to find the answers to their questions and, by so doing, uncovering or developing the *evidence* of the extent to which they are achieving their goals. This term is sometimes referred to as *product-based practice* and is one aspect of *learning-based practice* or *inquiry-based practice*.

executive director of education – Executive directors are collectively responsible for setting the direction for the department, effectively executing strategic priorities, and identifying and managing risks. *See also* **director of education**

generative communities – *See* **communities: generative**

generative dialogue – A specific, rigorous set of skills about how we converse with each other about professional practice for the purpose of clarifying and bringing into existence new ideas and thoughts that lead to more purposeful action. Further, it is a process of working with colleagues grounded in active listening; avoidance of criticism and judgment of others; trust and reciprocal respect; Socratic reflective questioning; and, ultimately, practical usefulness in achieving professional goals—leading to shifts in perspective, purposeful growth, and enhanced competence.

generative feedback – The type of feedback that leads to purposeful refinement of practice. The key factor in generative feedback is that both the provider and the receiver of feedback know what the desired practice is, know its component parts, and know its intended purposes.

generative leadership – A model of leadership where formal and informal leaders consistently and frequently communicate expectations of and establish conditions for purposeful, focused, learner-centric teaching supported by elbow-to-elbow instructional guidance.

growth – An organic process of gently sustaining and accommodating personal empowerment.

growth plan – A document that outlines a process that describes strategies for professional learning, and through which the answer to an inquiry question is evidenced.

initiative fatigue – A noticeable and palpable lapse of energy and willingness to engage in implementation of yet another cycle of change often described as "flavour of the month."

leader of learners – When a leader holds a primary responsibility of supporting, in various ways, the continued growth and learning of all those within one's sphere of influence.

leader-as-provocateur – A leader who subtly arouses curiosity and inquiry in the professional lives of educators; is humbly bold enough to construct structures that offer direct and sustained support for formal and informal school leaders; models and promotes a robust method that guides powerful collaboration around the most important work of schools and districts; and orchestrates and champions an elegant process for enhancing the likelihood of greater learning and growth in educators.

modelling – Modelling requires not only an understanding of what is involved in an actual process, but also the establishment of a mindset that will allow leaders and learners alike to be open to and indeed welcome ongoing reflection, feedback through questioning, and a commitment to the refinement of practice.

professional community – A group of people across a school who are engaged in common work; share a set of values, norms, and orientations toward teaching, students, and schooling; and operate collaboratively within structures that foster interdependence.

professional development – A training model associated with industrial programs that focus on increasing workers' performance through frequent external review that identifies deficits and areas in need of remediation.

professional learning – A model of increasing growth with 10 distinct characteristics based on self-identified learning goals.

provocateur – One who causes a healthy disruption by planting an irritant, causing reflection, a shift in thinking, and a variation in the course of action.

provocation – A niggling irritant that is relentless in requiring attention and causes reflection, a shift in thinking, and a variation in the course of action.

rationalist models of professional development – Based on the notion of the learner as tabula rasa, this type of professional development casts the role of the learner as one of passivity, with a locus of control for the curricula and process that resides in external sources such as gurus, experts, or titled leaders.

reactionary communities – *See* **communities: reactionary**

reconstructing understandings – After an idea or concept has been taken apart in a socially mediated process of reflection and dialogue, it is evaluated, reassessed, re-understood, and reformed with new facets, nuances, implications for practice.

reflection – An examination of practice that involves examining taken-for-granted assumptions.

reflection-in-action – One phase of reflection suggested by Loughran in 1996 to describe the adjustments and revised actions taken in the moment of action, based on assessment of the immediate effectiveness of practice. The prior stage described by Loughran involves reflection-*for*-action; the subsequent stage involves the more commonly understood phase reflection-*on*-action.

reflective practice – From the original work of Donald Schön, the idea that educators and other professionals can engage in continual inquiry into the impact of their practice. They reflect on practice, while engaged in practice, and after they have engaged in practice.

reflective practitioner – A term coined by social scientist Donald Schön in 1983. During his study of numerous professions, he posited that the most effective professionals rely on a process of intuitive, usually unarticulated, examination of their practices as a way to learn and improve.

relational trust – The extent to which there is consonance of expectations and priorities between and among teachers and school leaders.

resonant leaders – Resonant leaders have a high degree of emotional intelligence and a well-developed ability to connect personally with followers. They show empathy for employees struggling with life challenges. They are more likely to create harmony in a group and motivate workers to follow direction, even in tense situations.

shared responsibility – Groups of educators taking responsibility for demonstrating how their purposeful efforts on behalf of their students result in the outcomes they intended to achieve. This occurs when educators make a commitment to continuous professional learning where their own learning is as important as the learning of their students.

Socratic questioning – A systematic and disciplined form of questioning, most often focused on foundational concepts, principles, theories, issues, or problems.

Socratic questions – Questions that invite reflection on assumptions, goals and purposes, implications and consequences, as well as viewpoints and perspectives.

team – A grouping of men and women of goodwill working together toward the achievement of agreed-upon goals.

value-added leadership – A skillset used in differentiating support and pursuing individual and organizational goals that are unique to each member of the school community.

withdrawn communities – *See* **communities: withdrawn**

Author Biographies

PAMELA ADAMS, PH.D.

Dr. Adams was an educator in public schools in Alberta for 17 years before joining the Faculty of Education at the University of Lethbridge in 1996, teaching at the undergraduate, graduate, and doctoral levels. In 2005, she was appointed a teaching fellow in the Centre for the Advancement of Teaching and Learning, and went on to serve as an assistant dean in the faculty and a faculty liaison for the Alberta Initiative for School Improvement (AISI) for 10 years. Over the past five years, she has conducted collaborative inquiry research in nine school authorities and over 150 schools, investigating themes of school and organizational leadership, teaching effectiveness, school improvement, inquiry-based professional growth, and essential conditions for professional learning. Her publications focus on action research, site and system leadership, tertiary teaching effectiveness and enhancement, and conditions of school improvement.

CARMEN MOMBOURQUETTE, ED.D.

Dr. Carmen Mombourquette was a K–12 teacher, vice-principal, principal, and headmaster for close to 30 years. In July 2010, Dr. Mombourquette accepted an academic position with the Faculty of Education at the University of Lethbridge. Now he spends his time teaching primarily in the Master of Education in Educational Leadership program where, along with his colleagues, he is helping to educate the next generation of school leaders. His research interests include leadership at the school and district levels, school organization and its impact on student learning, student assessment and evaluation, and single-gender education. His publications and presentations include articles and book chapters on school leadership, instructional leadership, Indigenous school leadership, gender and its impact on student performance, parental influence on student success, and the impact of assessment policies on student performance.

DAVID TOWNSEND, PH.D.

Dr. Townsend was born in Sydney, Australia, and moved to Canada in 1967, where he worked as a classroom teacher, vice-principal, and principal. He later served as an assistant superintendent of schools and an educational consultant with the Alberta government. He became a permanent member of the Faculty of Education at the University of Lethbridge in 1985. David's research and scholarship interests include school and district leadership, school improvement, teacher development, staff and program evaluation, teaching and learning in higher education, and action research. Over the past 18 years, David has helped promote and refine a model of leadership growth that has contributed to measurable improvements in student achievement in several school jurisdictions. Retired from the faculty in 2014, David has continued his involvement in leadership research initiatives in Alberta, British Columbia, and New South Wales, extending a career-long quest to support and promote the vital work of public schools.

Index